INTERVIEW WITH A CANNIBAL

THE SECRET LIFE OF THE MONSTER OF ROTENBURG

ISBN-10: 1-59777-588-6
ISBN-13: 978-1-59777-588-5
Library of Congress Cataloging-In-Publication Data Available

Book Design by: Sonia Fiore

Printed in the United States of America

Phoenix Books, Inc.
9465 Wilshire Boulevard, Suite 840
Beverly Hills, CA 90212

10 9 8 7 6 5 4 3 2 1

INTERVIEW WITH A CANNIBAL

THE SECRET LIFE OF THE MONSTER OF ROTENBURG

BY
GÜNTER STAMPF

EDITED BY
PAT BROWN

Translated from the original
in German by Lewis Townsend

Introduction to the book

It is said that there are no longer any unexplored regions of the world, but you will find that Günter Stampf's excursion into the depths of Armin Meiwes's psyche will indeed take us into a land we will find as foreign and bizarre as any discovery of a heretofore-unknown primitive tribe deep in the jungles of a rainforest.

As Stampf approaches the boundaries of this unsettling and unsavory world of sexualized cannibalism, he does so with much trepidation and caution. But still, he moves forward, step by step, breath by breath, unsure of what he will unearth and how such disclosure will affect him personally. Slowly and carefully, he peels back the layers of Meiwes's hidden world, like a painted-over masterpiece of Michelangelo, only the more he scrapes away, the less refined and unpleasing are the uncovered areas of the underlying canvass.

We readers stand by him, looking over his shoulder as he delves deeper and deeper into this demented man's mind, and we find that he is not alone in his bizarre ideations. We learn that he is a product of his environment, his culture, and the online world of the Internet, and in doing so, we find that our worlds are not so far apart as we surely believed.

Hopefully, what we learn will contribute to our ability to improve the circumstances in our vastly changing world and prevent others from becoming the next Armin Meiwes or his victim, Bernd Brandes. We must recognize the immense impact the Internet has on disturbed individuals like these two men. Their bizarre ideations, that would once have received no stimulus or validation in one's own small locale, now gather strength and support, justification and validation, amidst the multitude of like thinkers in cyberspace. If these ideations within an alternate online reality stayed online, we might be able to ignore this perverse fantasy world. However, once these fantasies have been stimulated and obsessed upon for far too long, a human being may want the fantasy to become reality, and then we have an Armin Meiwes to contend with and a Bernd Brandes to mourn.

Günter Stampf goes himself like a lamb to slaughter, as he enters the world and mind of Armin Meiwes. An openhearted man, a seeker of knowledge, he does not bring with him the cynical, professional mind of a criminal profiler; perhaps this is what allows him to establish a congenial relationship with Meiwes and permits us to receive his story without a legalistic or psychological bias. The simplicity of the interactions between the two men and the honesty with which Stampf takes on his task make his journey into the world of cannibalism "palatable," and, dare I say, enjoyable.

Günter Stampf wanted this book to be, above all, a warning trumpet call for us to wake up to the seriousness of the increasing menace of cannibalism. In this mission, I wish him the greatest success.

—Criminal Profiler Pat Brown

Chapter 1
THE CANNIBAL

IGNORING THE "NO STOPPING" sign placed at the curb of the main entrance to the Kassel Penitentiary, the Turkish taxi driver named Ismail brings his vanilla-colored Mercedes 190 to a standstill to let me out. While writing out the fare receipt, he grins at me and wishes me a nice visit. "Ya know, Man-Eater is in there! He'd be the guy I would want to see!" His gallows humor that no doubt has sent shivers down the spines of dozens of passengers fails to amuse me. I wordlessly hand him a twenty-Euro bill and leave him visibly disappointed at my lack of response. Maybe my sense of humor wasn't kicking in, because I *was* going to see the Man-Eater.

Now I stand in front of his home, the Kassel Penitentiary, or KP for short. The prison is rated Number One, the highest security level available in Germany. The cinder block building, built back in 1873, stands on a birch tree-lined alley across from a single-floor apartment house in downtown Kassel. Unlike their neighbors on the opposite side of the road, few of the 500 inmates of KP will ever again travel down the street to engage in the rhythm of ordinary life.

To keep them apart from the rest of us, the walls measure five meters high and are topped with Nato wire—barbed wire with razor-sharp edges. Armed guards man the four watchtowers that flank the four floors of the four wings where the prisoners are housed. KP is a high-tech fortress where every square meter is electronically surveyed by cameras, so nothing goes unseen.

Even though the structure of the prison often reminds one of a Protestant cathedral, the male inmates who inhabit the small eight-and-a-half-square-meter individual cells have all violated one or more of the Ten Commandments, most of them earning life sentences for their sins. Cell 24—caving in his wife's skull with a hammer during a jealous fit; Cell 112—shooting a police officer during a bank robbery; Cell 376—strangling a little old lady when she surprised him during a burglary.

The most infamous of all, however, resides in Cell 1, Wing D, on the ground floor. His name is Armin Meiwes, known worldwide as "The Cannibal of Rotenburg." Technically speaking, the cannibal committed his horrific deed in the town of Wüstefeld, a little village five kilometers from Rotenburg on the Fulda in Hessen. This relatively unknown burg has an unwieldy name and, therefore, in favor of the spicier sounding and more recognizable Rotenburg, the media tabloids nonchalantly moved the crimes a bit to the west.

If the facts of Mr. Meiwes's crimes and sentencing were to be condensed down to a single paragraph for a simple news bite, they would read as follows: On the days of March 9 and 10, 2001, Armin Meiwes, an employee of Technologie Services, Inc., with the alleged consent of his victim, Bernd Brandes, computer engineer and division chief of the Siemens Company in Berlin, cut off Brandes's penis. Meiwes then slashed Brandes's throat, and when he was dead, butchered, disemboweled and consumed the man. In the first known case of "love-cannibalism" in the world, the court saw the actual crime as it occurred, for Armin Meiwes painstakingly recorded the penile amputation, the killing, and the butchering with his Medion video camera over the nine and three quarter grueling hours. The court sentenced Armin Meiwes to life in prison. He may apply for parole after thirteen years, with fifteen years being the earliest he can be released.

However, I was not entering the olive green steel turnstile of this imposing institution just for the barest of facts. I wanted the details, every one I could elicit, and today I would meet for the first time, a real cannibal—one who has declared his willingness, without conditions, to open his inner world to me. I walk as confidently as I can up to a bullet-proof window where I surrender my personal identity card to the official sitting behind it. At the next window, I am handed a small silver key and instructed to deposit all of my personal belongings—cell phone, keys, cigarettes—into the box. Then, I pass through a metal detector, and, in the parlance of computer gamers, I am ready to proceed to the next level.

I am escorted by a jovial, walrus-mustachioed official, who jokes as we walk though a series of electronically opening steel doors. "Let's go see the most famous prisoner in all of Germany, shall we?" he asks. He and the cab driver would get along famously.

After crossing through the long courtyard and another set of security stations, we reach the main penal facility. I realize that I have entered a world previously unknown and hidden to me, and as I climb the stairs to the second floor to the designated meeting place with Armin Meiwes, I hope I am prepared to plunge into the abyss of the human soul. "Mr. Meiwes is already on his way here," the official informs me, and now I know, there is no way to back out.

*

The life story of Armin Meiwes begins, in the opinion of the District Court of Kassel (File reference 2650 Js 36980/02) of January 30, 2004, as follows:

> *The defendant, who has no previous criminal record, was born on 12/1/1961 in Essen, the third child of his mother Waltraud Meiwes and the first child of her second husband, at that time Detlef M.* [Note: name changed by the author]. *The defendant has two half-brothers. Werner B.* [Note: name changed by the author] *was born on 1/15/1946, a child of Waltraud Meiwes's first marriage, to Heinz B. He is fifteen years older than the defendant. The other half-brother, Ilja B.* [Note: name changed by the author], *is issue of the relationship between Waltraud Meiwes and Ernst K., which Waltraud Meiwes entered after Heinz B. had abandoned her and the family. The defendant's half-brother Ilja B. was born on 6/2/1955 and is six years older than the defendant. The*

defendant grew up with his parents Waltraud Meiwes and Detlef M. and his half-brothers Ilja and Werner B. in Essen, where half-brother Werner B. soon (1964/65) left the family and moved to Berlin to study. The defendant's half-brothers Werner and Ilja B. got from their mother Waltraud Meiwes little information about their respective fathers. This stemmed from Waltraud Meiwes's particular position in regard to her previous husbands, who had abandoned the family, but also to her current husband Detlef M., the defendant's father.... The defendant first attended primary school, then high school until his ninth school year, when he had to repeat a year, having missed classes for six months because of an ear infection. In 1964, at the insistence of their mother Waltraud Meiwes, the family acquired a manor house in Wüstefeld with an outbuilding (former stables), which, with its forty rooms, reminded Waltraud Meiwes of the building in the Rhön in which she had completed her required year during the war. It was to serve on one hand as a retreat for the family during vacations, and on the other for Waltraud Meiwes to live out fantasies about life in the middle ages among lords of the manor.

*

The visitors' room in the Kassel Penitentiary has all the charm of an unoccupied railroad diner with its ten tables and wooden chairs bolted to the wall. I have been left alone, unguarded, eyeing the one lone table in the center of the room, one chair for the cannibal and one for the interviewer; such a small surface separating the two of us. The room is deathly quiet save for the low hum of the snack machine in the corner of the room. Next to it, there is an old coffee dispenser. I drop a fifty-cent coin into the slot of the machine and receive a cup of lukewarm, vile coffee that I drink anyway to pass the time and to calm my nerves.

Questions shoot through my brain nonstop. Will I be meeting a monster? Will he be like Hannibal Lecter in *The Silence of the Lambs*? Will he try to manipulate me? Can I remain objective after seeing pictures of the dissected corpse of his victim, Bernd Brandes? How will I be able to talk to a man who seasoned a human foot with rose paprika in a red wine sauce and then plated it with tomatoes? My stomach contracts and it is almost a relief when I hear the bolt of the door rattle. My man-eater is here.

Two security guards lead the prisoner into the room. Armin Meiwes doesn't arrive with a muzzle over his mouth like Hannibal Lecter; he isn't even in handcuffs. The horror scenario I envisioned of our first meeting with the cannibal is dispelled at a stroke. Armin Meiwes carries himself with dignity—tall, slender, and somewhat pale. He could be the quiet caretaker at an old folks' home, his appearance is so innocent. He is wearing the white cotton trousers and the cobalt-blue shirt of the laundry workers; his job is to spend his days washing and ironing handkerchiefs, blankets, and covers.

Armin Meiwes comes straight to me, offering his hand. "Hello. It is nice of you to come." His baritone voice, slightly hoarse but not unpleasant, is firm and persuasive. In contrast, his handshake is as soft as a ball of cotton wool. As we exchange greetings, I involuntarily find myself staring at his wide-open mouth, taking in the teeth that chewed up a man's flesh. He seems to have a strong bite. I hear the words of my biology teacher ringing in my head. "With the canines, we tear off the pieces. With the incisors we break them up. With the molars, we grind them." The meaning of "pieces" has changed forever in my mind.

A strange feeling comes over me that I am being watched—sized up. Armin Meiwes's eyes have the gray-green color typical of fifty percent of all German men. His close-cropped, dark-blonde hair is carefully combed to the right. His gaze is friendly, but disconcerting. I drop my eyes and note he has a brown soapstone pendant with some sort of geometrical figure on it. His left wrist sports a silver Seiko self-winding watch with yellow hands. I am trying to relax,

5

but failing miserably. I can feel Meiwes's gaze still upon me, waiting, and I force myself to move forward. After all, I am here to find out what is hidden behind those probing eyes. I look up and begin my interview with the cannibal. "Many thanks for talking with me."

I begin with an innocuous question. "Did you sleep well last night?"

"I was a bit nervous about today, but otherwise...." He seems a bit embarrassed and smiles awkwardly. I feel similarly and hope this is all I will find we have in common.

"What did you dream about?"

"I was in a house somewhere and the windows were painted over."

"Were they painted black?" I guessed, trying my hand as an interpreter of dreams.

"No, white," he says dryly.

I am no Sigmund Freud, but I remember that Freud believed dreams themselves are windows to the subconscious. Would the father of psychoanalysis find the whitewashing of this dream representation of a window an actual desire for the cleansing of the soul? Or could the painting it over be an attempt to shield us from seeing the truth of his inner being? I realized, perhaps, I should simply ask the questions for now and not stop to analyze too deeply what they meant.

"Are you bothered by dreams of this kind?"

"No, I actually usually dream of regular day-to-day activities. Well," Meiwes got a bit of a faraway look in his eye, "I dream a lot about my house in Wüstefeld."

Ah, yes, the house in Wüstefeld. Where the horror took place. Enough with this small talk.

"Mr. Meiwes, what is being a cannibal to you?"

"For me, I imagine that the person I eat stays with me forever. It's not about killing or butchering. It is about entering into a relationship. My main fantasy is finding that person who wants to be slaughtered and eaten. Then, I wish to disembowel and cut up the human body. I fantasize about the body lying on my table, ready to be sliced up. Then the belly is being cut open and the individual organs—the heart, the liver, and the stomach—are removed."

"Is a great part of your fantasy to search for that special someone?"

"Yes, my desire has always been to find a 'brother' whom I could assimilate into myself. I searched on the Internet, in the forums, and I found myself obsessed. The others in the forums and I stoked each other's fantasies. We shared our thoughts and our wish to either be dining on other humans or being the dinner. But, this longing, it did not begin on the Internet, but when I was a small child."

"Tell me of your childhood."

"What I remember most clearly is the time with my father. I was Papa's boy. I loved his magic tricks. I loved the way he started our old Opel without the key! He was my one and only. Then, he just up and left."

*

It is a day that changed young Armin Meiwes's life. He was eight years old. The date was September 29, 1970. His friend and neighbor, Manfred Stück, is hiding his face in his hands and counting slowly from ten down. "Ten, nine, eight…." and Armin has already found his place, lying in the field among the thistles. He doesn't hear the rest of the countdown. What he hears is the door to his house slamming and the loud voices of his parents arguing, the words unintelligible to him at the distance from the house to his hiding spot. It doesn't matter that he cannot hear the content of the conversation because he knows from experience that the words are not pleasant. The voices now become more vehement, and Armin feels a coldness wash over him.

"I see you! I see you!" Manfred has found him, but Armin pays him no mind. He jumps up and runs past him toward his house. But he is too late. Already his father, Detlef M. Meiwes, has left the house and jumped into the family car. The engine starts up and he is gone.

Armin sprints after the car crying, "Papa! Papa! Stop!" Tears run down the boy's suntanned cheeks, streaking them. For some reason, he knows that today is different and that if his father drives away, he will never come back. "No,

Papa! No! Stay here! Please! Stay here!" But his calls go unheeded, and Armin is left standing alone on the curve of dusty Highway 3336.

*

"Didn't your father hear you?"

"Yes, but he just stepped on the gas and drove away. He didn't even look in the mirror." The bitterness in Meiwes's voice was unmistakable. "It was only the week before that he wrote me a note that said—and I quote—'Armin is a good boy, our little fellow, so when he is with his Mama, then Mama shall not be so alone. Papa is sad he cannot be there.' I hadn't known when I read those words that they meant anything in particular. To Mama he also wrote, 'My dear little wife. Many kisses to you and our little fellow.' He wrote these words to us and then he left."

"Did your mother help you through this time?"

"My mother," he explained without emotion, "was simply bewildered. So all she said was, 'Papa is gone and will never come back.' It was my grandmother who later told me he had run off with a twenty-five-year-old girl who had lived with us in Essen as a tenant. Now, that I am an adult, I can look back and see that the marriage hadn't been going well, most likely because of the nineteen-year age difference between them. My father was then twenty-nine, and my mother was forty-eight years old."

*

The opinion of the District Court of Kassel of January 30, 2004, comments on this:

> Waltraud Meiwes could not accept men as independent individuals with their own interests and needs, and tried to shape them according to her own views, infantilized them, directed them or—after she had been abandoned by them—tried to annihilate them socially, and

erase them from her children's memory. In her attacks on the social existence of the men who had left her, Waltraud Meiwes did not shrink from drastic measures. Thus, after her first husband Heinz B. had sued for divorce, she reported his new living companion to the Health Office as a "hooker" with a sexual disease, and summoned the current husband of Heinz B.'s new living companion in order to report to him this alleged sexual disease.... In the year 1968/1969, the father of the defendant, Detlef M., also left Waltraud Meiwes and the family during the very same vacation sojourn on the Wüstefeld estate.... Waltraud Meiwes gave the defendant no reasons for his father's departure, as she had also not done for Werner B. and Ilja B. with regard to their fathers. Just as in respect to the fathers of the defendant's half-brothers Ilja and Werner B., the defendant's father was no longer mentioned after his departure. Although the defendant's father, before and also then, frequently asked about the children and especially the defendant in letters to his wife when he was away from the family on business trips, there was hardly any further contact between him and the defendant after his departure. Even in the divorce proceedings, Detlef M. did not refer to the defendant by name, but as "Respondent to 2)." Either shortly before, or shortly after, the father's departure—the exact point in time is so far unclear—the defendant's half-brother, Ilja B., left the family and was brought to Berlin and taken in by the other half-brother, Werner B. The half-brother Ilja B. had also been treated by the defendant as a person to whom he especially related, in whom he had confidence, and to whom he could turn for advice and comfort in time of care and need. The defendant thus lost in quick succession two positive male relationships, and during the ensuing period lived alone with his mother Waltraud Meiwes.... Now forsaken by a man for the third time, Waltraud Meiwes began to project her views of the position of the man in her life and in the family onto the eight-year-old defendant and make him a "self-object." She subordinated the feelings and needs of the child to her views of his duties, thrust him in a harsh tone of command into house and garden work and sent him, furthermore, to help acquaintances in their households.... The defendant, who felt abandoned after the departure of his father and his half-brother Ilja B., identified himself with his mother Waltraud Meiwes in her abandonment and bent to her wishes and needs, seeking thus to avoid falling out of her favor. The defendant had no close emotional connection with his mother.

*

Armin Meiwes stares at the half-full water glass before him on the table in the visitors' room of the prison, but I wonder that the landscape he sees around him is not his childhood home. When he is telling his story, his lips tighten, and when the bitter memories flow from him, his breathing is more labored, his nostrils flare, and his entire upper body stiffens. Sympathy is beginning to creep up inside me. I must remember he is a cannibal, a man who made a meal of another human being. His soul is a wasteland.

"What happened inside of you when your father left?"

"My perfect world was shattered. My younger brother already was living in Berlin with my adult brother to attend school. Since we were now broke, he wouldn't be coming home. He had always been the one I was closest with. We had shared a bedroom in the tower room of the house, and whenever I was depressed or sad, he would be there to comfort me. Half a year later—no, not even that—my grandmother died. So in such a short time, I lost three of the people who meant the most to me in life. At eight years old, I became the only man in the house. This is when I started to envision an imaginary brother who would never again abandon me."

*

As already mentioned in the court's opinion, the expert witnesses in both court proceedings found in Armin Meiwes a lack of emotional intimacy with his mother, Waltraud Meiwes. Rather, it was a subordination of self, a serving in order to please, and apparently his eager, anticipatory obedience that conceals his anxiety not to lose his mother, the only surviving person to whom he could relate.

"Those are assumptions of the expert witnesses," comments Armin Meiwes, justifying himself in a somewhat condescending tone.

*

I am curious if the mother is the real key to Meiwes's scarred, emotional world. I wonder if he will acknowledge this, or if I will have to read between the lines.

"After your father left, what was the rest of your childhood like? Were you sheltered?"

"I suppose you could call it that. In any case, my mother did everything for me. She even got me my own horse named "Polly" during the energy crisis of 1972. We could then ride in a coach behind our horse. The horse lived for eighteen years. So, I had a happy enough childhood, but I was also very, very lonely."

"Where did you go in the coach? To Rotenburg?"

"No, we stopped going to Rotenburg because of Polly's fear of church bells. I had taken a neighbor girl with me in the coach, and at twelve sharp, we passed the church. The bells rang, and Polly became frightened and shied off to the side of the road, damaging a parked automobile. There was a huge row over the accident, and from that day on, we no longer took the coach to town but instead enjoyed leisurely drives into the forest."

"Did you go to church as a child?"

"Yes, to several churches. I was baptized a Protestant. My half-brother Werner is a Protestant minister, and we were given a religious upbringing. No matter what city I drove to with my mother, on vacation or for business, we always first looked at the churches. We even went to the cemeteries to see if any of our relatives were buried in them."

"What of your mother's ex-husbands? Did she ever speak of them?"

"Very little. As for the first husband, Heinz B., I know that they fell in love at the hospital during the war. Then, according to my mother, he got into black market deals. More I don't know. I never found out where he ended up. As to the second husband, I did not know he existed until after my mother's death. All of us brothers had assumed the two oldest were from the first husband, Heinz. Then it came out that she was married to a boarder who briefly lived with us, and this is my middle brother's father. It seems he was crazy. He wanted to blow up the house and was promptly institutionalized. He died there from the effects of a war wound. After my father took off, my mother would have no more of men."

I shook my head with understanding. "Except for you," I reminded him. "So, then, how, in all, was your relationship with your mother?"

"It was a good relationship. She was a caring mother and a housewife. For sure, she had her own problems, but she never burdened me with them for the most part. She gave me love, certainly, but not in the way I would have liked. She couldn't take the place of a father. I lacked a male person to whom I could relate. This is why an imaginary brother became more and more important to me, along with the wish to have him inside me."

I was puzzled. "So are you telling me that at the age of eight, you already had a desire to consume classmates?"

"No, no, not at that time. Not really. The feeling was growing, and the fantasy of actually consuming someone and assimilating him in me came a few years later."

*

On this gray November morning, the primary school on the Margaretenhöhe in Essen looms before nine-year-old Armin Meiwes, a silhouette in the mist. The white air is damp. His warm breath comes in gusts from his mouth like the white steam from a locomotive. Armin is late; it is almost eight o'clock. The first biology class begins in two minutes, and still he has at least a four-minute walk, even at a fast clip, before reaching the classroom. Armin puts great store in punctuality.

Suddenly, from behind, he hears someone panting. Another boy, hurrying to class, he thinks. Armin Meiwes turns quickly and sees behind him a ghostly shape approaching. At first he does not recognize it. Then he sees it is his schoolmate, Frank. He is a year younger than Armin and attends the third grade, one level below him. He stands, transfixed, fascinated. The features of the boy are exquisite in the early morning haze. The boy has noble, almost fragile features. A lock of black hair escapes from under Frank's cap and clings gently to his forehead. The boy bafflingly resembles Armin Meiwes's half-brother, Ilja. At the sight, Armin feels an incredible tingling in his fingertips, a sensation that always comes when he feels intense, burning love, as he had once felt for his brothers or his errant father. Armin Meiwes makes fists inside his knitted mittens to stifle the pain.

"Armin! I am glad to see you! Now I am not the only one coming late!" Frank's words wrench Armin out of his solitary emotional world. Armin can barely speak. "Yeah, yeah." They walk together toward the school. Armin can only think of his closeness, how it feels when Frank hugs his body to him when Armin scores a goal during their soccer practices. He turns his head toward Frank, to smell his innocent breath, to suck it in through his nose. He feels the urge to touch him. Frank has become his "brother" in his mind, someone whom he can be close to, share his problems with. This feeling is new to Armin Meiwes, yet at the same time so familiar. The emotions overwhelm him, and he feels a need to escape. "Let's run!" yells Frank, and the two boys take off in a sprint. Armin feels a great relief, but those few moments when this desire engulfed him have left their mark. He is branded forever.

*

"It aroused me," admits Armin Meiwes, rubbing his eyes as though he might wipe out that moment and change the path of his life. But, there was, of course, no way to change the past, and that relatively innocent moment on the way to school gave way to more concerning fantasies. Eventually, he envisioned his school friends upon a long, rectangular table and slowly, with a sharp scalpel, cutting open their bellies and pulling out their entrails. He sees himself gently placing a piece of the innards into his mouth, slowly chewing the choice morsel, and delighting in the mixing of his saliva with the bits of the dead boy's organs. In this daydream, Armin Meiwes feels fulfilled.

*

In the psychiatric opinion of Prof. Dr. Klaus Michael Beier, Director of the Institute for Sexual Science and Sexual Medicine in the Berlin Charité Hospital, in the prosecution of Armin Meiwes, is the following passage of June 12, 2003:

> *He then imagined, he says, how he opened the belly of the boy concerned and extracted the entrails. This was mostly an image conjured up during masturbation, leading to an orgasm, even when he found that the consumption of flesh during further butchering aroused his fantasy much more. He thus came to orgasm before the "wildest" (namely the slicing up and arranging of the flesh) could be fantasized. Between his thirteenth and eighteenth year he recalls four specific fantasy victims (schoolmates) whom he ingested in this manner in his imaginary world. Moreover, at 14 or 15 years he had actual socio-sexual*

*encounters with a longstanding friend (Volker),
in which they performed mutual onanism.*

*

"These cannibal fantasies, at what age did they start?"

"I must have been about ten or twelve years old. I had seen a Robinson Crusoe film on television and this awakened the fascination of cannibalism within me. Well, actually it was a version of that story. In this one, two young men were sailing in a storm and one of them lost his life. So that he wouldn't just be tossed back into the sea and lost, the surviving man wanted to eat him, to keep him with him. But Robinson prevented him from doing so." Armin Meiwes then pauses and adds a detail that seems to fit with the story of the film he has just related. "I know that as a child I said to my parents who were watching the film with me, 'Look, that's real human flesh. It's much brighter than our Sunday roast.'" He goes on with his explanation of his developing cannibalistic imagery. "Then I started wishing that Sandy, the boy in the TV 'Flipper' series would be the one, my new brother, the one who would be in me. But this fantasy began to frustrate me. I wanted something more solid than an idea. I wanted a real person to be part of me."

"Did you talk to any friends of this desire?"

"Of course not. Not at all. That is obvious. You can't talk about wanting to make a meal of someone. Even with Bernd, my later victim, I could not even discuss this desire, not really. Oh, I also saw a film on public television when I was a child in which a woman serves her husband, as a delicacy, the roasted penis of her lover!"

Meiwes gave no discernable clue that he was fabricating this story, but, such a movie on public television? I found myself doubting him.

*

In its opinion of January 30, 2004, the Kassel District Court observes:

> *Since the defendant did not yet feel the presence of his imaginary brother Frank D. as perfect consummation of his desire for proximity and intimacy, there arose in the defendant's imagination, shortly before the onset of puberty, fantasies in which he sought to achieve his goal of having a person always with him and binding him to himself through a process in which this person became embodied in him. The object of this imagined embodiment was each time a younger male person. These imaginings went so far that the defendant, in his fantasy, relying on home slaughters he had witnessed, pictured to himself how he, as the slaughterer, would stab a person to death and then—this he regarded as a special moment—slit open the belly, extract the entrails of the imaginary subject, and then make a meal of him. The objects of these fantasies were actually existing persons such as classmates who pleased the defendant, but also models on television whom the defendant found attractive physically and in personality. With the onset of puberty, the defendant found pleasure in these fantasies, with the result that he invoked them for arousal during masturbation, experiencing the slitting open and disemboweling of the belly as a climax. His fantasy, as a rule, no longer proceeding to eating the slaughtered person, since he had already reached his climax. Afterward, the defendant sensed a feeling of inclination and belonging to the slaughtered person.*

*

Armin Meiwes places his folded arms on the table and leans toward me. He lowers his head as though he is in surrender to me. Then his sunken eyes look expectantly up at me, puppy-like, as if he wants me to pat him on the head and say, "Good boy." But, I do not give in to this psychological ploy. I need more facts.

"Were you allowed as a child to observe home butchering?"

"Yes, we children watched butchering in Rotenburg. I also often saw this in the home of our neighbors, the H family. The hogs always shrieked loudly before the butchering. When the shrieking stopped, I knew the hog was dead. The sow then lay on the butchering bench. Its blood flowed into a bucket and afterward the bristles were shaved off and the hide removed with a slaughter-knife. It wasn't anything unpleasant or awful, and there was nothing bad about it when it was hung upside down from a hook and slit in half. These animals had been part of the community, and they stayed with it after their death. It was a real village festival! People were happy! I enjoyed it very much."

*

Armin Meiwes's description leads me unwillingly to a long submerged memory from my own childhood. On a sunny day in July, my father Josef, whose descendants were farmers, put six young rabbits to play in a basket on the lawn of our garden. I was ten years old. I laid bath towels in the form of a cross on the grass and built the rabbits a kind of open-air structure. I stroked their soft fur and fed them fresh dandelions. It made me happy to see how their noses wriggled faster and faster in joyous excitement.

It must have been all of fifteen minutes when my father came and lifted one bunny after another out of my little rabbit arena by the ears and took it away with him, until only one was left, a white one. The remaining rabbit may only have been with me a few minutes more, but in that time I had given him a name, "Foffi." It was just the two of us, and a relationship developed between us instantaneously, as it is in the case of children. Suddenly, with the words, "Günter, come along," my father grabbed my Foffi by the ears and strode to the back of the garden. I went along happily, innocently unaware of any unkind intent. I was looking to see the rabbit hutch my father had built for the rabbits. I was a little boy, and what I imagined was happening, I expected to happen.

I was whistling, and then I stopped. From a pear tree, hung by chords tied around their necks, were the naked bodies of the rabbits. My father had slugged the animals with a wooden club and skinned them. Without a word, he shattered my Foffi's skull with three well-aimed blows. I stood appalled and numb. My father took the freshly whetted knife in his right hand and began to strip off the rabbit's skin.

I ran away from the garden and into our house and vomited immediately into the toilet. Tears streamed from my eyes and mixed with the fresh vomit spattered on the blue-and-white-checkered toilet cover. After a half-hour, my father entered the house and held out to me the stump of Foffi's white tail. "You can put it on your keyring if you want," he said quietly, and left, probably feeling a sense of satisfaction for having done something good for his son.

The rabbit's body was sealed in a blue plastic bag and stored in the freezer in the cellar. About a month later, Foffi was polished off by family and relatives in the form of a Sunday roast, complete with bread dumplings and red cabbage. I wouldn't touch the meat, and immediately after laboriously choking down half a dumpling, I threw it up on my mother's fine white tablecloth.

I cannot fathom any fascination or enjoyment one could get from the sight of a slaughtered animal. Even as children, I went one direction, and Armin Meiwes went another. Nevertheless, now we were here on a path together, and I must walk with him.

*

I thought about how my experience was hard to keep inside myself as a child and so I pushed Meiwes again on the issue of not discussing his "interest" with any of his friends.

"Did you never, ever, speak with anyone about your liking for human flesh?"

"I once told a schoolmate about it, but he only laughed at me and said, 'You are making that up.' I never told my mother outright that I wanted to eat someone, but I spoke about having someone become a part of me. As a child, I always thought, we have enough space; a third person could surely fit in my room with my brother and me. My mother didn't seem shocked at my comment. I looked like a happy child on the outside; in theory, I had everything I needed, only inside I was hollow and empty."

*

Armin Meiwes's father, Detlef M., a police officer, testified as follows, to expert witness Prof. Dr. Beier in the prosecution of Armin Meiwes:

Armin Meiwes was not a planned child but rather, in hindsight, one of many attempts by the woman he would later marry to bind him more tightly to her. This had not been so clear to him after Armin's birth, so that he agreed to marry her, although she would have to wait until he was 21 years old.... The purchase of the estate in Wüstefeld had been another of his wife's strategies to bind him to her, because from a financial standpoint this purchase had been "total idiocy"—the house was too dilapidated and too large, and offering it for sale (perhaps as a hotel) unthinkable for lack of investors. Then in 1965 he had finished a training course with distinction, and was therefore considered for further training. For one of these further courses he had to leave Essen for six months, which his wife, however, was able to prevent by taking extremely unusual measures, which, in his opinion, completely undermined the basis for a conjugal life. Then it chanced that in the training course completed in 1965 he had met a young woman he had known in a previous class. This drew a jealous reaction from his wife, who in an anonymous letter to the State prosecutor's office aroused the suspicion that this classmate had murdered her former husband. The proceedings were dismissed and Mrs. Meiwes denied having written the letter (although a handwriting expert was able to prove convincingly that this letter had come from her). But for Detlef M. the relationship had suffered a sharp rupture, which widened when his wife sent more anonymous letters to his superiors and asserted that he, Detlef M., was an unfaithful husband and was having sexual contact with other women—none of which was true and discredited him in his department. At the same time it was impossible to talk frankly with his wife about her apparent fear of separation, because—once cornered—she reacted with hysterical fits, in which, for example, she would faint. He remembers how she was once found "unconscious" in a park. The attending physician had told him the situation was like a "dance on the edge of a volcano." In any case, he had had too much, and decided in 1969 to separate, took a separate room and broke off all contact.... As he felt it, the earlier warm-hearted relationship had now taken, on her side, a turn in the direction of "hatred"—hatred because he had left her and she was now alone again. According to his information, his wife's relations with her previous husbands had had quite similar outcomes. Her first husband, father of Werner B., had likewise completely broken off the relationship, and the second spouse, whom he knew, a returnee from Russia (the father of Ilja B.), had tried to take his own life in Waltraud B.'s house and caused a gas explosion there; he had died shortly thereafter. His perception of his wife in any case was that, completely absorbed in her own needs, she tried to bind her emotional partners to her. That explained why in recent days she had had no friends, was completely unable to get on with her sister, who lived not far away in Essen, and in Wüstefeld had withdrawn into her own world. When in 1980 he resumed contact—partly for tax reasons (he needed a signature)—and visited Waltraud and Armin in Wüstefeld every year, she was, in conversation, completely preoccupied with her own concerns and had no time for other thoughts. He had therefore advised Armin to leave Wüstefeld as soon as possible, but— he had to admit—had not exerted an intensive effort to stiffen his son's backbone in these efforts at separation from his mother.

*

Waltraud Meiwes, apparently, was neither a good wife nor mother, but Armin Meiwes lacked either the resources or the wherewithal to break off his relationship with her. The boy was left to cope alone with his dominating mother, classified by expert witnesses as "psychologically disturbed." I needed to learn more about Mrs. Meiwes, even if Armin did not wish to go into that part of his past.

"Was your mother overbearing?"

"Well, my mother tried to have me with her always at home. When I was older, she even scared off my girlfriends. She never wanted me to leave her."

"Can it be that your mother had cannibal fantasies also?"

"There could have been a similarity in some aspects."

"In what way?"

"In that one wants to always have someone with him; otherwise...." Armin Meiwes's voice trails off. He cocks his head. Is he listening to someone? His eyelids begin to flutter nervously and he adds defiantly, "She was a completely normal housewife."

"Oh, yes? Then how would your mother have reacted to your deed if she were still alive?"

"My mother, if she had known of it..." says Armin Meiwes, thinking aloud, "she might have assented to the whole thing, but I don't know, I can't say."

"Would she have tasted human flesh?"

"Perhaps she might have tasted it, it's possible. As I said, my mother's and my imaginings had a commonality. She often read me gruesome bedtime stories like *Grimm's Fairy Tales* and such. They were interesting."

"What was interesting about the stories?"

"'Hänsel and Gretel,' for example. Hänsel is supposed to have been eaten by the witch. Decades later I exchanged e-mails with people on the Internet. You wouldn't believe how many people named 'Hänsel' are buzzing around out there in cyber land," Armin Meiwes smirks, rolling his eyes up until only the whites can be seen.

TRAIN UP A CHILD IN THE WAY HE SHOULD GO
AND WHEN HE IS OLD, HE WILL NOT DEPART FROM IT.

Proverbs 22:6

Chapter 2

ROTENBURG

*THE OLD WOMAN HAD ONLY MADE
A PRETENSE OF BEING FRIENDLY, BUT
SHE WAS AN EVIL WITCH WHO LAY IN
WAIT FOR CHILDREN, AND HAD MADE
THE COTTAGE OUT OF CAKE TO LURE
THEM. WHEN ONE FELL INTO HER
CLUTCHES, SHE KILLED HIM, COOKED
HIM, AND ATE HIM, AND THAT WAS TO
HER A FEAST DAY.*
    *—"Hänsel and Gretel," Grimm's Fairy
Tales, 19th century, Hesse*

*

THE LITTLE TOWN OF ROTENBURG lies nestled in the heart of Germany. To be exact, it's in the northeastern part of Hesse, on the Fulda, to the south of the Stölzing Mountains, where the hills are forested with red beeches, red chestnuts, and firs. With forty-two percent of its territory forested, Hesse has Germany's largest tree population. As soon as one approaches the area and reaches some fifty kilometers south of Kassel, the hectic pace of the Metropolis dies down without much resistance. Highways wind their serpentine ways through pretty valleys where many horses can be observed behind fences.

Rotenburg is the center of the "white industry," so-called because of its numerous clinics and medical facilities. Otherwise, the town is dominated mainly by small and medium-sized enterprises of a variety of businesses. The approximately fourteen thousand residents of Rotenburg have a happy, North Hessian sing-song in their speech. They are courteous and hospitable. In the saloons, simple fare is served, and at the center of town, three cafes and a smattering of snack bars stand one beside each other. Here, then, am I.

My first interview with the cannibal has led me to the core of his thoughts: his childhood in Rotenburg. I had found Armin Meiwes an open, serious man of average intelligence, a conformist, with a tendency to be overly sensitive. When one scratches but a little at the outer layer of his always courteous façade, one immediately meets head-on the trauma of his childhood, with its sense of abandonment, loneliness, and mental isolation which leads Meiwes to his sorrowful lament: "I was always alone, and I am still alone today."

But, I shall not allow this admittedly sad childhood of Armin Meiwes to pass as an excuse. I should think an absent father, a reading of a Grimm's fairy tale, a Robinson Crusoe film, a viewing of an animal butchering, and a domineering mother does not turn one into a man-eater—or does it?

"No, no" he concedes. "It wasn't that. There was something else."

I must agree with philosopher Friedrich Nietzsche that "Every profound intellect needs a mask." The human mask of Armin Meiwes must be a thick one, shielding the very dark soul where the truth resides. I must dig deeper. I believe it is not just *one* circumstance that can be to blame for his dreadful development into a monster. Presumably, many factors must have come together to make a man-eater out of him, to create the kind of being who did not shrink from cutting off a man's penis and roasting it.

My initial research into the environment of the growing cannibal leads me to the restaurant "Zur Gerichtsschänke" in Rotenburg City. From the entrance and smoking room, one passes through a swinging door to the dining room of the inn. It is furnished in rustic peasant style, with five oaken tables, including two long tables near the front window for larger groups of diners. Shortly after eleven o'clock in the morning, the place is as good as empty. Only one middle-aged man sits at the counter, staring silently at his glass of white wine.

I seat myself at the large table by the window. I am in desperate need of a Pilsner, freshly tapped from the keg. The young bespectacled waiter, whom one would guess to be a medical student earning his pocket money in this part-time job, turns out to be the cook and proud owner of the establishment. He recommends I must try the "Strammer Max," an open sandwich made of coarse bread, ham, and a fried egg, for the reasonable price of six-Euros-ninety. The bread slices are roasted in butter and covered with diced bacon and the egg is over-easy. He watches as I bite into the dish. "Taste good?" he asks, knowing I am a foreigner to the area and its cuisine. "Wonderful," I reply. He smiles broadly. "You should know that the term 'Strammer Max' comes from the Saxon German and it means 'erected penis'!" He laughs heartily. "It's probably because this sandwich has special qualities that strengthen you." The next bite almost gets stuck in my throat. The phrase "roasted prick" simply will not leave me. It is a black humor that tends to make one laugh in spite of oneself. The local residents have regaled one another, ever since Armin Meiwes's bloody deed became known, with the saying: "In Rotenburg, at Christmastime, instead of goose and turkey, we eat Santa Claus whole— complete with sack and prick."

*

"When did you first live alone with your mother?"

"It was in 1970. I was nine years old. We lived in Essen except for vacations. We spent these on our estate in Rotenburg-Wüstefeld, purchased by my parents six years earlier. When I finished my schooling in 1980, we moved to Rotenburg for good."

When he speaks, Armin Meiwes has a habit of mumbling toward the end of the sentence. He also swallows his words. S- and Z- sounds come out like "Sh," so that the word "gezogen" (moved) sounds like "getzhogn." At the same time, he pouts like a little schoolboy. Together, these habits give his accounts an almost innocent sound. His favorite clichés in speaking are "well then," "accordingly," and "seen thus."

"How was your mother able to afford the manor house?"

"Well then. My mother never learned anything of use. Accordingly, she worked as an Avon cosmetics consultant and sold electronic devices and vacuum cleaners for Electrolux. My father took all our money with him. It was only seven years later that she succeeded, through salary deductions, in earning our keep. It was a War of the Roses par excellence," he said grandiosely, referring to the movie of ultimate divorce nightmare. "We often feared for our existence and didn't know what we would have to eat in the evening. My grandmother, Paula, also had only a small pension and left nothing to us after her death. Seen thus, my mother's only recourse was work. She tried somehow to come up with money."

"How did she then?"

"My mother delivered newspapers and pamphlets at night. She didn't want anyone to see her having to do this. I often saw her weeping because she didn't know how we would get on. I also think she was lonesome, but we never talked about it. She had her problems and I had mine."

Armin Meiwes's eyes turn toward the barred prison window.

"Were you alone with your mother on the estate during vacation as well?"

"No, that is where she really blossomed because she didn't have to work. My school chums, Uwe and Berthold, often came along with us on vacation. We made a tree-house, played Cops and Robbers, Cowboys and Indians, sawed branches off trees—we did everything that was fun. That was really nice."

*

It was here in the idyllic setting of Hesse at the start of the 19th century that two brothers, Jacob and Wilheim Grimm, sons of a pastor, collected and published two hundred and seven tales including the well known "Hänsel and Gretel," "Little Red Riding Hood," "Sleeping Beauty," and "Snow White." The stories were originally intended for adults, but they made their way into the children's library. These were gruesome tales, like that of "Der Struwwelpeter" (Touselheaded Peter), in which children's fingers are cut off, or they burn, or starve to death. Even the lovely "Snow White" is supposed to choke painfully to death on the poisoned apple offered to her by her jealous mother-in-law. A public prosecutor would find in "Snow White" all manner of crimes: bodily injuries, torture, multiple attempted murders including fatal stabbing, strangling and poisoning. Finally, the story offers cannibalism as well. At the conclusion, the mother-in-law is thrust into live coals, where she dances herself to death, and then the happy townsmen eat her liver.

The bloodthirsty tales of the pious brothers arouse horror even today in millions of children when their mothers read aloud to them at night. Fearfully, they clutch Mommy's arm in their little hands until their eyelids close and sleep frees them from these terrifying misadventures.

*

The child Armin Meiwes can't get to sleep, although it's already after seven o'clock. The winter wind rattles the windows and doors of the lonely manor house in Wüstefeld. His mother, Waltraud Meiwes, has already put on her nightdress. Now she gently moves herself backward and forward, her eyes closed, in the rocking chair of her living room on the ground floor. At her feet sits Armin Meiwes with the open book of *Grimm's Fairy Tales*. He is reading to his mother the story of "Hänsel and Gretel": "Then she grabbed Hänsel with her claw-like hand, dragged him into a stable and locked him up, pulling the bar across the wooden door. Yell as he might, it was in vain. Then she went to Gretel, shook her awake and ordered, 'Get up, lazy-bones. Get water and cook your brother something tasty. I have put him in the stable and there he shall stay until he gets nice and fat. When he is fat, I shall eat him.'" Waltraud Meiwes giggles to herself without opening her eyes. Her belly, her right hand lying upon it, shakes along with her merrily. The story relaxes her, and at this moment, which Armin always waits for, he reaches for the night lamp and puts it out.

It is now pitch-dark. The boy leaves, as he does so often, without a goodnight kiss, and goes upstairs to his room.

His mother has named the room "Meadow," and there is a brightly colored wood plaque on the door with the name cheerfully displayed across it. With a single leap, the boy is in bed, pulling the covers over his head. He broods. What so confuses the lad is the fact that when he hears these fairy tales, he feels none of the fear the other kids do. No, he likes it when Hänsel is in trouble, caged, and about to be consumed. Armin Meiwes doesn't close his eyes for a long time.

Twelve-year-old Armin Meiwes finds pleasure in daydreaming of another person being absorbed into himself. The desire to slaughter and eat others grows stronger. The *Grimm's Fairy Tales* and the animal butchering he obsessed on left him feeling a lack, the one thing he was not getting for himself: the experience of killing and eating human flesh.

"That I read to my mother once I had reached the age of six did not seem unusual to me. It was normal."

For Armin Meiwes, much was normal that to other boys his age would have seemed strange. I recall an interview my wife and I conducted with the filmmaker and Oscar-winner Roman Polanski, and the experience occupied us for a long time.

Polanski, at the age of seven, was cruelly separated from his parents, brothers, and sisters by the Nazis. Roman Polanski had to grow up alone—apart from the SS-thugs who imprisoned him—in a concentration camp. To the question of whether his existence in those circumstances was dreadful, he replied, "For me it was normal." Like Armin Meiwes, he knew nothing else. The difference between the cannibal and the film director, though, hardly needs explanation; Roman Polanski worked out his trauma in films such as his acclaimed "The Pianist," while Armin Meiwes expressed his in reality.

"Mr. Meiwes, what is pleasing to you about the *Grimm's Fairy Tales*?"

"I would say that murder and manslaughter are everyday events."

"And cannibalism...."

"Yes, yes, like in 'Red Riding Hood.' The wolf wants to eat the girl. And in the story, the wolf eats six goat kids, leaving only one alive. The wolf isn't really a beast; he is a symbol for a wild man. The fairy tale veils this, keeps it secret, but still the truth is there."

"And that excited you?"

"Yes, surely. The fantasy films of today like 'Lord of the Rings' do not excite me. They are unrealistic and I get nothing from them. Fairy tales may be fantasy as well, but the earlier fairy tales held a grain of truth."

"Didn't you, as a boy, look for answers in these tales?"

"My mother never discussed the issues within the stories and I didn't bring it up with her. But yes, I thought about them. Why can't Hänsel free himself? Why does Gretel go along with fattening him up? And why does the witch want to cook Hänsel and eat him? My only explanation was that, through consumption, one person remains with another."

*

I wash my "Strammer Max" down with a double espresso with foaming milk—the highlight of my meal. I pay and leave the "Gerichtsschänke." I'm behind schedule. For me, as for many other Hessen tourists, Rotenburg an der Fulda has become a popular tourist spot because of Armin Meiwes's deed. People would like to know where this dreadful crime took place. "It is a source of incomprehensible fascination that the impossible became possible," explained psychiatrist Andreas Marneros during a TV discussion panel about the Armin Meiwes case.

The cannibal's attorney, Harald Ermel, has organized a private tour of the town. At the stroke of twelve, I step into the historic town hall square. I catch sight of the attorney's colleague, Michael Bock, who greets me from the distance with a wave of his arm. His vigorous handshake leaves a definite impression. His frameless glasses make the face of the fifty-five-year-old—if one's imagination smoothes away the wrinkles below his eyes—almost boyish. Ermel had read me off a laundry list of Bock's credentials over the phone, the admiration obvious in his voice. "Michael Bock is a former college instructor in tax law, he was in the CDU (political party) until 1997, and he was town councilor and the head of the cultural department in Bad Hersfeld."

Mr. Bock starts up the conversation in a grand manner. "You're lucky to have caught me. Yesterday, I was at the Shania Twain concert." A typical politician, he speaks amicably. Still, I did not understand his connection to the matter. He starts right in with the facts, speaking tirelessly, his brown mustache moving up and down on his upper lip like a little furry animal. "Rotenburg has a long history," he begins his lecture. "It was first mentioned in documents in 769 A.D., with six estates and ninety acres of land. Here, on the steps of the town hall, is the town's historic coat of arms, a branch with three linden leaves." On it is engraved a little verse:

> *Rotenburg on the Fulda—the town*
> *On the shield three green leaves hath.*
> *The mountain is red, the shield white.*
> *He thrives who lives by honest work.*

Rotenburg is known for its well-maintained half-timbered houses, the lawyer informs me. The jewel of the little town is the Landgraval Rotenburg Castle, an architectonic mishmash thrown together over several centuries. After the original structure from the year 1470 burned down in a fire, it was reconstructed in 1570 by Landgrave Wilhelm IV and his son in renaissance style. In 1750, the west wing was built in baroque style, and, finally, forty years later, the north wing was completed in empire style. Since 1953 the castle has housed the Hessian Land Finance School and the Training Offices of the Hessian Street and Traffic Administration.

Another symbol of Rotenburg is the late-Gothic St. Jakobi Church, whose predecessor was already recognizable on the town's coat of arms in 1248. It too fell victim to the great fire and was rebuilt and enlarged in the following century. The last great reconstruction was the renovation of the steeple in classical style in 1819.

Overall, the setting of the bloody deed resembles the landscape picture on a cheap carpet. On the hill to the south sits the Heart and Blood Circulation Center, HKZ for short, a mighty concrete hulk with two hundred and thirty-three beds. Because of its modern techniques and good physicians, the center enjoys an excellent reputation beyond the borders of the Land. When the doctors are out of sight, most of the patients permit themselves a draft beer in one of the numerous inns, like the "Gerichtsschänke" already mentioned, or behind a chestnut tree on the Fulda River bank. If they wish to be even naughtier, they secretly puff on a cigarette. Meanwhile, young mothers push their strollers along the river and chat about the weather. Retired people shuffle across the road with their dachshunds. A policeman stands at the pedestrian crossing and doesn't know what he's supposed to direct.

Up to the moment when it became known that Armin Meiwes had consumed the engineer Bernd Brandes, most Germans had never heard of Rotenburg an der Fulda. The most notorious crime the town had been able to claim to that point occurred in 1982 when Ulla von Bernus, the so-called "Witch of Berlingen," allegedly harried a couple of people to their deaths. A crime of this magnitude managed to merit a five-page article in the magazine HÖRZU. The residents of Rotenburg reported to me that the woman had only wanted to earn a quick mark with her hocus-pocus. Rotenburg was regarded, it must be said, as a sleepy provincial community.

The address, now become sadly famous, stands a little outside, however; that is exactly where I want to go. My city guide, Michael Bock, now takes his leave and wishes me all the best. I make off, driving my rented car out of the town center past the famous half-timbered houses. Here Bock would surely have wanted to explain further details. In Germany, there are over two million such houses, eighty percent of them plastered over or disguised. Those buildings in which the half-timbering is still visible give, even from the outside, a glimpse into the historic development of building styles, the formation of tows, the economic and social position of the man for whom the house was built, as well as its former utilization. When you drive along Regional Highway 3336 in Rotenburg, which after five kilometers leads in the direction of Niederthalhausen, you see rising up on your left, at the end of the street, a three-story half-timbered house with a fully-developed attic. Its many corners strikingly recall the house of Norman Bates of Alfred Hitchcock's "Psycho," where he lived, like our cannibal, with his mother.

The Meiwes house is located on a three-thousand-square-meter plot of land at the edge of the residential section of Wüstefeld. It is surrounded on all sides by seven neighboring houses, two belonging to farmers engaged mainly in growing cattle feed and farm products. The Meiwes family estate, though showing signs of neglect, is the real attraction of Rotenburg. The manor house stands powerful and ominous before the visitor. The iron gate at the end of the driveway, which branches directly off from Highway 3336, is secured with a pink-colored child's bicycle padlock.

As if taken from a film scene, an old children's swing gently moves in the garden with the wind. A gold-colored Mercedes Benz 280SE, an old concrete mixing machine, and a collapsible aluminum ladder are rusting away in the garden next to an apple tree. Between the Mercedes and the house, an unpaved path leads toward the horse stable, then peters out in a meadow. Boards with wood carvings adorn the fifty-six windows. On the north gable of the house, toward Highway 3336, a covered balcony is attached to the second story. On the west side, left of the front door, a winter garden projects from the front of the house. On the oaken double front door, with rectangular barred glass sections in its upper portion, a shiny bronze lion's head with a knocker beckons visitors to announce their presence. The "Wüstefeld Estate" structure was built as early as 900 A.D. as a border station between Hessen and Thuringia. In 1266, the building was mentioned for the first time in a document. In the course of circling around the house, I indulge in fancy: If the house were a face, it would show a grinning toothless mug. In truth, it's an old hovel where you can hear the fleas cough. It is a very quiet, spooky place.

Suddenly, a cobalt blue blur approaches from the countryside. A tractor chugs in my direction. Farmer Manfred Stück is on his way to our appointment, traveling in rustic fashion. He is the cannibal's neighbor and has known Armin Meiwes since childhood. He stops his machine directly in front of Armin Meiwes's spook house. Only after the engine dies down, does he begin to speak. "Awful place, isn't it?" he says in greeting, jumping down from the John Deere tractor.

"To be honest," I tell him, "I wouldn't like to spend my vacation here."

Farmer Stück scratches his head. "Yeah. As a hotel it probably wouldn't do," he concurs.

We tramp across the field surrounding Armin Meiwes's house, past the terrace where piles of wood are being seasoned, where among other things, a grill, a flower vase, and a circular saw are lying about. After a few minutes of silence, we begin chatting.

"Burglars have been here already looking for money and computers. But the police took anything of value a long time ago. What annoys me and my wife, Meike, are those devil-worshippers who come after midnight in black robes and pale faces and bury skulls in the ground. Often you hear this awful rock music when they park in front of the house. Then we can't get a wink of sleep. I have to leave at five a.m. to take care of the cows."

"Why don't you call the police?"

He shrugged his shoulders helplessly. "Oh, by the time the cops get here, they are long gone."

He tells me now and then that tourists passing by wind down their windows and ask about the old jalopy in the garden. "They always use the same words," the farmer goes on. "They say, 'It's a shame about the old Benz. Do you know who it belongs to and how we can buy it?' They have no idea that the owner is a cannibal and will be sitting behind bars for the next fifteen years." In a way, neighbor Stück seems a little proud to know Armin Meiwes.

I ask why he thinks his school friend became a cannibal. He reflects for a few moments. "Oh, an explanation—what can I say?" He pauses to ruminate some more about the question. "An explanation? I can't fathom why someone becomes a man-eater, feeds on humans, and eats them." Farmer Stück doesn't think too much of philosophical or psychological analysis. As a native of the area, he believes in what he sees; seed and harvest, good and bad. Since his son at the age of seven developed a brain tumor the size of a hen's egg, he doesn't think so highly of God anymore either. "My son never cursed, never said a bad word, and got sick just the same." So it's better to talk to him about the past and better times. Farmer Stück changes the subject himself and points toward the hill. "There is where I have my new stud farm. Nice, isn't it? Forty horses are stabled there—that's where Armin and I, when we were boys, always ran around in the field."

Abruptly, he stops short on the graveled road between Armin Meiwes's house and the field, his mind searching backwards in time for the beginnings of his relationship with Meiwes. "I was born in March of 1962, Armin in December of 1961. I'm only four months younger. People get odd ideas because the newspapers say Armin had an unhappy childhood. Well, he had the kind of childhood many people can only dream about. He lived here in Wüstefeld and he had a pony. I still know its name; it was 'Polly.' He harnessed her to a little carriage and trotted about Wüstefeld in it. He had chickens and sheep and the like. For a boy, you couldn't grow up better, could you?"

As we walked across the soggy ground soaked by the February rain, his rubber boots made sucking noises as he sunk deeper and deeper into the mud. My gym shoes felt as if they were pulling off my feet. Not letting myself get distracted by the physical obstacles of our walk, I go on the attack.

"A happy childhood, you say? What of his mother?"

"His mother, his mother," he repeated. "I knew his mother, of course. As a small boy, I was in that house of theirs. His mother was a bit odd. She had an affair with a sheep farmer who lived here by the name of Vladimir D. At that time, in divorce matters, the issue of guilt was still a deal breaker. That's why Detlef M., her ex, didn't have to make support payments, not even for Armin. He walked scot-free." He waved dismissively with his right hand and then put it quickly back in his pants pocket.

"That was surely hard for Mrs. Meiwes to accept?" I venture sympathetically. He lowers his head, swings it from left to right like an ox, and drawls, "We-e-l-l-l." Farmer Stück fills his cheeks with air as if getting ready for a big response.

"Frau Meiwes had no connections here in the village. She lived there in the big house, you might say, twenty-four hours a day. She didn't even care to go to the door. Only on Sundays they went out in their carriage. She preferred wearing a dirndl with frills, and she wore enormous, funny hats. She looked like somebody from another century. Armin sat next to her like a timid little mouse." He seemed lost for a moment in the memory. "In general, Armin was, at least on the outside, friendly, pleasant, and forthcoming, like many murderers. They don't let others know what is really in their minds. My father always said it's hard to get a person to drop their defenses," declares Farmer Stück, now playing the amateur criminal psychologist, but hardly convincingly.

*

Son of a neighboring farmer, Manfred Stück is fifteen years old and his world overlaps with that of his friend, Armin Meiwes. On this warm September afternoon, shortly before two p.m., Manfred is feeding the horses in their paddock when he notices Armin about a hundred meters away, pulling a lawnmower from the woodshed. He is wearing a shirt with orange and blue stripes, neatly tucked into his tight blue jeans. Around the boy's waist, a brown leather belt is draw much too tight, making his upper body appear squeezed off. Even though the temperature is hitting the mid-eighties under the glaring midsummer sun, Armin is intent on his work. He fills the tank with gasoline and begins going back and forth with the lawnmower, neatly trimming the grass.

Then, from out of the house, comes Armin's mother, Waltraud Meiwes, striding onto the lawn. The bitterness of recent years has made her body shrink. Her skin is wrinkled, her voice thin and screeching. Her tone is so shrill she seems a nasty old maid to Manfred. Waltraud Meiwes wears a frilly skirt, so unfashionable she looks a porcelain doll that sits behind locked doors in the dining room hutch. Suddenly, Waltraud Meiwes yells imperiously, so that Manfred Stück can hear her all the way from the paddock. "Armin, stop mowing now! And bring out the chair to me." Stolidly, Armin does what his mother has ordered. He goes back to the house and pulls a white basket chair into the garden. His mother seats herself without a word and sits, watching her son. Then Waltraud's voice screeches again. "Armin! Bring me some coffee and a slice of cake, and use our best china and silver. And don't forget the side table."

Armin Meiwes stoically turns the motor off and goes back into the house. A few moments later, with visible effort, he lugs over the heavy little stone table, its upper surface tiled in the Florentine style with a chessboard pattern. He returns to the house, and shortly after, he is back again with the Meissen porcelain plate, a cherry tart upon it. The neighbor boy Manfred Stück knows the little drama as it is repeated every weekend in the Meiwes family garden. Manfred suddenly feels sad as he watches, and thinks to himself, "Forever ordering him about. In his place, I would have, I don't know—said something, done something. His mother really has Armin under her thumb. Apparently, he is afraid of her."

*

"Oh, yeah, the way she ordered him around," continues Farmer Manfred Stück, then he catches himself, not wanting to say too many bad things about Armin's childhood. "Perhaps it is normal, when one lives under the same roof alone with an elder, to be constantly ordered around. But does that destine you to become a man-eater? I mean, just because of an overbearing mother? I don't know...."

To neighbor Manfred Stück, Armin Meiwes's bestial deed is just as incomprehensible as it is for other people all over the village of Wüstefeld. To further his frustration at such a turn of events is Stück's emotional connection to the

Meiwes manor. "It is a shame," he fumes. "That house once belonged to my grandparents, but was sold off under a period of financial distress. Now, look at it, in ruin, and in shame, all because of Armin Meiwes."

Farmer Stück suddenly changes his tone and becomes downright angry, as if his brain had shifted gears from kindness to hostility. "Armin and his mother never had enough money to maintain such an enormous house. It's a crumbling old wreck. Thirty-six rooms and just two people to live in it. But they held on to it. Look over there!" He gestures furiously towards the front of the house and rants on. "I tell you now, the old jalopy he's got parked over there, the Mercedes 280, why not even a half-wit would drive it. Twenty liters of gas, but Armin was proud as a peacock of that car."

I try to calm him down. "When you look at the house as it stands today, what do you associate with it?"

"Proud as a peacock when he sat in it," Farmer Stück won't let himself be diverted. He sticks firmly to his train of thought. "There in the Mercedes he felt like a king. I said, 'Armin, what are you going to do with that pile of scrap?' Yet he didn't consider it so and when he and his mother went shopping in it, you might as well have watched the king and queen drive off. He loved that car and he loved the house. If you look in the telephone book, you will find not just 'Armin Meiwes,' but 'Armin Meiwes, Wüstefeld Manor House.' He wouldn't ever leave here, not until they took him away."

His anger won't die down. Manfred Stück takes a deep breath, hisses, and declares, "Right now, I don't care one way or the other what happens to him," although clearly he does. "I try not to waste my time thinking about it, but I have three children and when Armin gets out of jail, maybe he will want to eat more people. That's what worries me," Farmer Stück emphasizes. "In the news they said, if someone eats bull's meat and can't get veal, the veal becomes all the more delicious in his eyes, especially if you have tasted it and liked it better. I don't know that this won't be the same for Armin."

Farmer Stück goes on unloading repressed anger. "Armin has as yet only eaten Mr. Brandes, who was age forty-four. Maybe the day will come when he says, 'Oh, hmm, my, maybe a twenty-four-year-old will taste better,' or he goes even further and wants the most tender of meat, the young ones, maybe my children."

I must stop the farmer's rage. "Armin Meiwes only eats people who want to be eaten," I protest. "He is not like the witch in 'Hänsel and Gretel.'"

"Oh, yes, that is what I have always said," he conceded. "But, still, no one would have expected Armin to do what he did. That he was a bit odd and withdrawn and perhaps had homosexual leanings; that is nothing bad. But what he got up to there..." His voice trailed off as his eyes traveled over to the manor.

I let him gather his thoughts and calm down. He says nothing for a minute.

"What I object to," says the farmer finally, "is that Armin ate Mr. Brandes. I mean, Brandes wanted to be killed; that is clear. He wanted it and Armin carried it out. But, that he then grills him! Sits down and eats the flesh? That is too much!"

This is true, I think. "What would Manfred Stück say to his neighbor Armin Meiwes if Armin stood before him now?" I ask.

"'Armin, I would say, what kind of shit did you do there?' That's what I'd say to him! I've already thought about it several times. So, if he came here, I'd stop my tractor and ask him to his face, 'Just what got into you to do such a thing?'"

Our conversation was over. Bidding me farewell, the farmer's firm, heavy hand crushes my writer's fingers like a fruit press.

*

As I arrive the following week at the Kassel Penitentiary, prisoner Armin Meiwes awaits me—again in his starched blue-and-white penal uniform—in a small visitor's room, a whitewashed cubicle measuring one hundred and fifty square feet in size, with a wooden table, two chairs, and a barred window. On the left, by the entrance, is a washbasin. At the other end of the room, a forlorn rubber tree despairingly holds out against withering.

"Hello, Mr. Stampf? How did you like Rotenburg?" he asks politely.

"It's quite romantic," I respond. "It must have been nice for you when you were a child."

"Well, yes..." he hesitates and then starts the sentence over. "You could say so."

"I met your neighbor, Farmer Manfred Stück," I add truthfully to test his reaction.

He smiles and doesn't seem surprised. "I once asked Manfred if he thought I was homosexual. He ducked the question. He said, 'Armin, you must know yourself what sex you are attracted to.' Then we dropped it and did not discuss it again."

"Are you homosexual?"

Armin Meiwes bristles and answers somewhat heatedly. "Now, wait a minute! I am bisexual." He considers this important. "That is really something quite different. In regards to sex, I am chiefly oriented towards women. When we are talking about friendship and affection, I don't care what body it lives in."

"We'll come back to that later," I say, firmly dropping the subject. I will come back to the topic another time, for I have noticed since the outset of our interviews, Armin Meiwes needs to have clear preparation for deeper discussions. He is used to it from childhood.

I confront him with an old black-and-white photograph showing his mother, Waltraud Meiwes, in her mid-twenties.

"When you look at your mother, what do you feel?"

He hesitates a little in responding. "Well, in principle, fine, it's my mother. As a young woman, she was a very pretty woman."

"But this picture radiates an emotion, don't you think?"

"Yes, it certainly does."

"But, what emotion, Mr. Meiwes?"

"I know the photo from our photo album. For sure, as she looks upwards at the photographer, she has the radiance of a princess."

"Did your mother keep this look?"

"Well, later she changed, of course. Being abandoned hardened her and left her really embittered."

When Armin Meiwes talks about his mother, it is without the slightest emotion. The child Armin Meiwes, who now sits opposite me as a grown man, grew up under a domineering mother, lost in a thirty-six-room house. The boy didn't rebel, but chose inner isolation. Never did anyone see Armin Meiwes cry. "A man doesn't cry," his mother used to say. All his life he had hidden his emotional world from the eyes of others.

Armin Meiwes says, "She thought she could control me. But she couldn't control my thoughts."

*

His mother taught him, "You don't say anything bad," but she forgot to instruct him that he shouldn't *think* anything bad as well. There lies a great difference. That was how the abnormal thoughts of the son, always outwardly obedient, could develop undisturbed. In the questioning of the defendant in the East Hessen Police Headquarters (File No. ST/0132109/2002) on December 10, 2002, Armin Meiwes states to the police officials, in answer to the question as to when he first noticed his cannibalistic leanings:

> *As a boy, between and 8 and 12 years old.... It seems to be related to the full moon. Sometimes it's so strong then that I'd like to take someone's life. I would say it works in a cycle of six to eight weeks. That's also what others have said who are inclined that way.*

Therefore, Armin Meiwes fully admits that he was, in his mind by the age of twelve, "a fully realized cannibal."

"Was it coincidental that your room and your mother's were so close to each other?"

"No accident," he stammers. "It was that way on purpose. It made sense for our rooms to be on the second floor right by the stairs and not at the end of the long hallway. If anything happened, we could quickly go back and forth. And, at the time, there was only one bathroom upstairs, so it was practical for both our rooms to be near it."

"Did you ever talk to your mother about sexuality?"

"Relatively seldom. I didn't really, no, not at all, of that I am absolutely sure. But now, I wouldn't know if others at the time did so with their mothers."

"Who told you about sex then?"

"They told us about it in school. In sexual instruction and the like. But nothing was discussed as to what should be talked about in the home."

"Have you ever thought of consuming your mother?"

"No, I always wanted only to have a brother inside me, a man; this is what I was missing."

"But your mother was always sweet and kind, wasn't she?"

Armin Meiwes is silent.

"Did your mother hug and kiss you?"

"Well, when I was a boy and fell down."

"Hugged you—when you fell down? How often does a boy fall down? Twice a year?"

Armin Meiwes is silent again.

"Did your mother ever take you in her arms?"

"When I was sick or in pain."

How often is a child sick? Once, at most, twice a year? Armin Meiwes, in purely statistical terms, got caresses four times a year! Here begins for me the split in Armin Meiwes's boyhood emotional life. According to Sigmund Freud, his father—"the creature the boy admires"—is no longer there. The consoling breast and caressing hand of his mother—these he never received. Waltraud Meiwes was embittered and coarsened at heart. The abandonment by his father combined with the coldness of his mother left Armin traumatized. With no help in dealing with his feelings, he moved into adulthood with a paralyzing fear of permanent loss. Such a lack of growth allowed his confused childhood fantasies to remain as such and become full-fledge sexual aberrations as an adult—perversion, fetishism, inversion. In Armin Meiwes, all of these are combined and there is no counterbalance in his life. Sexual abuse has been widely studied by experts, but abuse in the mother-son relationship has gone largely ignored. "I had friends aplenty," says Armin Meiwes, "but I could not speak of what I imagined, that of having another boy inside me. And I could not speak of it with my mother either. I was left alone with my fears and worries."

"My relationship with my mother," notes Armin Meiwes in his statement on the forensic sexual-medical opinion, "could have been described as love-hate." Further, he declares, "I despise my father. Things might have turned out differently if it hadn't taken him ten years to speak with me. He might, perhaps, have written a long letter letting me know that he loved me, and that way, he would have been able to counteract my extreme fear of loss and perhaps even have prevented the act itself."

The picture Armin Meiwes has imprinted in his mind, to this day, is imbued with hatred and contempt.

*

The judgment of the Kassel District Court in the penal case of Armin Meiwes (AZ 2650 Js 36980/2) of January 30, 2004, offers this observation:

> The defendant, who felt abandoned after the departure of his father and his half-brother Ilja B., identified himself with his mother Waltraud Meiwes in her feeling of abandonment, and bent to her desires and needs, seeking thereby to avoid falling out of favor with her.

*

Overall, the result of these unfortunate circumstances left Waltraud and Armin Meiwes locked in a relationship of little to no communication. Both lived alone with their fear of loss and each had taken refuge in an inner world. "My mother had completely withdrawn. Apparently, she feared if she began another relationship, she would be abandoned again," declares Armin Meiwes. Mother and son hovered next to each other like two connected atoms—until three decades later, upon the death of Waltraud Meiwes, the bomb exploded.

"If you were to describe your mother's attributes, what would they be?"

"Oh...."

"Was she controlling?"

"Yes."

"Dominant?"

"Yes."

"Decisive?"

"Yes."

"Wounding?"

"Yes."

"Hurtful?"

"Now and then."

Expert witness Prof. Dr. Beier believes that Waltraud Meiwes even invented illnesses to bind her son to her.

"Mr. Meiwes, have you ever thought of doing away with your mother?"

"Oh...."

"I am not a public prosecutor."

Armin Meiwes reflects for a few moments, and then it bursts out of him.

"Well, yes. Once, after my mother had complained to me of pain in her legs because of her osteoporosis, I had to help her down from the third story to the ground floor. We had to take the wide staircase in the manor house with a total of forty-eight steps. For one moment, as I supported my mother and she hung on to me, I thought of Gretel finally taking action against the witch who wanted to cook her brother and pushed the witch instead into the oven. I thought to myself, one good shove to my mother and it's finally over." Yet fifteen-year-old Armin does not push his mother down the stairs. Instead, he swallows his rage, which from now on begins to grow like a cancerous ulcer in his body.

AN UNBROKEN HORSE BECOMES RESTIVE,
AN UNRESTRAINED SON BECOMES UNPREDICTABLE

(Jesus Sirach 30:8)

Chapter 3

THE MEAT

"**D**ON'T GET EATEN," jokes my attorney on the telephone this summery May Wednesday as I start out from Hamburg on the way to Kassel, three hundred and eight kilometers away.

The sentence, capped by a "heh-heh," pursues me since I have been working on this book like a bad joke no one can resist, each jokester expecting to get a laugh from me out of it. "Thanks so much," I answer once more, slightly annoyed. How can my friends truly understand that the subject more and more "devours me?"

While they make jokes about the cannibal of Rotenburg, he pursues me into my sleep. Like the hum of a refrigerator always present in the background, Armin Meiwes rattles in my head unceasingly. My research is leading to surprising revelations as certain ideas recur in my dreams again and again.

I am plagued by nightmares. One dream has Armin Meiwes holding a pistol to my chest. Twenty meters behind me stands, in support, the Editor-in-Chief of RTL, who has Armin Meiwes in the sights of a shotgun. "Put your weapon down," I beg the Cannibal. He ignores my request. Armin Meiwes is threatening me, but instead of hating him, I feel pity. I weep. No, I wail, and am sad. Why? After all the Cannibal has told me of his childhood, I am suddenly sorry for him. Do I have the right? Can one feel sympathy for a butcher? Yes, one can. But I remind myself I must remain neutral for an objective appraisal of the case. That alone requires my professional ethos, and now more than ever, I am morally guilty.

Unavoidably, however, these nocturnal thoughts mingle with reality, and I am again at their mercy. In the dark of night, the man-eater is again up to mischief in my sleep. Armin Meiwes is making sausage with a meat grinder out of the bloody remains of his mother. As he works, his mind is tranquil and smiles to himself with satisfaction, as if he has just buttered a slice of toast for breakfast. In the morning I wake up with a pounding headache. I'm so exhausted and soaked in cold sweat that I can hardly get out of bed.

On this trip to my next interview with the Cannibal, I try to appraise the nightmares in conversations with myself. For a man, the very thought of having his penis cut off is simply the most disgusting, repulsive, horrid, yes, "ugh"-inducing of all notions. This movie in my head hurts physically and makes me afraid.

Psychoanalyst Sigmund Freud speaks of the fear of castration that is already present in small male children. "As soon as boys discover that many human beings have penises and many (women, that is) do not, they assume the latter have lost their organ by castration and thus, fear the loss of their own sex organ." This fear of loss has planted itself over millennia deep in the male genes. The reason may go back to prehistoric times, when clans were ruled more often by women than generally assumed. This in turn led men to brandish an erect penis as a symbol of strength and fertility. In ancient Greece and Rome, the god Priapus was worshipped and immortalized in order to emphasize the dominance and strength of men. A vestige of phallic symbolism is the setting up of the maypole: a twenty-meter-high wooden organ with rings, representing the vagina.

For me, the unmanning is like chopping off the roots of a tree. The sap of life is taken away.

*

Three and a half hours later, the butcher Armin Meiwes and I are once again seated opposite each other on the ground floor of the Kassel Penitentiary. The duty officer has assigned us to "Conference Room 1," which, soundproof as it is, ordinarily would be used for confidential consultations between inmates and their attorneys. The glass box has an area of four-point-eight square meters, and in the center stands a simple wooden table, ninety-by-sixty centimeters. Three conference chairs made of chromium, covered with anthracite-colored cloth, are placed close to it. I feel like a chicken in a coop. It seems as if with every breath, the temperature of the glass case rises. Droplets of sweat are already forming on Armin Meiwes's forehead. His cold Marlboro breath wafts into my nose.

"I just smoked a cigarette," he says apologetically, as if he has read my mind.

"No problem," I lie. "I had some chewing gum with me, but the officers at the door took it away. They probably don't want you to get Spearmint between your teeth."

Armin Meiwes grins broadly. I look at his bared incisors and I immediately regret encouraging thoughts of eating.

"I dreamt of you," I say, opening today's interview.

He looks up, surprised.

"About a meat grinder you were using to convert your mother into ground beef."

He isn't shocked.

I want to find out if my dream has any basis.

"Have you a meat grinder at home?"

"The meat grinder," he says after thinking a moment, "I always saw at the butcher shop. I often went there as a boy. I liked the technique they used to grind up fresh meat."

Well, there you are. Now we're getting warmer.

*

In September, 1977, Armin is sixteen years old and nearly five-foot-eleven inches tall. His body has grown unusually large for that height, making him a bit of a Frankenstein. His outward appearance, however, is nothing compared to the monstrous ideas sprouting within his frame. On this afternoon, he hurries downstairs from the third floor of the apartment house at Hohe Warte 19, in the Holsterhausen section of Essen, where he is living with his mother Waltraud until the move to Wüstefeld in 1980. The trade school student jumps onto his grass-green bicycle and pushes down hard on the pedals. His destination is located about a seven-minute ride away in Gemarkenstrasse: the "Siebenand" butcher shop. Armin leaves his trusty bike at the entrance to the shop, but not in the bicycle stand, and enters the building. "Hi, old pal," the gangly youth calls out politely as he goes in, and, going up to a boy his age, he happily hugs his former schoolmate, Uwe, with whom he attended secondary school.

Uwe began a training course in the butcher shop a few weeks earlier. Armin stands in front of the board where current offerings are written in chalk—"fresh blood sausage, 100 grams, 70 pence"—but his attention is now fixed more on the butcher's apprentice, Uwe, and his activities. "Well, what have you learned then?" Armin asks.

"Right now, I'm removing the legs and cutting up the meat," answers Uwe. "Look!" The boy takes a piece of beef weighing about three kilos off a silver hook, lays it on the blue-and-white tiled counter and goes to work with the big meat-carving knife. Slowly, the sharp blade slices through the butter-soft meat and separates it from the bone. Armin watches every move.

While the apprentice butcher filets and hammers the chunks of meat into cutlets, Armin stares into the display case. He sees the fresh livers, kidneys, and tongues, and in one corner of the display, he admires a pig's head. He gazes at it for a long while. Then he discovers the fresh beef sections laid out. They come from young bulls, heifers, oxen; they are bright- to medium-red, stringy, powerful, thin, and marbled with veins of fat. White plastic signs announce the various meat parts: filet, hip, neck, upper rib, lower belly, breast, shoulder, upper belly. The thin pieces of pork lying ready to sell on glass platters are bright pink and gleam with moisture. "Fresh cutlets for sale," reads the plastic sign stuck in the meat. Lost in thought, Armin, at the sight of the meat, gives in to the longings in his mind. He imagines he is looking at human flesh. In his mind's eye, he sees the names and photos of his school friends on the descriptive signs. It would be better if, on the meat sections, there could be something like: "Michael, 16, blond, lightly muscular, charming and friendly, likes playing football and doing handicrafts." Perhaps a fellow like Sandy in the TV series *"Flipper."* Armin Meiwes would give his life to taste such a morsel.

"And how are things with you?" asks the apprentice butcher for the second time.

"Oh, everything's okay. Tomorrow we have a German test and I am in good shape for it. Now I've got to go."

"Give my best to your Mom," the apprentice calls after him. But Armin is out of earshot. He grabs his bicycle and pumps hard back to the apartment in Essen. There he tiptoes up the stairs and locks himself in his room. Armin fantasizes how he would sniff one of his school friends, as one would a freshly blooming flower. How he would cut him up and hold his warm entrails in his hands. He longs so much for a boy who voluntarily would allow himself to be slaughtered, and whom he might take into himself.

*

These harbingers of the act he committed nearly three decades later are discussed in the opinion of the Kassel District Court, dated January 30, 2004 (AZ 2650 Js 36980/02):

> *Killing the person to be slaughtered by cutting his throat was part of the defendant's imaginings, but did not arouse him sexually. Rather, the thought of killing was for the defendant associated with the imminent fulfillment of his longing for bonding through consumption. Along with these fantasies, the defendant experienced to a reduced degree imaginary sexual contacts with men, as well as to a reduced degree with women, during masturbation. After graduation from junior high school, the defendant attended a trade school in Essen, until Waltraud Meiwes and the defendant moved in 1980 from Essen to Wüstefeld.*

*

Meanwhile, the glass cell in the clink is as steamy as a tropical hothouse.

"I'm really thirsty," says Armin Meiwes.

"Your whole life long you were also thirsty for love and sexual fulfillment," I respond, resuming our interview and taking pleasure in having successfully made such a clever segue.

"Mm, mm," is all he can answer. Armin Meiwes picks up the water glass and drains the two-tenths of a liter in a single gulp.

The prisoner sets down the glass, not in the middle, but on the outer right edge of the table. The move is as unusual as Armin Meiwes himself. He is always outside the box. And then for the first time, I notice his hands, which he places stolidly on the table, clasping his fingers together. The backs of his hands, with their eight knuckles sticking up, and the areas from his wrists to the fingers, are wavy and hilly from the veins that stand out. The hands of Armin Meiwes resemble, in miniature, a landscape of foothills.

His very skin is of parchment-like color and seems as fragile as paper. He has the pallor of a prisoner who has been too little in the sun. Once or twice a week at most, Armin Meiwes takes part with the other inmates of Kassel Penitentiary One in a half-hour walk around the inner courtyard under the watchful eyes of video cameras. "I work mostly in the laundry and I'm much too occupied with ironing. Furthermore, I would rather be alone with my thoughts."

His intertwined fingers are thick, long, and powerful. They can surely be strong gripping tools. There's no other way to put it: Armin Meiwes has the paws of a bear.

"How did you go on developing into a butcher?"

"The first highpoints of my cannibalistic fantasies surfaced when I was sixteen. Since then, there has hardly been a day when I haven't been preoccupied with the assimilation of another person. Sometimes more so, sometimes less. Over and over, I've imagined how I would cut open the belly, let the blood run out, and pull out the innards and intestines."

When Armin Meiwes talks about his abnormal tendencies, his fingers suddenly start drumming nervously on the table as if performing Tchaikovsky's First Piano Concerto. He actually hammers on the surface of the table. Is it a sign of arousal?

"Did these imaginings lead to sexual acts?"

"Yes," he says embarrassed. "I often, as we say politely, jerked off."

"When was it that you began working killing acts into your fantasies while masturbating?"

"When I was sixteen or seventeen. I imagined how I would rape a schoolmate, drug him, and take him into myself."

"Describe to me your first sexual experience."

He looks at me wide-eyed, as if he hadn't understood the question. "Don't remember," he mumbles.

"So many?"

"No, actually fewer." He squirms in embarrassment.

"Please answer more clearly. Did you have sex with boys or girls?"

"Well, naturally, I had acquaintances I grew up with. One of them was Volker. We've known each other since we were two. We explored each other's bodies and we mutually masturbated, but you can't describe that as a sexual act."

"But that is certainly a sexual act!"

"All right, yes, as far as I am concerned. At fourteen, I made my first approach to a girl in my school. We had set up at our home in Essen, a rumpus room in the cellar, and there were the wildest parties, and they led naturally to such things."

"Tell me about the wild parties."

His icy features soften and a smile plays about his mouth, as if he is glad I am leading him back to that bright moment in his life's memories. "Well, then," he goes on in a much brighter tone, "at home in Essen we had a large cellar, which as a teenager I converted into a party room. The room was twenty square meters in size, with an old side buffet of walnut, a commode, a desk, a washbasin, and several chairs. With my friend, Volker, I painted a sign with the word "Bar." Then we furnished our party room with plywood. With record player and speakers, we turned the cellar into a club, and then we partied and danced. The whole gang rocked with everything that was modern in the seventies. Kiss, Abba, Tina Turner; these we played the most."

Armin Meiwes bobs up and down against the chair arm as if he were rocking in memory at this very moment at that party. For the first time in our talks, there is a tone of pleasant frivolity, and for a few seconds, he is a happy man. "Then, my world was still fine...or halfway," he murmurs, toning down his exuberance.

In any case, he finds it easier, in his almost euphoric mood, to speak of his first kiss. During one of these "wild parties," the young people open a spontaneous competition: Who can make a real French kiss? Ute K. is the "kiss sacrifice" who joins the game eagerly. A blond, slender girl with a freckled nose, she seats herself on the desk below the window and awaits the "kisser kings." Armin is the first to have a go. He touches her lips and she leans further and further back until the two are entwined on the desk. The other kids whoop and clap at the sight. Armin canoodles with the girl for a good two minutes.

"How was the first kiss with a girl for you?"

"The first French kiss, the canoodling, were really nice and pleasant."

"You got on well with girls, then?"

"Yes, yes, yes," he says in hearty agreement.

"Describe your relations with women in more detail."

He answers immediately, without much reflection, and again in dry terms. "I didn't really feel especially drawn to women. During my school days, I had close friendships with several girls. Some edged closer to intimacy, to kissing and petting. But at that age, there were friendships with several boys. With them, too, I had intimate contacts, including petting."

"What did you think about during sex?"

"Well, during sex, I concentrated on the person in bed with me. I never trusted myself to let my slaughter fantasies influence me during sex. I was always a real guy. Ask about me!"

I do.

At Bad Hersfeld Police Headquarters, Armin Meiwes's schoolmate Berthold S., during interrogation on December 19, 2002 (Proceedings No. ST/132109/2002), gives this portrayal:

> *I have known Armin Meiwes since junior high school. That was the Kepler School here in Essen.... My first impression of him was that he was nice and perhaps a bit shy and inhibited, a typical country boy. It showed in his clothing, too. He wore a white shirt with polka dots and leather shorts. We all wore jeans.... They lived there in a small apartment, and part of it was sublet.[...] During school days we were a threesome: Armin, I, and Volker K.... Armin was a good student, especially in math and English. He was also well integrated in our class group. He didn't have friends other than Volker and me, mainly, I think, because he hardly had time. He had to do many chores at home. His mother was indisposed on occasion and complained of pains in her bones. Whether she was really sick I cannot say.... Mrs. Meiwes had taken on the care of two older women. ... For them, Armin had to do the shopping two or three times a week, wash windows or things like that. Even at home, he had many domestic chores, like doing the dishes, taking out the trash, gardening, or cleaning. His mother at that time sat mostly on the sofa and gave him orders. Many times, she said: "Minchen" was bad today; he has to keep to his room and can't come out to play.... I can't remember his ever speaking about his father. The same is true for his brothers.... For Armin, his family consisted only of him and his mother. When we were about in the sixth to eighth grades, I often went with Meiwes to Wüstefeld during vacations.... This house had*

interested us kids greatly; it seemed a bit like a haunted house. Yet all the rooms were orderly and furnished. All the beds were always made. One room stood out especially: it was the so-called wedding room. All the furnishings were pink and red. That room was only for show and wasn't occupied even by Mrs. Meiwes.... When we were between about fourteen and sixteen years old, we here in Essen wanted to give a party on the top floor at the Meiwes's. It had to be cleaned up first, of course. Volker and I started in alone, and Volker accidentally found a pile of porn magazines, but only with naked men. We suspected right away that Armin might be gay, since he always came stag to our parties and never brought a girl. When Armin came upstairs a little later, he got furious that we had found his magazines.

That was the first and last time, when I was there, that he got furious. We never after that dared to ask him if he was gay....

It must have been between 1982 and 1983 that we went with the whole gang to Wüstefeld.... We talked and recalled old times. Then it came about that Armin began trying to get closer to me and went so far as to kiss me. But I told him in no uncertain terms that I was not inclined in that direction, and that I would erase this attempted approach from my memory.... It occurred to me during our visit [Author's note: Easter, 2000], that Armin was leading two lives. One was his life outside of his estate. Here he was forthcoming, polite and at ease in company. His other life began behind the garden door. He was of course always nice and polite, but considerably more dominant. Here he was master of the house, and everything went according to his ideas. He wouldn't accept help. We couldn't touch anything, let alone move it one centimeter.

*

According to the testimony of his schoolmate Berthold S, his friends suspected that Armin Meiwes as a teenager was a shy homosexual. Much more interesting, however, is the fact that the split personality of Armin Meiwes was apparent to his friends. Outwardly he was, just as he is today, friendly, forthcoming, and nice. As soon as he was in his own world, however, within the "four walls" of his manor house, he changed, according to the statements of the witnesses, into the "strange, pedantic being who takes pleasure in deciding just how things are to be done."

Because of his inhibitions and inability to love, Armin Meiwes goes farther and farther into his inner world, in order to live out his fantasies undisturbed.

By his own statements, Armin Meiwes never experienced the "first great love," for either a girl or a boy. In talking with Armin Meiwes, one thing becomes clear to me: His dominating fear of loss has from the outset excluded a close relationship to other people and understanding the value of love. It was not that Armin Meiwes didn't want to love or that he didn't want to experience the emotions other human beings shared. He simply could not feel these emotions because he had not received love in his upbringing. He kissed girls and boys, felt it to be "pleasant," but a feeling deep in his heart, as felt by other young people his age, was beyond him. This also affected his sex life.

"Have you had problems with sexual fulfillment?"

Armin Meiwes hesitates this time before answering, so that nothing will be lacking in clarity. "I had and have problems when I am with a person for the first time and am about to introduce my organ into the vagina or anus. Then I have erection problems, but only the first time, not afterwards."

"Have you ever thought of assimilating with your female friends?"

He is incensed at my question. "Women? Consume them? Slaughter them? Nah, I only wanted to have a younger brother. That was the desire that really took root in my heart. But a woman in lovemaking, never, no. I always wanted only men to eat."

I show Armin Meiwes a somewhat faded photo of him at sixteen years old. He stands like a gasoline pump in front of the manor house in Wüstefeld, arms folded. His expression is serious, except for a wry smile that suggests to the viewer a hint of emotion. The prisoner pulls his rimless reading glasses from his left shirt pocket and puts them on. "I have to see it in sharper focus," he says. "I'm farsighted, one-point-five- and two- diopters. Without glasses, I can't see it." His eyes can now make out every detail of the photo.

"I can remember," he says, "that one time Berthold and I, with Volker and Uwe, raced one another on our bikes to Rotenburg. On a hill, I told Berthold I would like most to eat someone up. Berthold didn't take it a bit seriously and laughed. 'If you want to eat someone, then eat our teacher. You'd be doing all of us a favor.' I answered, 'No, I'd prefer a friend, a brother.' But Berthold just passed it over."

"Did you speak seriously at that time with anyone at all about your fantasies?"

"Exactly, exactly," he mutters to himself. Then he removes his glasses and puts them back in his shirt pocket. "I wasn't ready for it then. It's just like when you have to go to the dentist with a toothache. In the waiting room, your tooth suddenly doesn't hurt any more. I was afraid to open up to anyone, because at that time, I could sense my feelings were not right. That was why I could never develop more intimate contacts with people I liked and who meant somewhat more to me. Instead of 'I love you,' I would have had to say, 'I'd like to cut off a slice of you.' Whoever it might be, he wouldn't have understood that."

"Why did you never reveal yourself to someone like a therapist, to get a reaction?"

"I was ashamed of my feelings. I became a prisoner of my soul. I was—how should I put it—at the time, my own enemy."

I would not like to become Armin Meiwes's protector, but let's be honest: With whom was the teenaged Armin Meiwes to talk? His domineering mother? A Catholic priest? The farmer boy? His teacher?

Having grown up in Essen and the little town of Rotenburg an der Fulda at the end of the seventies, he probably would have been ostracized because of his homosexual inclination. How was he to confide in someone and tell them, "I want to eat a person"?

*

In the psychological assessment by Prof. Dr. Beier, the respected psychiatrist of the Charité Clinic of Humboldt University, Berlin, which was also cited in the first court opinion, Armin Meiwes is described thus:

> *At the level of self-classification, the defendant himself feels...with reference to his fetishistic-cannibalistic leanings, "already disturbed," but sees no feasible way to the realization of his desires with exclusively willing partners. On the meaning of the term "fetish," the specialist says persuasively that in the fetish (from the Portuguese "feitico" = magic) an "object" is chosen as the "pseudo-thou," behind which the beginning of a relationship with a real "thou," consequently a real person, retreats into the background. [Translator's note: The German familiar form "Du," meaning "You," is used in addressing those whom one knows well, in contrast to the formal "Sie," meaning "You," used in addressing those not well known.]*

"Fetishism," in western culture, is understood as meaning that a person feels sexual desire, and is capable of sexual activity, only in connection with certain objects— even parts of the body.

In 1905, Sigmund Freud presented, on the basis of clinical experiments, a psychological theory in which he sought to make understandable the occurrence of perversions. For him, abnormal thoughts in morbid fashion were an emotional problem which Freud understood as a radical emphasis on sexual desires. The perverted symptom, according to Freud, is a modified "normal." It arises from a mistaken—as is always the case—treatment of normal, unavoidably recurring conflicts in development. This was the first introduction of the concept in literature and later was elaborated upon by numerous psychoanalytically oriented authors, whose studies have in common that their reports centered almost exclusively on men who display perverse symptom formations.

*

The ensuing days I spend reading theoretical literature on cannibalism and books dealing with spiritual subjects. The Rotenburg Cannibal is now firmly convinced that the person consumed lives on in him, and, thereby, experiences love, similar to the millennia-old rites of primitive peoples, as practiced today in Papua-New Guinea. There, too, the fleshy parts of the deceased (mostly brains) are eaten, so that part of the beloved person remains in the community.

To my surprise, I find not a single chapter on the subject "Love-Cannibalism." At the World Health Organization not a single category includes the likes of Armin Meiwes. He apparently eludes all hitherto internationally recognized "categorizations." Armin Meiwes is, therefore, the first of his kind to practice "love-cannibalism," and can thus give information about a perversion that might otherwise be incomprehensible. At two o'clock in the morning, I finally come upon the work of British clergyman and psychologist Selwyn Hughes (1928-2006). The Welshman founded the mission and spiritual welfare work "CWR," and became known for his "Every Day with Jesus" prayers. George Carey, the late Archbishop of Canterbury, described him as a "giant of the faith."

Selwyn Hughes explains the sequence of obsession and sin in a unique manner, which seems to me clear and logical: the thought leads to tolerance—leads to inclination —leads to appetite—leads to hunger—leads to insatiable longing—and finally, to action. Accordingly, the one necessitates the next. He also has a sentence I underlined in red. "When a fight is lost, it is most often lost in the first decisive minutes." That coincides exactly with the statements of Armin Meiwes that as a twelve-year-old he was already a "completely developed cannibal," and from feelings of shame, could turn to no one. Conditioned throughout by his surroundings (dominant mother) and experiences (loss of his father), he cannot summon the courage to seek change (therapy). Wherever on this planet Armin Meiwes flees, he carries with him the burden and joy of doom, like Sisyphus, his rock.

FOR I KNOW THAT NOTHING GOOD DWELLS
WITHIN ME, THAT IS IN MY FLESH. I CAN
WILL WHAT IS RIGHT, BUT I CANNOT DO IT.

FOR I DO NOT DO THE GOOD I WANT, BUT
THE EVIL WHICH I WOULD NOT, THAT I DO.

(Romans 7: 18-19)

Chapter 4

THE ARMY AND THE FIANCÉE

JANUARY 1, 1981, FALLS on a Thursday. On this day, nineteen-year-old Armin Meiwes begins a new chapter in his life; he leaves home. He volunteers—at first for four years—as a candidate non-commissioned officer in the Budeswehr (West German Army). His training for Supply Sergeant begins in Kassel. Three months later, he is transferred to Rotenburg, to the 52nd Armored Infantry Battalion. There he is assigned to 1st Company in the supply group. From time to time, he is promoted. Later he attends the Noncom training course in Bremen. Armin Meiwes extends his enrollment to twelve years.

His army life serves a number of positive purposes. He has a bit of freedom from his mother's domination, he is in a position to exercise more authority over others, and his urge to slaughter other human beings is temporarily suppressed. To be sure, he is regarded by many colleagues during this period to be a "homebody" because, in the evenings, he always goes home to his mother in Wüstefeld. It is home leave, however, that causes Armin Meiwes to revert to his old behavior pattern, bowing to his mother's pressure and subordinating himself.

His fellow soldier, Hartmut M., offers the following observations to investigators during the interrogation of witnesses on January 1, 2003 (Proceedings No. ST/0132109/2002):

> *I came to Supply Group S 4 as a civilian. There I got to know Armin Meiwes as a staff noncom. He was my superior.... I can say of him that as a superior he was a hundred percent, and one could go to him with any question or problem. He always tried to help.... We noticed, though, that he took his mother along on trips by the Noncom corps, while the*

*others brought their girlfriends and wives. We
formed our own opinions about that.... The way
other men shielded their wives, he shielded his
mother. She was his One and Only.*

To that, Armin Meiwes says, "In these gatherings
and trips, there were always several retired people with their
wives, and they got along well with my mother."

His neighbors, Karl and Herta S., testified to the
police on December 12, 2002 (Proceedings No.
ST/132109/2002):

> *Mr. Meiwes's mother was very
> embittered.... I can still recall.... We had the
> impression he didn't have an opinion of his own.
> He always did as he was told. We attributed this
> to his mother's influence. This impression was
> strengthened in the following ten years and
> became even more pronounced.*

*

In my next interview with the Cannibal, we go on
leafing through his photo album. We embark on a journey
back in time through his life. A particular picture draws his
attention. It shows Armin Meiwes in the Army in the midst
of a dozen fellow soldiers. Armin Meiwes has a thick
moustache two centimeters long and dense blond hair and
wears an olive green uniform.

"How old are you here?"

"In this photo, I'm about twenty-three years old. The
photo was taken in the sergeant's training course in 1984 in
Bremen. I was a soldier for twelve years."

"Why did you become a soldier?"

"I wanted to defend my country. Furthermore, jobs
were very scarce in Rotenburg and Wüstefeld."

"Was it a good time?"

"Yes." Pause. "Carefree." Pause. "Nothing to worry
about."

After several training courses in Sonthofen and Unna in 1986, Armin Meiwes graduates from a course of higher training as an administrative employee. "I had no professional education and used the opportunity to get a proper graduation certificate." Most recently, he is a Master Sergeant and shares responsibility for the supply group. He has twelve men, including four Noncoms and two civilian employees, under him.

"About my time in the Army, I can only say that there were no problems of any kind," continues Armin Meiwes in a solemn tone, as if he had memorized it, "with my superiors or with my subordinates."

In the order and clear-cut hierarchy of the military, Armin Meiwes earns, for the first time in his life, something like recognition. He wins respect from his superiors—as mentioned, he gets several promotions—as well as from his subordinates. They accept his leadership and have trust in his orders. His desire to assimilate another person can thus retreat into the remotest corner of his subconscious mind.

"Did you have homosexual contacts during this period?"

"During my Army service I had more contacts with women. I was even engaged—to Petra K."

*

"Armin, just go to Mrs. M.," counseled his fellow soldier, Albert B. "She always has a few babes ready to go." Armin takes Albert's advice. Twenty-two-year-old Armin Meiwes meets with this dating broker in Kassel-Oberzwehren. Mrs. M. operates her little agency in her living room. Her workstation consists of a mahogany desk, a blue filing cabinet, and a telephone. He tells his mother nothing about his visit. Armin registers in the client file and next to his personal details writes only "Looking for a nice woman my age." Preferences? "None." Appearance? "Not important." Mrs. M. promptly arranges a first meeting by telephone, but only after he has paid a cash deposit of one hundred marks. If an arranged relationship holds up for six months, another two hundred marks will be due. The broker puts the money in her brown leather wallet and gives him the candidate's telephone number. Mrs. M is done with her job after only forty minutes. "You'll have to do the rest yourself. Good luck!"

After Armin arrives back home in Wüstefeld, he pulls the slip of paper out of his pants pocket. Two telephone numbers are written on it, one for Petra K. and one for Petra A. He decides spontaneously to go with the Petra of the "K" and dials her phone number: zero, five, six, nine, two....

"Hello," answers the party on the other end of the line decisively.

"Yes, this is Meiwes, Armin," he stammers shyly into the receiver. "I got your number from Mrs. M. and..."

"Yes, yes, Mrs. M.," interrupts Petra K., "got it. Shall we meet this Sunday at one p.m. on the Königsplatz?"

"Love to, super, 'til then," Armin replies happily. "Oh, yes, how will we recognize each other?"

"Take a red carnation," Petra K. tells him, as if the Wüstefelder were the nth candidate of many.

"Will do! 'Til then, looking forward to it." Somewhat too abruptly for Armin, Petra K. hangs up.

On this cloudy Sunday afternoon in April 1984, Armin Meiwes leaves the manor house wearing blue jeans and a white shirt, and climbs into his gold Mercedes 280. Half an hour later, the twenty-two-year-old soldier stands erect on the Königsplatz in Kassel. He waits calmly and with alert eyes for his blind date. He has bought the identification symbol—the red carnation—at the Esso filling station, and holds it as instructed, in his right hand.

At the stroke of one, Petra K. comes toward him, walking briskly. Armin's first impression of Petra K.: five-foot-six-inches tall, brash, blond, curly-haired, strong, and sturdily built.

"Yes, hello," he greets her.

"Nice it worked out."

"May I invite you to have coffee and a piece of cake?"

"Sure, love it. Let's go then."

They go to a dimly lit café on the square and drink a coffee with milk. Petra K. tells him about her life. Armin will never remember those details. While her words pour out, his eyes scan her body. Petra K. has beautiful, firm large breasts, which stand out under her beige-colored blouse.

After scarcely half an hour, Armin settles the check, and after a short constitutional, the two agree to see each other again. Armin escorts his new acquaintance to her black Opel Kadett. Petra K. says goodbye in front of the car with a kiss on the cheek. As she drives off, Armin thinks to himself, "I'm going to introduce Petra to my mother."

*

In the forensic-medical opinion of Professor Dr. Beier, specialist in Psychotherapeutic Medicine, one finds the following:

Discussion with Petra S.:

Petra S. (born K. in 1962) comes from Berlin and moved in 1982 to Wolfhagen, near Kassel (the previous year her parents had moved there); she is now married and has a 13-year-old son. Around 1984, she met Armin Meiwes through a marriage institute; she remembers him as a "gentleman," always forthcoming, courteous, and friendly. Unfortunately, she says, his mother so dominated him that she was always present in his imagination. She, therefore, had not been able to develop the feeling of being the most important woman in his life; nevertheless, she noticed that he was interested in a solid relationship—but recently his mother had managed to prevent it.

Thus, she had called at the house in Wüstefeld on one occasion, and been promptly driven out "in disgust" by the mother. Then he had presented himself once to her parents in Wolfhagen—but his mother was with him, which had seemed odd to everyone, especially her parents. For her, in any case, it had been clear that Armin could not stand up to his mother, and thus he had become less and less interesting to her as a partner for life.... She cannot confirm Armin Meiwes's statements concerning the sexual interactions between them. There had indeed been kissing and necking, but hardly sexual intercourse. The detailed description of the situations alleged by Armin Meiwes did not trigger any recollections. Thus he had alleged that the first sexual intercourse had occurred in her parents' house (this she categorically denies); the second sexual intercourse had occurred on the back seat of his car on the return journey from Wüstefeld (on this point Petra S. recalls that there had actually been sexual interactions, but only smooching and necking, and not coitus); and the third time had been on the occasion of the engagement of two friends in their apartment. She could not remember that couple and added that she was incapable of having sex with her boyfriend in the apartment of other people, especially when they were present.

She had also not been engaged to Armin Meiwes. Such an occasion she would celebrate lavishly with all her relatives and friends (it had been that way with the man who later became her husband); she recalled, however, that Armin Meiwes had given her a ring and might have considered this in his own mind as an engagement. She interpreted his allegations as wishful thoughts arising from their relationship. Finally, they had lost touch with each other. In any case, she was of the opinion that he had been in love with her and had wished for more for himself. Finally, she had not doubted that he was sexually oriented toward women.

*

I confront Armin Meiwes at the Kassel Penal Institution with the testimony of his alleged fiancée. For the first time, the prisoner gets angry and his voice trembles in rage. His eyelids begin to flutter nervously. "What rubbish," he hisses.

"How then was your relationship with your fiancée?

"She wanted me totally for herself alone. She wanted me to move to her place, but I had a large house and didn't want to leave it. I always had to visit her and she was less and less inclined to come to Rotenburg. Even today, she lives not a hundred kilometers from her parents' house. I had the feeling that she needed a living Barbie—shall I say a Ken, actually—and not a husband. That's why the relationship failed."

"Weren't those your mother's words? She is said to have meddled in your relationship."

Armin Meiwes immediately defends his mother. "My mother, from the beginning, received every woman well."

"In the records, there is something very different, Mr. Meiwes. Your mother, it says, drove your lady friend 'out in disgust.'"

The tone of his voice shifts back to "calm," and he tries in his mind to approach the truth.

"Well, all right. When things got serious between my fiancée and me, my mother naturally tried to prevent it diplomatically in this manner. On the other hand, any woman I sought for myself would have had to be prepared for life alone in the country and also get on with my mother. This, then, was problematic."

"Did you want to start a family?"

"Yes, I did want to. Especially with Petra. And my mother was eager to have grandchildren. But, even later, the right woman never materialized. The second woman from the partner agency, Petra A., couldn't have a child. So, for me, she was finished. And after the failed engagement, I said all right, I don't need it any more."

The opinion of the Kassel District Court of January 30, 2004 (File No. Js 36980/02) has the following to state concerning Petra S.:

Since the defendant, because of the slaughter fantasies he regarded as unusual and bizarre since their onset, yearned for conformity in an outwardly experienced and lasting relationship to a woman who above all would fulfill his desire for a child, he registered with a marriage brokerage in 1984 at the age of twenty-two. Through this marriage brokerage, the defendant became acquainted with the witness Petra S. Author's comment: [previously K.], whom he regularly dated for several months and with whom he exchanged tenderness (kissing and necking). It is still unclear whether the relationship between the defendant and witness S. also reached the point of sexual intercourse. The defendant's mother, Waltraud Meiwes, perceived witness S. as endangering her possessive relationship with the defendant and treated witness S. in a chilly and hostile manner. Waltraud Meiwes tried to talk defendant into breaking off with his friend S. For witness S., her contact with defendant became thereby unacceptable. As for the defendant, witness Petra A, she did not represent the desired partner in an intimate relationship, because a closure in her Fallopian tube made it impossible to fulfill his wish for a child. Although these reasons for leaving the relationship were never expressly mentioned by either witness Petra A or defendant, they both broke off contact.

*

Armin Meiwes's relationship with a woman had fallen through, and his dream of becoming a father and leading a completely normal family life had evaporated. Soon thereafter, his professional career in the Army hits a snag.

It's hard for Armin Meiwes to talk about it. Before he begins, he takes several deep breaths as if he had just climbed a mountain 6,000 meters high. Finally, he starts. "After a

Christmas party on December 16, 1986, with a one-point-four milliliter alcohol level, I crashed into a telephone pole." He compresses his lips as he often does when discussing an unpleasant subject, and shrugs. "It was shortly before midnight, between Mündershausen and Wüstefeld. I was shocked and called the police myself. My old Mercedes 280 was a total wreck, my driver's license suspended for nine months, and I had to pay a fine of fifteen hundred marks. For me, it was the beginning of the end of my career as a soldier."

That, however, was not Armin Meiwes's only accident. Barely a year after getting his license back, on May 9, 1987, there is another collision. Meiwes is about to turn from a track across a meadow onto the Wüstefeld highway. In the blinding afternoon sun, he fails to see an approaching car with two female passengers. He rams the vehicle and it turns over and skids into a ditch. In the judgment pronounced by the Rotenburg Municipal Court on October 6, 1987, the judge, based on external circumstances, and finding "slightly heightened fault," sentences Meiwes to twenty days at a daily rate of sixty-four marks. In the processing, Meiwes for the first time engages his defense attorney, Harald Ermel of Rotenburg an der Fulda. Exactly fifteen years, two months, and four days after this judgment, Meiwes will consult his attorney in another, highly delicate matter.

These two accidents lead to a serious breakdown in confidence on the part of his superiors in the Army. Further promotions are out of the question in the coming months. His inebriation and the accidents arising from it are duly noted in the Army's internal "LBS" point system. In spite of his training courses, Meiwes no longer reaches the number of points required to continue his Army career. "Three times I applied. All three times I was turned down. In the point system of applicants for the Army, I was no longer on the top of the list for the top thirty men who could be accepted. That completely stymied me."

Hurt by the humiliation, but also disappointed because no one was willing to pardon his faux pas, Armin Meiwes plunges into an adventure:

In 1988 the defendant met a man by the name of Frank, from Coburg, continues the opinion of the Kassel Municipal Court of January 30, 2004, (AZ 2650 Js 36980/02), during military exercises in Shiloh, Canada. With this Frank, there were also sexual contacts. Defendant did not draw Frank into his slaughter fantasies, which at this time, when defendant had a partner, were again present only in a somewhat subdued and latent fashion. Defendant's relationship with Frank from Coburg ended when the latter left the Army.

*

The nineties are the decade of the computer, the Internet, and the World Wide Web. Typewriter and telex are out of date. A global revolution begins. Computers become more affordable for everyone in the western world. The globe becomes more and more interconnected. In the course of a few years, our entire communication system changes. In 1981, there are only 200 active Internet users worldwide; in 2006, there are 439 million. Not until August 2, 1984 is the first German e-mail received. The term "Internet," which every child knows today, is invented in 1987. In March 1989, Tim Berners-Lee writes the first English version of his plan for the development of the World Wide Web ("Information Management: A Proposal").

In 1991, the World Wide Web is installed in the European Nuclear Research Center (CERN) near Geneva. In the same year, Apple, IBM, and Motorola agree on the PowerPC Platform. In 1993, Intel puts the Pentium processor on the market. The Internet brings not only blessings, but also curses. Abnormal users suddenly have direct access to one another through a "port."

Armin Meiwes is one of the first in Rotenburg an der Fulda during the nineties to become fascinated by the world of computers. "I had already worked with computers in the Army. It was fun. As a lover of technical things, I bought every magazine on the subject. Computers were my hobby. I simply had to have such a thing, a calculating machine, with me at home," says Meiwes. "It was clear as sunlight to me that I wanted to make it my profession."

So, as a transition to civilian life from military service, in 1993-94, he takes a two-year training course as a PC service technician in the Army's professional training service in Göttingen. "There I began a daily development course in personal computers," he goes on in a monotone. "After a year and a half, I did my on-the-job training at the Cooperative Accounting Center in Kassel. I went by train every day to Göttingen and back in the evening to Wüstefeld."

But what effect on his personality does the return to his mother's home full-time bring? Do his childhood traumas rise up to plague him? Do the feelings of abandonment and loneliness resurface? How does he behave towards his mother and his friends? I am curious to know the answers. Next time I see the Cannibal, I shall ask him.

*

On Sunday morning, the center of Rotenburg an der Fulda is practically deserted. I walk along the main street. A grayish-brown cat, licking its paws in front of a kiosk, sees me, the sole pilgrim, and flees. The little side street, the Hofweg, into which it runs, is my destination.

There I am awaited by Klaus Nölke, who came into the world in 1951 as the elder of two sons of a worker's family in Eschwege, and who, as he informed me beforehand on the telephone, has been on friendly terms with Armin Meiwes since their time in the Army.

As soon as I ring the bell at house number 2, the wooden door of the multi-family home flies open.

There stands Klaus Nölke to greet me. He wears a mouse-gray woolen sweater with a greenish-brown fishbone pattern on the front, and under it, a black-and-white striped polyester shirt. One might think he had fished the upper parts of his ensemble out of the closet expressly to attune me optically to the 1990s, the time when he became more closely acquainted with Meiwes.

The man is around five-foot-seven inches tall and looks somewhat like a goblin. His disheveled hair stands straight on one end, as if he just got out of bed. On the left ear glints a little silver earring, a relic of wilder times.

"Good morning," says Klaus Nölke, sounding as if he had a cold or is a chain-smoker. "Come in." My host limps. He pulls his left leg back and notices my look. "That was a stroke in 1999, but I am still alive."

The three-room apartment is rustically fitted out with furniture that you can buy in a large furniture store like "Möbel Kraft," directly off the autobahn at exit A3. The wooden beams in the ceiling lend the apartment a cottage-like charm. The antique mahogany wardrobe in the living room is much too bulky for the seventy-square-meter apartment. I observe the wardrobe as I pass by. "Nice, isn't it? I inherited it from my grandmother," says the pensioner. On the other side of the room, oil painting replicas of archways and half-timbered houses grace the whitewashed wall. Under them, on the wooden side buffet, stand several yellowed pictures in silver frames of Nölke's wife, Elisabeth, and Elisabeth with her parents. In the glass cabinet stand three bottle-ships and porcelain pitchers decorated with southern-state motifs.

Klaus Nölke offers me a seat on the dark blue velvet couch in the living room, and we drink freshly brewed coffee.

"That Armin," he begins our interview without being coaxed, "what an incredible story. That he eats a man...." He drags deeply on his cigarette, inhales the smoke, and immediately coughs it out.

"How did you get to know him?"

"We got acquainted in the barracks, around 1984-85. Armin was always nice, forthcoming. Not a know-it-all. Quite a normal guy and you could really get on with him fine. Unbelievable that he did such a thing." He shakes his head five times, one after the other. Since the age of twenty-three, he thinks, he has known Armin Meiwes as a decent friend. As young soldiers in their early twenties, Klaus Nölke was in the Air Force and Armin Meiwes was in the Army. They were both stationed in Alheimer Barracks in Rotenburg, in the years 1983 to 1988.

"About him being attracted to men, there were rumors. There were no details," he says. "To the general public, and to the GI's in the barracks, he hid it well. After work, he was always up to something. As the old saying goes, 'Service is service and liquor is liquor.'"

From my black briefcase, I pull out a couple of photographs from former times. Klaus Nölke picks one picture out right away. It shows Armin Meiwes at the helm of a sailboat. "Yes, here you see Armin at the rudder," he comments on the snapshot. "There were six of us, from May 26 to June 6, 1990, on the Baltic. From Burg on Fehmarn, we sailed on past Denmark to Norway."

"You have to know," he declares, his voice soft and subdued, "Armin told his mother nothing of our sailing trip. He sold the old lady the story that he was attending a one-week training course in the Army. So he made a secret of our trip."

"Why did he have to do that?"

"Well, we had the feeling he was under tremendous pressure at home from his mother. We had to agree among ourselves that we would keep our mouths shut when his mother was around. To discuss the sailing trip, we met with the skipper, Mr. B. He also promised not to speak of it so that it would not get back to Armin's mother. She was the absolute boss and he was under her heel. Nobody would have changed places with Armin. His mother had all the charm of a poisonous snake. He was like a guinea pig in the cage with something that would eat him."

"So how was the sailing trip?" I want to know.

The frail, much too tender man, who is almost sinking down in his couch chair, tries to get up, can't quite make it, and falls back into his original position. For the next ten minutes, he reports on the "adventure with Armin Meiwes on the high seas." He exerts himself frankly to give me the most detailed information possible. Excerpts:

"We had no problem at all. Not a bad word was spoken. So there were never any fights."

"Armin did our cooking out of cans—lentil soup, noodle soup, sometimes noodles and sausages."

"When we had a party, he washed the dishes in the kitchen."

"I even have a video that Armin took."

Klaus Nölke now rises with difficulty from his chair, pressing on the couch arm. He supports himself on his cane, which was lying on the floor beside the couch, and hobbles to the mahogany cupboard. From the bottom of the second drawer, he takes a videocassette and puts it, as if in evidence to support his testimony, into the cassette player.

During the following forty-three minutes, I see the Cannibal of Rotenburg on the model "Dehler 420" sailboat named "Seespiel." Armin Meiwes laughs, jokes, suns himself, and announces to his fellow vacationers at the helm the current course ("three hundred degrees, speed five-point-five knots!"). Meiwes flirts with Klaus Nölke's ex-girlfriend, sings sailor songs like "Boy, Come Back Soon," plays cards with his pals, throws dice, and toasts the cameraman in a beach restaurant with a glass of white wine. Once he laughingly feeds bread to swans ("Yes, now you have to dive, swan!"). Mostly however, Meiwes himself is behind the camera. He wisecracks and utters outrageous nonsense in the film.

Klaus Nölke speaks to the camera. "Hey, hey, hey, Freddy, can you name me a few types of spices?"

"Carnations, cinnamon, marjoram, and, and, and...."

"You forgot an important one. I will give you a hint: what does your father put on his balls in the morning?"

"Hairspray!" Meiwes calls out.

There is laughter.

The friends' nonstop nonsense continues boisterously on land. The men bob up and down on a child's rocking horse with a coin slot. The camera ranges over the beach—the filmmaker, Armin, records a couple of unknown youth, muscular and suntanned, rubbing lotion on one another. He has them much too long in his viewer.

Yet, no one, probably not even Armin Meiwes himself, would bet a nickel that this innocent vacationer, nine years and ten months later, would kill a man and eat him.

"What was it like, the day you learned that Armin Meiwes, your sailing friend, with whom you shared your cabin during that voyage, was a man-eater?"

He shrugs at the question and can't take his eyes off the television, where the vacation video is still running. "It was a shock! When a friend called to tell me, I thought he was pulling my leg." He presses the stop key of his player and turns his whole upper body towards me. His gaze is clear and direct. The simple man chooses his words carefully. "In my opinion, Armin was two persons in one. One Armin was the friendly, kind, next-door-neighbor and good friend, and the other Armin was, in private, not so correct, to put it politely."

"Two persons in one." The words still echo in my mind. Until now, I have spent my time at the prison facing the "friendly, kind next-door-neighbor." At this moment, I have no idea if, one day, I will find myself inside a room with the no longer "so correct" Armin Meiwes.

I must return to Kassel for my next interview with the Cannibal.

Klaus Nölke gives me, as a parting gift to his guest, the man-eater's vacation videotape.

"Don't you need it anymore?"

"No, no," he says dismissively, "go ahead and take it along."

"The subject is perhaps repulsive," he says, as he follows me in the narrow hallway to the door of the apartment. "People in our area have never had to face cannibalism; it is unknown territory. That is why opinions differ. One person says what Armin did is bad. Another says it's much worse that someone like Mr. Brandes allowed it to be done to him."

He waves and calls after me. "Supply and demand, that's what I say!" Klaus Nölke laughs at his own joke and shuts the door.

*

After my conversation with Meiwes's friend, Klaus Nölke, and the testimony of his ex-fiancée, Petra S. (formerly K.), I sum up the situation once more.

Following his soul-refreshing time in the Army, it's back to the "tragic entwinement with his mother" and the "infantile-mother-link (Sigmund Freud)." His wish to lead a normal life is broken by his mother. He even has to lie to her when he goes on leave with friends. "She didn't have to know everything," says Armin defensively. "I was old enough to go and I went along with them because someone dropped out. It was nice on the boat, going to such beautiful places, and the whole thing for two weeks cost less than two hundred and fifty marks."

Waltraud Meiwes would not tolerate her son near any woman she didn't like and thus prevents him from feeling love for anyone other than her. Armin has social contacts, but deep inside he is lonely. Often he has the feeling that he not only resembles his mother, but that he is only an extension of her life. Armin cannot feel like a "real man" under her decades-long dominance, let alone develop manly character traits.

*

Prof. Dr. Beier concludes, in his forensic sexual-medical opinion of June 12, 2003, about Armin Meiwes:

> *"Everything happens [with Armin Meiwes] on the fantasy level, where control over the fetish and its magical significance describes the inner connection existing between Armin Meiwes and his fetish—the meat issuing from understanding men; he has the fetish completely under control when he prepares it and assimilates it.*

The following passage is especially instructive:

> *Simultaneously, the fetish bestows power on him and instills in him its own male identity. From the psychoanalytical standpoint, this would be consistent with the assumption that Armin Meiwes has not freed himself from his "first love-object" (his mother). In this connection, it has to be taken into consideration that his mother assumed in his development a*

"supremacy" under which her own (feminine) thinking and acting was seen as authoritative, and male acting and thinking as unsuitable and insufficient.... Armin Meiwes hardly had available—and then only negatively—male identification material, since the father image he got from her was negative, which by itself led to the expression that one did not speak about his father. For the development of male identity, it might have been significant to release himself from his mother using male identification materials (coming from the father), in order to build his own stable male identity. This is classed as "disidentification" from the mother." Armin Meiwes carries out this buildup of male identity by means of a quite archaic experience and behavior model: the incorporation, that is the assimilation and absorption, of the object of his desire, a process which he himself regards, in the sense of a magical way of thinking, as lasting. Psycho-dynamically, therefore, it is only through the cannibalistic assimilation of the man in Armin Meiwes that he achieves the development of male identity.

*

This unhealthy mother-son connection is reinforced, according to expert opinion, by the mother's maladies, such as disturbances in the rhythm of the heartbeat or attacks of weakness, in order to control and "assimilate" the son. She employs her ever-more-frequent need for assistance as an instrument of her power. What must not be forgotten in light of all these scientific reflections is that his mother is also the only security in Meiwes's life. This control, nonetheless, oppresses and irritates him deeply. Armin Meiwes did admit, "We quarreled and argued when there were problems." He says he tried to show her his own true self. In one of our conversations, he says of this," I always had to be there for her. I put on again my mask of devoted son and lived with this lie. I hated myself for not being as I wanted to be."

From this unsatisfactory life, he always wants to take refuge on the other side, the fantasy world of shamelessness, of the fetish, of spiritual abysses. It is his boundless paradise.

The slaughter imaginings move from the background to the center of his thoughts.

"Did you, at that time, feel rage toward your mother?"

Armin draws a deep breath, stretches his upper body, and says clearly and precisely, "In such an old house, there must be constant renovations. Instead of doing something in the bedrooms, she wanted to extend the roof. Below, the house was falling apart and the top floor was covered with new boards. I would have loved to take my mother and nail her to the front door." Pause. "But, no, no, that I would never, never have done."

THEY HAVE EVIL IN THEIR MINDS, BUT THEY KEEP THEIR PLANS SECRET. THEIR SOULS ARE CORRUPT TO THE CORE, AND THEIR HEARTS ARE AN ABYSS.

(Psalm 64: 7)

Chapter 5

THE DEAD

"OLIVER, OLIVER," ARMIN MEIWES sighs at our next meeting in the pokey, "that was a shame. The evening before, we had such a good time chatting and now the..."

"Oliver? Who is this Oliver?"

He tells me his story in a subdued, monotonous singsong.

"Well, it was Oliver from Cell 27. He made a fraudulent claim on an insurance policy. Yesterday, he got a letter from his wife. She's suing for divorce. Last night, just a few hours ago, he hanged himself in his cell—with his black belt." As if holding the belt in his hand, Meiwes lifts it above him and jerks his head upward like the dead man hanging from the strap. "He croaked."

"Does his suicide upset you?"

"Yes, I am extremely upset by it—especially by the coarse indifference of the other inmates and workers. One of them said only, 'Now we have an empty cell again,' and laughed. And the warden shrugged and said, 'I don't care one way or the other.' How can people be so unfeeling? Even if I didn't know him intimately, a man has died in despair who knew of no other way out. He, too, had no one he could talk to."

Meiwes has voiced his emotion. Would that he had been so compassionate with his victim, Bernd Brandes, and sent him home.

"And what else upset you?"

"Well then, Oliver was a nice, polite young man. Years ago, when I had been at liberty, I could have imagined Oliver as 'brother.'"

There he is again, the "other, not so correct" Armin Meiwes.

*

In 1994, Armin Meiwes is thirty-two years old.

George W. Bush is elected Governor of Texas. Nine hundred people are drowned when the ferryboat "Estonia" sinks off Finland. The railroad tunnel under the English Channel is opened. Nelson Mandela becomes the first black President of South Africa. Race car driver Michael Schumacher wins the Class One World Championship in Australia. Germany rejoices over Markus Wasmeier's two gold medals in the Winter Olympics ski events. The Kelly Family is Number One on the charts. Roman Herzog becomes the first President of the unified Republic of Germany, and Helmut Kohl becomes the Chancellor for the fifth time. The great actor Heinz Rühman dies.

Back in the solitude of Wüstefeld by Rotenburg an der Fulda—a village of twenty-five inhabitants, among them fourteen children—Armin Meiwes is trying, after the abrupt end of his military career, to get his feet on the ground again. "My brother Ilja and I wanted to set up a computer school. I think it was a good idea at the time. All the companies had junked their typewriters and bought word processors. Their personnel needed training," explains Meiwes on the idea of founding his start-up enterprise.

The headquarters of the Meiwes computer school would have been his mother's estate in Wüstefeld. "Ilja was an Information Technology technician and had a professional license. At the time, we had still had 386 and 486 processors. We bought the parts from a wholesaler in Paderborn and assembled the computers ourselves. Altogether we invested 30,000 marks (roughly 7,500 dollars). Ilja wanted to do the teaching, while I would be responsible for drumming up new business. Then we gave a few courses. Do you want to know why it didn't work out?"

"Could it have been because in little Rotenburg only a couple of dozen people had computers?" I ventured.

"No! We gave two courses, and then a former neighbor complained. That's how things go in the village! The sheriff came and shut down the shop. My brother went back to Frankfurt, where he lived with his fiancée, and found a job as a programmer. I said to myself, Armin, you can't always have plums. Sometimes you have to suck lemons. So I went on with the sale of the PCs I had assembled myself. Fortunately, a former trainer at the Professional Promotion Facility in Göttingen called me up a few days later and asked if I could begin helping out in the Kassel Accounting Center of the Volks-und Raiffeisen Banks in Kassel. Most recently, I earned fifteen hundred Euros net and made a very good living on it. In addition, my mother had a small pension of 600 marks. I was very happy doing my job, right up until my arrest. It was a solid, responsible assignment which kept me busy every day."

*

In 1998, at exactly five a.m., Armin Meiwes's digital radio alarm beeps in his bedroom, "Meadowland," one of thirty-six rooms in the Wüstefeld manor house. Meiwes is an early riser. In his dark-blue, two-piece cotton pajamas, he stands in front of the washbasin in his bedroom to the right of the door. He turns on the faucet, holds his washcloth under the cold water and rubs it with scented soap. Then he rubs his face with the washcloth and cleans his armpits. He shaves, combs his hair and dresses. The whole process lasts exactly seven minutes. As he does every day, he goes down the eighteen steps from the first floor to the kitchen on the ground floor. He puts on the coffee. Next, he pours milk on his corn flakes. A knock on the ceiling yanks him out of his daily routine, and right afterwards, his mother calls out hysterically, "Armin? Armin! Where are you?" From her bed, Waltraud Meiwes has pounded on the floor of her bedroom with her crooked walking stick. Ever since she has constantly feigned illness, she has used the stick to summon Armin, like ringing a bell for the butler.

"Coming!" he calls back, responding immediately. On most days, his mother sleeps until nine o'clock, but today she has wakened earlier than usual. As he rises, he wipes his mouth with a napkin and hastens to his mother on the first floor, taking the stairs two at a time. The only room lacking a name, Waltraud Meiwes's bedroom is directly opposite that of her son. His mother lies in her frilly white nightgown under a down quilt, in an old oaken double bed with night cupboards on either side. Below the bed on the left, lined up in a row, are twenty pairs of worn ladies' shoes. In front of the bed stands a round wooden table with three wooden chairs. The room has a single window measuring twenty-four inches by sixteen, with wooden pegs. Against the wall shared with the next room, "Flower Meadows," stands an artistically carved armoire whose right door doesn't close properly. On the commode next to it, on a wig stand, is draped a hairpiece woven in dark brown, black, and black-brown colors. There is also a Chinese vase, a tin plate, medications of every kind, two bottles of eye drops, and a photo showing Waltraud Meiwes as a woman of twenty.

"Good morning, Mama. Is everything all right?" asks Armin.

His mother looks at him seriously. "I just wanted to know if you're finished and if you've got everything tidied up in the kitchen," she says instead of a good-morning greeting. Usually Armin has to wake his mother up before leaving.

"Yes, I have cleaned up. I still have to do the dishes and then I'll leave," he answers. He gives his mother a quick kiss on the forehead.

"When will you come home today?"

"I'll be back around six. Be careful climbing the stairs and have a really good day."

"My days are all the same," grumbles Waltraud Meiwes to herself. "Come on time! And call if you're going to be late!"

Armin Meiwes walks down the hallway on the first floor. He glances fleetingly at the landing that he had paneled in wood a few days ago at his mother's express wish. Then he goes down, finishes washing up, and leaves the house shortly before seven o'clock.

In his new Lancia, Armin Meiwes sets off on the thirty-six-mile drive to Kassel. In Number 41 Falderbaumstrasse, punctually at eight o'clock, he settles into his job in the large workroom of the business office in the Kassel-Waldau Accounting Center. He shares the six-hundred-and-forty-eight-square-foot room with four colleagues. His repair corner is spartan: table, telephone, office chair, and on a side table, his tool kit. Meiwes gets his work orders by telephone. He is regarded as an industrious and always genial collaborator. His colleagues and former customers describe him as "calm, pleasant, courteous, cooperative, and even-tempered." By the end of the morning, he finishes the drudgery of writing.

Around one o'clock, Meiwes sits with other employees in a small restaurant near their office. The midday menu, at ten marks—soup, main course, dessert—is paid half by the company. After the noonday break, he packs his tool kit into the white service vehicle, a VW Golf diesel, and drives across the district, to service or repair four or five automatic teller machines. Often he advises one or another bank director on ways to improve technical efficiency in the bank branches. But toward four o'clock, he gets nervous. He looks more often at his silver quartz wristwatch. At six-thirty sharp, he's returned from his outside service to the business center, puts the car key in his desk drawer and takes leave of his colleagues: "OK, 'til tomorrow. I'm off for home to my mother."

*

His business colleague Matthias W., born in 1964, comments:

> *During work hours, Armin and I got to know each other better, and understood each other immediately in our work, and this extended then to the private sphere. I also visited him at home. He was in my home, and my mother was with us in Wüstefeld. I became acquainted with Armin's mother in this way. If I am asked how the relationship between mother and son seemed to me, my belief is that his mother had the upper hand.... Armin and I*

shared a hobby—going to saunas. We tried to meet regularly, which now and then didn't work out because of our jobs. We always went to the thermal baths in Kassel.... I would like to mention here that Armin used to comment on the appearance of women who were present. We didn't talk about men.... I didn't notice [any homosexual inclination in him] and he never tried to get intimate with me.... If I am asked how Armin behaved toward ladies at home with us, I can only say that his behavior was very relaxed and friendly, but he never tried to take liberties with any of our female colleagues. It occurs to me that Armin once, at a party where a lot of drinking had gone on, somehow made a comment, which made me think he might be sloshed. Thereupon, I answered accordingly that I didn't care, so long as he didn't get fresh with me. Finally, I would like to say that in Armin Meiwes's house there are flowers belonging to us, to my mother rather, that are to stay there through the winter because we have no room for them. If possible, I request that these flowers be delivered to me.

(Source: Witness interrogation on 12/17/02, East Hesse Police Headquarters, Proceedings No. ST/0132109o/2002).

*

Leaving work at five o'clock at the latest, Armin Meiwes stops regularly on the way home at "Aldi" in Rotenburg an der Fulda. He buys bananas, sausages, marmalade, toilet paper, soap powder, and miscellaneous provisions for daily use. Then he drives back to the Wüstefeld manor house, where his mother impatiently awaits him. By way of greeting she barks at him, "Well, then, what kept you so long?"

"I never answered and just cooked a quick dinner," Meiwes tells me. "Usually my mother and I would eat together in front of the TV in the living room: vegetables, sausages, rice and the like. We also drank coffee together. We didn't talk much. And then I took the vacuum cleaner and vacuumed, did the laundry and scrubbed the bathrooms. I tidied up the kitchen and mopped the floor."

*

A house tells much about the people who live in it. The Wüstefeld manor house was mentioned in documents as "Wusthevelt" as far back as 1266. Over the centuries, from six to eight families have resided and lived on the estate—all under one roof. The half-timbered structure was a big business for this neighborhood. A former owner, Elias Stück, was known far outside the district in the '30s. As a leading farmer of the district, he was a representative in the governing bodies of the town and the savings bank. Elias Stück was the driving force behind the erection of the little church in Wüstefeld.

The partly cellared manor house, with a living space of over sixteen thousand square feet, and thirty-six rooms distributed over three stories, is designed for far more than two persons. Twenty-five rooms of the half-timbered house are designed for guests, but are rarely used as such. In the summer, however, there are occasionally a few vacationing guests. These rooms were fitted-out by Waltraud Meiwes and her ex-husband, who bought the place at auction when it was falling apart, intending to rebuild it as a boarding house. The plan failed, like so much in the life of this family. The guest rooms are still maintained, and each has a washbasin with soap and a gray face towel, a double bed and a two-door armoire. According to the current hotel category, the manor would presumably rate a "one star plus." The aging guest rooms could all stand a thorough cleansing. Cobwebs and bits of fluff lie about in the corners of the rooms, each bearing its own name: "Sunbeam," "Early Dew," Pine Forest," "Green Corner," "Evening Calm," "Under the Linden," and so on.

The actual living quarters of Armin and Waltraud Meiwes are located—except for the two bedrooms and the bathroom on the first floor—on the ground floor of the building. Altogether, they consist of twelve rooms.

From the elegant 430-square-foot parlor, there is access into three areas: to the right are three rooms, among them one named "Paradise," which is crammed to the ceiling with old furniture. Here and there on some walls of these three rooms, bare bricks are exposed and white telephone cables hang from the ceiling, conveying the impression that alterations are underway.

Exiting left from the parlor, one goes through a wooden door with a window inset, and enters the handsome living quarters, consisting of a living room and a dining room. To the left of the dining area is the winter garden.

The furnishings of these rooms are a mixture of antique wooden closets from the time of the original builders and domestic utensils that can be bought cheaply at flea markets. Here are two couch sets in gray and beige with side tables flanking them, a few odd chairs, brass standing lamps, a stereo set, a blue dial telephone, a tarnished, illuminated globe, and an old, out-of-tune piano. Also, an antique cupboard with wood carvings, crystal bowls, two flower vases, copies of oil paintings in gilt frames, upholstered chairs, serving tables, wall clocks, porcelain figures, and much more. The entire living area is completely overloaded. It could be said that the rooms are a collection of junk and old furnishings such as one finds in the storeroom of an antique shop.

In the old kitchen, at the far end of the parlor and to the left, is a mini-window with red and white curtains. The kitchen unit is equipped with an electric stove and a washing machine. A deep-freeze chest stands next to the sink. Beyond the spacious kitchen, through a small corridor, one reaches another, smaller kitchen with another stove and a refrigerator. Going on down the hall, one passes two bathrooms and finally arrives at Armin Meiwes's two "workrooms," where with his brother Ilja, he had wanted to run the computer training courses. The office space consists of one room with an area of 250 square feet, and another smaller one, 150 square feet. The larger workroom is crammed with diverse furnishings and a plethora of computer parts—monitors, hard disks, plastic boxes, and PC tools. Against the left wall stands a steel container with several operating units lying on it. On both a mahogany-colored cabinet and an L-shaped table are piles of PC documents, housings, and operating units. Even the entire polyvinyl floor is strewn with PC parts. Here is where Armin Meiwes assembles his own computers, which he sells privately.

The two workrooms are the realm of Armin Meiwes.

As soon as his mother goes to bed around nine-thirty p.m., he turns on his highest-performing computer. In the desk drawer below, he has hidden a pile of porn magazines: "Gay Boy," "Playgirl," "Model Men." With a pair of scissors, he carefully cuts out from the magazines the handsomest male bodies and files them in a blue folder.

"At that time, in any event, a change came about," declares Meiwes matter-of-factly. "I think that in 1996, after the automobile accident with my mother, I bought a PC video card with which I could process and alter the particular photos in any way I wished. The men-magazines, these I bought in porno shops in Kassel. I looked especially for issues in which the entire bodies were shown, so I could work on them. It wasn't at all that simple, because mostly only the genitals were displayed. I spent a lot of time in the shops, leafing through the magazines. I regarded my representations of the dissection and cutting up of a man as artistic work and took great pains with it. I was proud of my creations."

*

The District Court of Kassel, in its judgment on January 30, 2004 (File No. 2650 Js 36980/02), writes in official German concerning this decisive phase in the life of Armin Meiwes:

From 1996 on, the defendant began to live out his fantasies by altering photos and videos and rearranging them in the computer, acting evenings in secret when Waltraud Meiwes sat in front of the television, or at night when she slept. In the process, he retouched homosexual representations of naked male bodies in the computer, in such a way that they looked as if the abdominal cavities were opened, the heads cut off, and the like.

The police had in their possession the original works of Meiwes from his computer. As the saying goes, I obtained photocopies of them "in a roundabout manner." I wanted to know what there was in the pictures that was so important to the investigating agencies. What did Armin Meiwes show in them?

I spread out the pictures before me like a puzzle on the parquet floor of my office. I put each object under the magnifying glass. I am bewildered by what is revealed before me. As a supposedly hard-bitten journalist, I have already seen many bloody, obscene, and tragic things in my career. But what I am now viewing surpasses anything I have ever imagined concerning good and evil. These photos were more than simple images of naked men with a few creepy alterations. What Armin Meiwes created in these pictures was mind-boggling.

I ask myself seriously for the first time, why I am doing all this to myself? But this is the wrong time to look for an answer, because suddenly, a thought like a lightning bolt flashes in my mind: the photographs have a special significance to them! Feverishly I line up the photos, picture by picture, in a specific order. The twenty photos are now like pieces of a puzzle fitting together to make a recognizable image. The photos were altogether disturbing and gruesome just as they were, but, when lined up in this way, I had stumbled upon something more.

*

I must confront Armin Meiwes with my discovery. I drive to the Kassel Penitentiary, the photocopies in my pocket. I want him to tell me what took place in his mind at that time. The prisoner is brought to "our" conference room, which this time, thank God, is not a sweatbox. I can't start right in though, for today above his left eye there is a blue-black, bleeding sore.

Suppressing my impatience to get an answer to my questions, I try to be polite and ask, "Were you attacked by a fellow prisoner?"

"Oh, no. A wooden slat fell on my head," he recounts. "I was trying, with a prison colleague, to set up the new tables in the television room. He was a bit clumsy, so that the slat whacked me over the eye."

"Sorry to hear it," I respond.

Meiwes makes a dismissive gesture with his right hand and says waggishly, "Oh well, I'm not having my picture taken today, anyway."

Meiwes is vain. Aside from his gashed forehead, his appearance, as always, is neat. He is fragrant with Nivea Cream and Axe deodorant. Axe costs eight Euros here in the prison store. Eight Euros! The prices here would make any pharmacist turn green with envy.

The psychiatric finding of the expert witness offers the following comment on Meiwes's appearance:

> His dark-blond hair is cut short, and thinning above his forehead. He is clean-shaven and wears half-spectacles, through and over which, in conversation, he makes and maintains eye-contact. His manner is generally neutral to cheerful. No signs of dullness or impairment of mental faculties, reaching the level of depression or suicidal tendencies, has been observed.

I ask Armin Meiwes if he will agree to comment on the first photographs, which date from 1995 and 1996. He consents with a firm, "Yes, certainly," and I extract them one after another from the file.

"Where did you get these?" he asks, visibly astonished.

"Contacts," I answer curtly.

I have had each picture enlarged to eight by twelve inches and inserted in a folder. Meiwes has taken the photos himself with a VHS video camera or with a Polaroid 2000 speed camera. They were taken seven or eight years before he turned his fantasies into reality with the crime against Bernd Brandes.

I hand him the first photo.

Picture One shows Meiwes in the smaller, 130-square-foot workroom of the Wüstefeld manor house. He is standing in front of the wooden table and pointing to a model made of cardboard and paper.

"Here I put together a slaughter-room myself. In it, I laid naked, male Ken dolls on the dissecting table and photographed them. Later, using the PC card, I exchanged the dolls with the altered photos. These photos were intended for me alone and I sent them to no one."

Picture Two: Meiwes holds an artificial penis in his hand. "This is a plastic dildo I packed into an airtight bag. I am representing a freshly cut-off penis I would want to freeze in a plastic bag."

Picture Three: Meiwes is standing in the "balcony room." He has tied his hands together with a cord and hung himself on a hook in the wall. "I arranged this photo so that it looks as if I were hanging on the hook. I tried it before with handcuffs, but it didn't work so well."

Picture Four: Meiwes lies, eyes shut, in the blue lacquered bathtub without any water. "The placement in the bathtub is supposed to represent a slaughter victim, that is, a man already dead. He is to bleed dry in the bathtub. I processed this photo in the computer. I brushed out the hands and feet so that in the picture, these body parts have already been cut off. Those were the first things I rearranged in this manner."

Picture Five: A naked young man is locked up behind bars. "Here I wanted to represent a young man in a cage. I cut the photo out of a porn magazine and laid it behind the bars of a refrigerator."

Picture Six: Model of a male body lying on its side. Hands, head, and feet are missing. The stumps are blood-red. The body is being flambéed and something is stuck in its posterior. "I modeled this body out of marzipan and painted it with cocoa powder mixed with water. The two tin sticks in the posterior area are supposed to represent knife and fork. The flame was used to make the surface of the body smooth and shiny. By that, I mean I didn't intend to set fire to the body."

Picture Seven: Armin Meiwes is lying stark naked on the wooden floor, holding a ketchup bottle on the area between his chest and belly, where he has dripped a red line twelve inches long. "I wanted to show how I would have disemboweled and cut up a body. The ketchup was supposed to represent blood to make it look more realistic."

Picture Eight: Meiwes is dangling like a show-window mannequin from cables in the air. His head hangs to the right, as if his neck were broken. His eyes are wide open, staring blankly. The jaw hangs slack like that of a corpse. "The photograph was taken in front of the former children's room on the ground floor. I pulled myself up on the door frame with a block and tackle I had used for the renovations in the house. I wanted to show how a slaughter victim looks hung up."

Meiwes describes each photo the way other people do the snapshots of their latest Mallorca vacation. He never pauses and leaves no answer incomplete. On the contrary: he speaks soberly and factually about all the details, like a physicist explaining quantum theory. Thus, Meiwes states precisely his reason for making each one of the pictures. He is not in the least embarrassed.

"Didn't you find it absurd to create these photos of yourself while your mother was sleeping in the next room?"

Meiwes grins. "I had fun with these pictures and they got more and more realistic. It was really artistic. I don't mean they aroused me sexually. It took real study to mold a substance like marzipan and make it look like a body."

"Did you practice and study your slaughter operations that way?"

He takes a sheet of paper from my pad. With a silver ballpoint pen he pulls from his left shirt pocket, he draws a table on it. "Well," he explains, "that's what you could call the beginnings. We lay the victim on the table." He now draws a body—or rather a stick figure—lying on a table. "Then we cut the victim's throat, cut off the head; next we castrate it, and, finally, we cut off the penis." Meiwes starts to illustrate the description he has just given.

"You don't have to draw me a picture. Thanks. I can imagine it," I say, before he can put the severed genital on paper.

"All right, then." He puts the ballpoint pen back in his shirt pocket. "Now we slit open the belly, more or less like in the photograph where I'm lying on the floor and have colored the area around my belly red with ketchup. Then we disembowel the victim, cut him in half, and hack off his hands and feet. After that we can divide up the body."

"Did your mother sense that you had an inclination towards cannibalism?"

"No, she didn't catch on at all," he declares. "Neither about that or "the other." Although, one time, Frank, my Army acquaintance, thought my mother might have peeked in on us and saw us having sex at night. But I don't think so."

His brother Ilja testified, however, in his interrogation on December 13, 2002 (Proceedings No. ST/0132109/2002, East Hesse Police Headquarters) as follows:

> I know that Armin also informed my mother of it at some time unknown to me. I know my mother did not tolerate his homosexuality.

If it had been only a matter of love between two people of the same sex, I would not have needed to reveal his behaviors. Armin Meiwes led an irreconcilable dual existence between external appearance and his sick emotional life.

"How did you manage to hide your double life?"

He replies with the sure superiority of a perfectly camouflaged soldier. "You know, I did it at times when no one could look on; when there were no visitors. I also didn't boast about it and I didn't show my works to anyone. Many people blab when they have a secret like that. I learned to suppress my emotions completely in company. Always be nice and polite and don't talk too much. That way I get along without stumbling into a trap. None of my friends or colleagues got wind of my pleasure in cutting up a man. Not one."

I hand him Picture Nine. Meiwes is holding an eight-inch butcher knife to the left side of his neck, close to the throat. In this photo, too, is seen a cut, apparently bleeding. Meiwes examines the photo calmly. After a few moments he takes a deep breath and says, "Oh yes—well, sticking the knife into the neck and cutting the throat are hard even for me to think about. That's the necessary evil before the assimilation."

Suddenly he laughs out loud. "Here, for this object I pepped up the ketchup with spices. Paprika and cinnamon. That way it looked even more realistic than blood and stayed on better. The spices made it thicker and it didn't run down from the neck."

If we didn't know where these unusual representations were leading, we could laugh over them: paprika, cinnamon and ketchup as substitutes for blood—like a school play.

In the next ten photos that I lay out on the table, there are enlarged depictions of a bare male breast, a right leg, various pieces of flesh, and a modeled chunk that looks like a lower belly cut open.

"What did you want to achieve with these photos?"

Deliberately he picks up one of the photos—the one of the breast.

"This one here turned out very well! For this scene, I rubbed sunflower oil on my own chest so as to make it look realistically oven-roasted. In my scenario, the breast was to be prepared with French fries as a meal. I also snapped and filmed my legs and thighs several times, because in my opinion, these parts can give the juiciest roasts."

I pick up the "open lower belly" photo. "And what about this open chunk with the little spheres in it?"

"I put together this wonderful creation out of marzipan. The photo is supposed to represent a human underbelly filled with potatoes. That's the reason for these little balls in the open part. They're the potatoes."

With every succeeding photo, Meiwes reveals to me his once deeply hidden perversions, which now lie before us in the glare of daylight. Without a word, I add the last picture to the row of photos.

Picture Twenty: Meiwes, standing, inserts a broomstick into his anus. He is grinning broadly.

I confess that at this moment I feel ashamed for him. But he laughs aloud when he sees the photo.

"You have that one with the broomstick, too? Good. The photo is supposed to show a man on a roasting spit. I used it mainly as a model for a montage. I put together other male bodies with the broomstick. I had altogether thirty or forty different men on the spit."

"Why did you make these photos, in which you degrade yourself?"

"I made them for myself! I've never found such photos anywhere, not even in any porn magazine. They were my ideas and my inspirations. I staged these pictures like a director so that they would look as realistic as possible. I was really proud of my works."

Speechless, I realize that Armin Meiwes is clearly still proud of his "works," these heaps of garbage.

"Does something strike you as rather interesting when you view these pictures, Mr. Meiwes?"

He reflects. "What do you mean?"

"In that these photos were a prequel to something?

"Oh yes. Most of the photos were taken in 1996, shortly before the automobile accident with my mother. It was really quite hard to make sure she didn't catch onto something when I made the photos."

"Anything else?"

"Hmm."

"Think hard."

"I must say, now that I think about it, when I examine these photos..." Meiwes pauses for a few moments. "I think Bernd Brandes, who came to me five years later...Yes!" Now he realizes the context of the photos, which had so struck me when I studied them in my office. They were the exact script of the events to come. "Oh, yes. I 'butchered' and prepared Bernd almost exactly in the same order as in these photos."

"Thank you, Mr. Meiwes. That will do for today."

I pick up the photos from the table, put them back in my folder, get up and leave.

WHEREFORE IF THY HAND OR THY FOOT OFFEND THEE, CUT THEM OFF, AND CAST THEM FROM THEE: IT IS BETTER FOR THEE TO ENTER INTO LIFE MAIMED OR LAME, RATHER THAN HAVING TWO HANDS OR TWO FEET TO BE CAST INTO EVERLASTING FIRE. AND IF THINE EYE OFFENDS THEE, PLUCK IT OUT, AND CAST IT FROM THEE: IT IS BETTER FOR THEE TO ENTER INTO LIFE WITH ONE EYE, RATHER THAN HAVING TWO EYES TO BE CAST INTO HELL FIRE.

(St. Matthew 18: 8, 9)

Chapter 6

THE MOTHER

THE COUNTRY OF LEBANON is about half the size of Hesse and has a population of three and a half million people. Unlike many other countries of the Arabian world, Lebanon is not—I'll use a word appropriate to this book—"devoured" by the desert. The narrow 155-mile-long coastal plane is fruitful, a favored land, with hot summers and mild winters. In the fields, citrus fruits, bananas, and date palms flourish. Covering the mountains, whose highest peak rises to over ten thousand feet, are pine and cedar forests, as well as groves of olive trees and fruit gardens planted on the terraces carved out by the inhabitants. The mountains are covered with snow into April and look, here and there, much like the Tyrolean Alps. Vacation spots such as Broumana, Aley, and Damour appear to have been transported from Austria or Switzerland to this unlikely location in the Middle Eastern landscape. In an easterly direction, the Lebanese Mountains descend steeply to the Bekaa Plateau, nine miles wide, and seventy-five miles long. It is the country's granary. Here lie the vineyards of Kasra and Kefraya where an outstanding Blanc de Blanc and the "Chateau Kefraya" are produced, as well as the easily digestible Arak. Arak is the national schnapps of the Lebanese, pressed from grape skins and supplemented with anise in the second distillation. This lends it its unique flavor.

In the Lebanese capital of Beirut, the thermometer, on this June day in the year 1996, reads ninety-three degrees Fahrenheit in the shade. The city, with its million and a half inhabitants, stews in the scorching noonday heat. The sunny skies would lead one to believe the land below must be a paradise, yet Beirut has been for decades a hell on earth, a land where civil war rages unendingly. The city's deep wounds are visible in every street. Shell holes and bombed-out houses are silent testimony to previous attacks. The people of Beirut have coined the proud saying, "Beirut died a thousand deaths and was a thousand times reborn." It is a ravaged land.

Burning houses, torn up streets, wailing ambulance sirens transporting the dead and wounded. These are the terrible symbols of the fifteen-year civil war (1975-90) that destroyed Lebanon—the "Switzerland of the Near East."

In 1996, while the usual unrest and assassinations plague Lebanon, Armin Meiwes stands in the steaming heat of Beirut in the front yard of a two-story, whitewashed residential house. Around him, five dark-haired children are romping about. The Wüstefelder is playing tag with them. The children laugh. It is his third visit to this country. Meiwes is taking a three-week vacation in Lebanon. His neighbor in Wüstefeld, the Lebanese-born German citizen Maarouf Y., is his host in this foreign land. Y. is a security official of the Deutsche Bahn Co.

Maarouf Y. shows Meiwes his homeland. They visit the majestic temples of Baalbek, whose cornerstone was laid four thousand years ago. The temples, because of their tremendous size, are included among the most significant holy places ever built in the Near East. The remains of the Temple of Jupiter, with its six columns—originally fifty-two—are numbered among the landmarks of Lebanon. Even the smallest temple of Baalbek, the Temple of Bacchus, is mightier than the Acropolis of Athens. Meiwes also goes to the world-famed "Cedars," another historical site of the country. Biblical King Solomon knew the quality of cedar wood and had his temple and palace built of it. In the first Book of Kings, Chapter Five, Solomon asks Hiram of Tyre for help in the building of a temple. In the Bible, we read in verse twenty [Translator's note: in the King James Bible, verse six]: "Now therefore command Thou that they hew me cedar trees out of Lebanon; and my servants shall be with Thy servants..." The Pharaohs used the costly wood in building their sun boats and sarcophagi. Many centuries later, there remain but a thousand cedars in the ancient forest stands of Lebanon. Some of these trees are over fifteen hundred years old and of great size and beauty. Tourist Armin Meiwes snaps dozens of pictures of these beauties of nature. By means of a delayed shutter release, he photographs himself in front of them. Later, he films the same scene again.

*

Armin Meiwes's host, Maarouf Y., in his interrogation by the Police in Alheim (Proceeding No. ST/0132109/2002), gave the following testimony concerning the perpetrator:

> In June 1988, I moved into a house at No. 5 in Wüstefeld.... The house was situated quite near Armin Meiwes's house.... Armin lived there with his mother. We had a very good relationship with them both. We helped one another and I found it wonderful that Armin and his mother helped our children with their homework.... I can also say that Armin helped tend the garden. He came to our house quite often and used his big tractor to mow the entire lawn. And he volunteered to repair my cars. He didn't even accept money for it. So it was a very warm, neighborly relationship.... Armin was with me altogether four times on vacation in Lebanon. He went to Lebanon with me in 1994 and 1995, 1996, and also and lastly in 1998.... He mostly flew with us to Lebanon and stayed there, as a rule, for two weeks.... I still own a house in Lebanon, and Armin always stayed in our house. There I have a family with about 200 relatives. I think Armin got to know almost all of them. They liked him a lot, because he was such a nice fellow.... He didn't have a real hobby. He liked to tinker with old cars. He still has an old Mercedes sitting behind his house, and two Trabbis. He also has an old Wartburg. As a second hobby, you might say, he was always fiddling with computers.... Armin told me he often went on the Internet, but I don't know what he meant by that.... I had absolutely no objection

to Armin playing with our kids. He got along well with children.... If everything I read about him in the papers is true, then he has totally disappointed me.... For practically 14 years, I've been deceived by him.

*

"It was a real bomb of a mood in Beirut," laughs Meiwes, winking over the stale joke during my next visit to the Kassel Penitentiary.

"Did your mother release you and let you go on vacation?"

"I decided whether and with whom I went on vacation," he says firmly. "My mother had nothing against it because she treasured her family. She was fond of her children, so she made no great objection. All she said was 'If you want, just go ahead. It's too hot for me over there.'"

"Excuse me for saying so, but Lebanon isn't only hot. It's not exactly recommended as a vacation spot by the Foreign Office."

"Ah, anyway I really enjoyed going there." Meiwes is unshakeable. Not even the danger of bombs deterred him. "That there was war there a few years ago and an occasional attack during my visit, this didn't bother me. Besides, I did a lot of thinking there."

"What about?"

"The bomb and grenade craters made me think of how many dead there must have been. It became even clearer to me how quickly life could end. Poof! A second and it's over!"

Death might almost have caught Armin and his mother Waltraud Meiwes, too, on Sunday, April 14, 1996. Just after rising, Waltraud Meiwes says to her son, "Armin, dear, I haven't been out of Wüstefeld for a long time. Let's drive around the area a bit and see where our ancestors lived."

Armin, his face still tanned after his vacation, readily agrees. He wouldn't have dared to refuse. He sits down at the wheel and his mother takes her seat next to him. She buckles herself in as usual. At nine o'clock, the golden Mercedes 280 moves off from the manor house toward Rotenburg. With no particular destination in mind, mother and son want to visit some of the cemeteries in the surrounding villages in order to search the records for the names of deceased relatives. But on this Saturday morning, most parish offices are closed. Only in Thuringia is their quest rewarded. In this little village, they meet the priest, whose name Armin forgets right after the introductions. The clergyman offers to give them some information about the inhabitants of the surrounding area. He leafs through the files gathering dust in the archives of the parish. He now looks specifically for the ancestors of Waltraud Meiwes. After a short interval, he announces to his waiting visitors in tones suitable to the pulpit, "Dear Sister, on your relatives, the Meiwes and Vetter families, I have unfortunately found nothing in the death notices. God bless you!" Of her own family, there were no survivors, since her own brother, Helmut Vetter, had been killed in France on March 2, 1943, during the Second World War. Cancer had taken away her sister, Gerta, at the age of fifty-eight, and her mother had died in 1971, at eighty-five. She had broken her back. Of this large family, only Waltraud Meiwes was left. Her mother, born in Essen as Waltraud Siegfried Lydia Vetter, wrote a little book entitled "The Plate," in which she referred to the "historic significance" of her family from 1790 on.

For Armin Meiwes, this day is wasted with another one of those senseless Saturday excursions on which he chauffeurs his mother about the region without goal or purpose.

Already getting on in years, the now somewhat senile woman says, "Well then, they're all buried together in Essen." Armin supports his mother on his arm and gently propels her out the door. Very nearby, he sees the village tavern. "Come, Mother, let's go in." Since the sun is shining, they decide to sit under an umbrella on the open square. His mother orders her favorite dish, beef stew with rice, and Armin allows himself half a duck with blue cabbage and a fat potato dumpling. Both have a small glass of Burgundy. During this late noonday meal, they don't converse much other than to say politely, "Taste good, Mother?" and "Yes, fine thanks, and yours?" "Mine too, yes, yes." "Shall we go home, then?" she states more than asks, "I'm tired."

Armin leads his mother to their parked car, opens the passenger door, and helps her in. He hands her the safety belt and shuts the door. He goes to the driver's side, takes his seat behind the wheel, and turns on the ignition. They drive off.

After about six miles, around four o'clock in the afternoon, Mother and son are in their Mercedes on a winding country road, enmeshed in a sluggishly moving column of vehicles. Ahead of them creep a truck and a VW flatbed. Behind comes a black Porsche 911, uncomfortably close to Meiwes's vehicle. Just after a local exit, on an uphill curve, the Porsche driver suddenly pulls into the left lane, passing Armin's car, the truck, and the flatbed at eighty miles an hour. Down the hill comes an Opel Kadett headed straight for the Porsche in the midst of its risky passing maneuver. Just at that moment, Armin thinks, "He's going to crash." The Opel driver tries to veer, but the Porsche sideswipes its fender at full speed. There is a loud, metallic gnashing. Next to Armin, his mother gasps, "What's that?"

The Porsche lurches but comes quickly to a stop on the left side of the lane. The Opel Kadett skids, rolls over, and stops about a hundred yards farther on, diagonally on the narrow road.

Armin feels as if he had watched this scene in slow motion detail. He jams on the brake. The tires screech. His car collides at around thirty-five miles an hour with the radiator of the besieged Opel, crashes fifteen feet deep into a ditch, and ends up positioned sideways against a tree. The force of the collision knocks the windshield out of its frame and it shatters into a thousand tiny fragments of glass.

Then there is dead silence.

Armin turns immediately to the passenger side and looks at his mother. Waltraud Meiwes's breath rattles. She is taking shallow inhalations and says not a word. She is unconscious. Her son tries to get out of the car to rescue her, but both front doors are jammed. Armin crawls onto the back seat and manages after two or three minutes to get out by the rear door. Completely self-controlled, he goes immediately for help. Climbing out of the ditch, he sees, as if by a miracle, an ambulance returning from a mission. He jumps into the road and hails it. The medical aides carefully lift Waltraud out of the car. She is given oxygen on the spot.

Armin, also, is given a checkup. Except for a few scratches and shock, he is completely unhurt. The driver of the Porsche and the three occupants of the Opel Kadett have also escaped with only slight injuries. Waltraud is diagnosed later in the hospital in Bad Hersfeld; the seventy-two-year-old has broken all her ribs above the safety belt and suffered serious internal injuries. No organ is intact—the spleen is ruptured, the lungs crushed, the kidneys bruised.

For almost three months, Waltraud Meiwes lies in the intensive care unit, her life sometimes in the balance. On top of her multiple traumas, she has been diagnosed with thrombosis, a vascular condition in which a clot (thrombus) forms in the circulatory blood vessels. This in turn can lead to a fatal embolism, the complete blockage of a blood vessel by an errant blood clot.

Waltraud has to take the medication Markumar. This chemical preparation serves to thin the blood, thereby preventing further thromboses. Its main drawback is that a pinprick or a small cut can cause hemorrhaging.

Patients on Markumar have to be tested regularly to determine the clotting rate of the blood. If it is too low, there is danger of fatal internal bleeding.

In September of 1996, Armin brings his mother back home to the Wüstefeld manor house in the repaired Mercedes 280. She lives out her days as a needy, bedridden woman, for Waltraud will never recover from this accident. She can't even cut a slice of bread or wash herself. From this time on, Armin, besides his other tasks, must take over all the domestic work.

*

In the meeting room of the KP, Armin Meiwes puts his elbows on the table and hides his face in his hands. His cheeks are creased in a pattern like a harmonica.

"How did your mother cope with this accident?"

"After that, my mother wouldn't leave the house at all," he says, keeping his elbows on the table. He seems melancholy speaking about this episode. "She was like a child. I had to keep an eye on her twenty-four hours a day. Besides that, she was subject to mood changes because of having to lie in bed so long and because of the need to take the blood-thinning medication. She was very unhappy about her physical condition. Unfortunately, it made her even more demanding and eccentric. The worst part was her constant fear of hemorrhaging. She was always calling me up, in the shop or wherever, because she was so afraid. I hardly got home, and it was, 'Armin, do this, Armin, do that.' It was awful. I hardly had time to meet anyone. Not even friends or women."

"What burdens did you have to carry on your shoulders during this period?"

"Get up, cook, clean, do the laundry, take care of Mother, go to work, call Mother on the phone, go shopping, serve her meals, change the wet bedclothes, and help Mother into bed. I would turn on the computer to calm my nerves. Even at night, I couldn't go out."

*

Ali Y., oldest son of his Lebanese friend Maarouf Y., in his interrogation on January 2, 2003, (Proceeding no. ST 0354238/2002) offers this recollection of the time:

> She was very dependent on Armin. This dependence extended even to financial matters, since she didn't get much of a pension and, as far as I know, didn't even have health insurance. I had the feeling that Armin could never bring a woman home with him. Mrs. Meiwes had very decided views on a wife for Armin. Anybody else

would have been out of the question for her, and she wouldn't have tolerated any woman who didn't meet her requirements....

Mrs. Meiwes was very bossy. She treated Armin like a child. The two of them also argued frequently. Armin did defend himself orally, but Mrs. Meiwes always had the last word.... After Armin and his mother had the collision in the car, she couldn't move about as much as before. For example, Armin had to help her in and out of the car, or when she wanted to get up from a chair. Besides that, he had to do all the domestic chores—the laundry and the cooking. That probably bothered him a lot. He didn't complain directly to me, but it could be seen from his behavior that the whole situation weighed on him.

*

These oppressive consequences of the accident meant for Armin Meiwes de facto house arrest. One could say he received a suspended sentence with probation. His mother now shuts herself up in the half-timbered house and Armin gets away from the estate only when he goes to work or buys food. He cares lovingly for his mother despite the hard work, and does all the domestic chores. In the daytime, the son functions much like a machine.

When night comes, Armin hunches for hours in front of the computer in his workroom. He occupies himself with the assemblage of photo collages in which naked men are portrayed in torture scenes. Or he makes pencil drawings of young boys tied to wooden bars with their bellies cut open. "Abducted by Cannibals," he titles one such "work."

For his employer, the Cooperative Computer Center of the Volks- und Raiffeisenbanken in Kassel, Meiwes must dispose of two gray bank safes, each four feet six inches high by two feet deep. He installs them, however, with help from an office colleague, in his computer room in the Wüstefeld manor house. Both safes, of security level C, have several compartments. Electronically safeguarded number combinations hide his secret "treasures"—gay porno magazines, photos made with self-timers, his own slaughter sketches and pictures, dildos, and imitation body parts made of marzipan.

Long after midnight, Armin sits at his Grundig TV in the living room, secretly watching films of corpses, documentaries on injured people, reportage on cannibalism, and gay porno films he buys in sex video shops in Kassel. "These films fascinated me and distracted me from my overwhelming loneliness," Armin states.

Such films to deal with "overwhelming loneliness?" He could also have read the Bible, Goethe, or Shakespeare— even Stephen King. He could have watched BBC nature films or painted landscapes. He could have kept busy growing orchids or running his miniature railroad on the top floor. But Armin Meiwes has decided instead to focus his sick thoughts more and more on cannibal-fantasies and dead bodies. It is his hobby, his passion—and his ruin.

"Mr. Meiwes, among the confiscated videos, there was a series of porno films that belong in the sadomasochistic category that feature brutal 'shackle games.'"

"You won't believe it, but those videos did not arouse me sexually."

"No? Do you think I'm stupid? Pardon my cynicism, but you can hardly have used the porno cassettes as covers for beer glasses."

"Please believe me. I wanted those films, not for the sex scenes, but for the video of entire bodies, from head to foot, for the purpose of processing them better with the PC video card. Before, I altered the still photos, but now I could put together my own little illegal slaughter films. The best suited for these were the filmstrips of the American filmmaker, Tom 'Ropes' McGurk, which I found in the sex shop in Kassel."

On the Internet, one also finds on a Swedish home page, a trailer of McGurk filmstrips. A DVD costs 29.90 Euros [about forty-five dollars], and these DVDs have names like "Keep Sucking," starring Master Bondi & Caeden, "No

Way Out," and "Raped and Waxed." The films can be sold freely to persons eighteen years or older. The illustrated DVD envelopes show nothing but men in perverted, homosexual activities. The main actors are muscular, covered with oil, and wearing leather garments and chains. In the stills, the actors flagellate themselves in cages, tie themselves with ropes (bondage) to the diagonal cross, and are chained with handcuffs to iron bars. In these, McGurk is always the "master," and the other actor, the "servant." Master and slave.

"Did these sadomasochist pornos inspire you in some way, if not sexual arousal?"

"The films led me to probe deeper within my thoughts. A man's fantasies are as infinite as the universe. I became specialized in the artistic illustration of slaughter and looked for source materials to improve my creativity. I became a real master at it."

"And a slave to your sick fantasies," I commented. "Why didn't you at least include 'normal' sex films?"

He gazes at me for a long time, as if the answer were in my eyes. "Oh...well," he says at last and only half answers my question, "it was just so thrilling. I had created my own world."

"What a world. Were you able to sleep soundly after seeing this rough fare—we'll call it horror-porn?"

Somewhat embarrassed, Meiwes scratches his upper forehead. "Well then, in bed, before going to sleep, I enjoyed reading Mickey Mouse magazines."

"That's a giant leap—from sadomasochistic illusions to kids' comic books."

"I love Mickey Mouse," he says, beaming like Columbus after discovering America. "I had a whole collection of Mickey Mouse comics that I bought during my Army service. And even afterward, I bought every new Mickey Mouse book in our supermarket at Wüstefeld."

A grown man who reads and collects Mickey Mouse books. That is another side of Armin Meiwes: concentrated cuteness.

"Didn't you ever have any nightmares?"

"No. I have never once had a bad dream, either of corpse parts, or of blood, or anything like that. I have always slept soundly. And I still do today."

"Didn't your fantasies or later actions ever enter your dreams?"

He shakes his head. "It's the truth. The slaughter representations and everything I've experienced to this day—including the Bernd Brandes part—I've never seen any of it in my dreams. Not even for a second."

I still cannot believe that Armin Meiwes, after his bloody deed, can slumber like a well-fed baby. I myself can no longer sleep without the possibility of Meiwes, in the form of a demon, appearing in one role or another. For Meiwes to sleep peacefully is but further proof that for him, his actions are "normal" and to this day, his conscience is clear.

*

At the end of 1996, Meiwes establishes, through Tiscali GmbH, Robert-Bosch-Strasse 32, 63303 Dreieich, an Internet connection for his telephone number, 06623-7579. His IP address is 62.246.25129. The access number is 62.246.25.129. The connection is in his name; the address is 1 Wüstefeld Estate, 36199 Rotenburg. The subscription charge of 19.90 marks, as well as the connection costs, is charged monthly to his account under the notation "Tiscali online."

"I came to view the Internet as further liberation," Meiwes explains. "At first, I surfed it in a quite normal way. On the World Wide Web, I looked for subjects that had always interested me, and I looked for male action photos. I also read stories, such as the one about Jeffrey Dahmer."

Yes, Jeffrey Lionel Dahmer, known as the "Monster of Milwaukee." Beginning in 1978, the blond, bespectacled man killed at least fifteen—in any case, that was the number that was given in court—mostly black young men, in Wisconsin. The heads, limbs, and genitals of his victims, he kept in his refrigerator. Dahmer, as he explained in court, wanted to make the men mindless sex slaves. On November

29, 1994, the mass murderer was killed by a fellow inmate with an iron bar.

"And this sick criminal interested you, Mr. Meiwes?"

"Among other things, although I was repelled by his actions. I hate violence, which is why I never used it. I also looked for male action photos in order to download and save them so I could process them later. I now had a lot more material for my evening hours."

Later, Meiwes plows through the World Wide Web in his search for photos and videos of corpses, body parts, slaughtered animals, and torture scenes. Within the rapidly growing Internet universe, Armin Meiwes, the always nice and polite computer technician, begins to show his other side, Armin Meiwes, the butcher. The photo collection of Meiwes takes a more drastic turn towards even more extreme perversion.

Picture One: Meiwes stands completely nude in front of a bookshelf covered with plastic film. His arms and legs are stretched out from his body. He looks like a big X.

Comment by Meiwes: "I presented myself as a hanging corpse. I later put the photo in my 'Yahoo Group' on the net—that's a kind of exclusive club for like-minded friends."

Picture Two: Meiwes has wrapped himself naked in transparent film. He crouches, bent over in front of the bookshelf.

Comment by Meiwes: "This presentation is supposed to show a person packed in cooler wrap. He is to be frozen and then seasoned and consumed."

Picture Three: On a carving board lies a three-inch-long organ, and next to it, in a frying pan, an imitation penis. "That's my cock," says the prisoner happily, "the one on the left," he explains, pointing to it with his index finger. "The other, the penis on the right, I put together out of pigskin and pork. By exhibiting the two genitals side by side, I could show how well I succeeded with the imitation made of pork. I found these imitations more realistic than the photos I made with the dildo. The penis in the frying pan was to be eaten. Got it?"

"Did you eat the penis made from pork?"

"Yes, of course. I seasoned it with salt and pepper, added a little garlic, and broiled it nice and juicy."

Picture Four: A life-size show-window mannequin lies on a greasy grill.

"That one really needs no explanation: a man is to be grilled."

Picture Five: I try to help him define it: "It looks like a backside made of marzipan."

"Absolutely right! A human behind, from which I'd like to prepare a roast ham." He stares me down reproachfully because I laughed sourly. The next pictures are also grotesque and absurd, which he has recorded on celluloid: a broiled pork leg in handcuffs, a doll on the roasting spit, a show-window mannequin on a hook, and so forth.

Comment from Meiwes: "Oh yes, the pork leg in handcuffs. It looks like a man's lower arm. I know all that stuff quite well because I carved up some animals for my neighbor. The huntsman, who rented her forestland, gave her, from time to time, a wild boar, a deer, or a hare. So I had lots of experience handling meat."

*

Armin Meiwes interrupts his work at the computer only when he hears the doorbell or the tapping of his mother's cane in the Wüstefeld manor house. As his mother's condition worsened, Meiwes found his creative time dwindling.

"And it was endlessly nerve-wracking," Meiwes says with emphasis in a disgusted tone. "In those last months, I didn't have a quiet moment to myself. On New Year's Eve of 1998, my mother had a very bad fall on the way to the bathroom and injured her hip. From then on, she couldn't control her bladder. I had to pull on her adult Pampers for her." He grimaces with disgust.

"I changed my mother's soiled diapers and washed her. She couldn't get out of bed any more. I even had to carry her downstairs because she could hardly walk. Her mind was still active though, which meant she was just as demanding, if not more so. Caring for her was a physical burden, but, worse than that, was the extremely heavy psychic burden that weighed on me. I was hardly out of my room and she would tap with her cane. She would bleat, 'Bring me another cup of tea,' 'bring me another bowl of soup,' 'bring me more something or other.' She never dropped her bossy tone. It was dreadful, simply dreadful."

*

Nicole Agaficioaei, née Wurmnest (she gets the complicated name from her second husband, a Rumanian), has her brown hair pulled back on her neck with a clip, a fringe of bangs on her forehead. Mrs. Agaficioaei wears silver eyeglasses with blue-toned lenses and silver earrings. The overall impression the forty-five-year-old woman makes is one of a quite young and vivacious woman. One would not imagine, from looking at her, that she has borne and raised four children.

I called her after she slipped me her number at one of the trials I attended. "I'm a friend of Armin's," she said then. "If you want to find out something, I can help you."

Now we're standing in a drizzle on the bank of the Fulda River in Rotenburg. When she speaks, she inclines her head to the left, and sometimes her head begins to nod back and forth. Her voice reaches the volume of an operatic diva, a bit too loud for my taste.

"I met Armin in September, 1998, at a private celebration in the 'Landcafe' in Rotenburg. We liked each other from the beginning. I had a computer in which something didn't work right, and we got on the subject of computers quite by accident. He told me he was a computer technician and would be glad to help. Armin also said he was living alone with his mother, and that she had something against women he might bring home because she was very domineering. Anyway, Armin repaired my computer a few days after we met. My youngest son was also born around that time."

"How was that again, Mrs. A-g-igu-la—oh, Nicole?" I interrupt the flow of her words. "Your son was born when Armin...?"

"No, no, what am I saying? It just happened that in that same year, my youngest son was born," she says, correcting herself.

"I remember Armin being fascinated by the baby and admiring him. I handed him the baby to hold. He held him quite lovingly. In the summer of 1999, I went down to see Armin with my baby, and we drank coffee—I mean Armin, his mother, and I. On that occasion, I saw the entire house with Armin, from top to bottom. He showed me all the rooms, including his bedroom on the first floor. The house fascinated me immensely and I thought of what one could make out of it. At the same time, it rather depressed me because all the rooms were crammed with furniture and you couldn't get a good view of them. Also, it smelled very musty."

"And his mother?"

"His mother was very nice to me and my children. One could sense that she loved her son very much, but also very much needed him. Mrs. Meiwes somehow dominated Armin's life. She wanted him to make her dreams come true, that he live her life for her. To live a life that she hadn't created—that's how I see it. Armin, of course, had a hard lot with her. That woman just sat in her chair, and when she became ill, she only lay in bed. He was alone with her in that enormous house. He attended to his mother before work. He came home in the evening, washed and dressed his mother, and took her downstairs. He cooked, did the laundry, and tried to keep clean the rooms he used. His kitchen, for example, was immaculate. I was often down there when she was still alive. She was quite taken with my baby, and you could see that this was also her wish to have family, children, living in the house.

"Once we drank coffee outdoors in the garden, and Armin had set the table and served cakes. Then she said, 'No, not this set.' And Armin said, 'Well, I've got this set already on the table.' And she insisted, 'No, I'd like the other set, with such and such colors.' Armin was clearly upset and irritated.

But he went in and got the other set. Those naturally were things that grated on him; that has to be understood. He had a pile of things to do, and when his mother dwelt on such petty details, it exasperated him. You have to understand this woman, too, who sits there and can't help herself, can't move and is reduced to the point where someone has to take care of everything for her. But after that summer she went quickly downhill."

After Nicole Agaficioaei has related all her meetings with mother and son, she embraces me warmly and whispers in my ear, "Just between us, I would entrust my children to Armin even today." Then she looks deep into my eyes before saying, "You understand what I mean. Armin, as I know him, is a good man. He is no monster."

*

It is Thursday, September 2, 1999. Armin Meiwes is on the telephone at his workstation in Kassel. He's distressed. The PC of a client in Bad Homburg has fallen to the floor. Besides that, the ATM of a bank in Kassel has been reported out of order. If the customers had their way, he'd have to solve both problems at the same time. Meiwes is exhausted. For weeks, he has slept hardly more than three or four hours a night. Today, shortly before noon, an indefinable, queasy feeling in the stomach area creeps up on Meiwes. At first, he can't imagine where it comes from.

"It was weird," he recalls.

Meiwes tells of one of the worst shocks in his life, if not the worst. "Well, my mother was no longer a young girl. She was seventy-seven years old and had been very ill in recent years. On the night of September first, she seems to have had a slight heart attack, because in the morning she felt really awful. She said, 'Armin, my right arm hurts.' I asked her, 'Shall I call a doctor?' She answered, 'No, it must be this damned hot weather. Just go on to work.' I gave her another aspirin and started to leave. Going out, I said, 'Mama, I'll make sure to come home quickly from work.'"

"After I had repaired the ATM, I tried to call her. But she didn't answer. The weather was still fine, and I thought, well, maybe she's sound asleep and doesn't hear the phone. I got home about four-thirty. I opened the door and called out to her. No answer. Then I went upstairs to the first floor. Her bedroom door was open.

"I saw how she was lying in bed. I went to her. My mother's eyes were wide open, and the blanket hung halfway down to the floor. Rigor mortis had already set in. 'Mother is dead'—that was clear. There wasn't a spark of life."

"What did you feel at that moment?"

Meiwes stares at the water glass in front of him. He blinks. It even seems as if his eyes are wet. A hint of feeling? But he says something unexpected. "I thought only, 'Shit!'"

"Did you caress your mother?"

"No. I was in shock, and for the moment, didn't know what to do. After trembling a few moments, I called our family doctor, Mario K., and then the hospital. The doctor came right away. He stated that she had died around noontime, exactly when I had this indefinable feeling in the stomach."

"What was the cause of death?"

"She probably had a second, and this time fatal, heart attack. The way she laid there—well, it wasn't the first corpse I'd seen. I saw my grandma on her bier. Anyway, our doctor took care of all the necessary formalities and notified the funeral parlor. When the doctor and the body were gone, I broke down and cried uncontrollably. It was clear that I was now completely alone. They were all gone: father, brothers, and mother."

"I don't want to seem unfeeling, but there's a pressing question on my mind. Did you, at that moment, think of assimilating your mother?"

"I didn't give it a thought. I wanted to assimilate a brother. But maybe it was because I was convinced in my heart that my mother would not have wanted it. Besides, she was a woman."

"Oh, if your brother had died, would you have eaten him then?"

Meiwes reflects a moment and answers with a complacent smile. "If it had been my brother, and he had wanted it for himself, then I would have eaten him. My father would have been much too tough." He grins ironically.

"Well, five days later there was the burial," he continues. "My mother didn't receive the last rites and was not laid on a bier. She didn't want all that."

"Who gave the graveside homily?"

"My brother Werner, who's a Protestant priest. He organized the funeral service accordingly in the little chapel at the Atzelrode Cemetery."

"How did the burial go?"

"Well, Wüstefeld isn't very big, and we were at that time, I believe, thirty-five residents, including fourteen children. They were all there. From the Atzelrode locality, some of the one hundred and eighty residents had come. We had brought along a cassette recorder and played music by Johann Sebastian Bach. The sermon my brother Werner gave was really very moving."

This is how the parish bulletin announced it:

> "Waltraud Meiwes interred. Rotenburg-Wüstefeld. With representatives of the local community taking part, our sister Waltraud Meiwes (aged 77) was interred in the Atzelrode Cemetery. 'At the final moment, she was once again the little girl she had been before. We will never forget our mother,' said her eldest son and Protestant minister from Berlin, Werner B., in the moving, hour-long burial service in the presence of 50 guests. Heart failure was given as the cause of death."

*

"We recorded the whole burial service with a tape recorder," Armin Meiwes tells me.

"Why did you do that?"

"That was the drama! On the very day when my brother Ilja set out for Egypt on his honeymoon, our mother died. I didn't know what to do, call or not. He couldn't cancel the honeymoon or fly back. For him, I had the sermon, the sounds in the funeral service, and the lowering of the coffin recorded by a lady friend, and then we all listened to the cassette together."

"The idea never would have occurred to me, Mr. Meiwes."

"Well, it was all nicely organized. Nicole [Nicole Agaficionaei, nee Wurmnest] and the other ladies of the neighborhood arranged the funeral meal, with coffee and chocolate cake. We held it at the manor house in the rooms where the computer courses were planned. There was plenty of room there."

"Do you still recall what you thought when you tossed a rose to your mother at her grave?"

"I wished her luck now that she could live in peace and quiet."

"You mean...could rest in peace," I corrected.

"Or something like that."

"Were you also relieved by her death?"

"Shocked and relieved at the same time. Somehow, I was glad it was all over."

*

The Atzelrode Cemetery lies today in the shade of its mighty pines, especially the older part of the cemetery, with its steep slope. Here are the majority of the graves, numbering around seventy.

Twenty days after the death of Waltraud Meiwes, side by side with his brother Ilja, Armin Meiwes kneels this morning at the gray marble gravestone with the lily carved on it. The resting place lies at the side of the cemetery; seen from the street, it is the third grave above on the left. Armin holds a package with two tubes of special glue in his hand. His brother Ilja, back from his honeymoon in Egypt, places the granite figure, twenty-eight inches high, on his mother's grave. The figure looks like a dog. It is a representation of Anubis, the Egyptian jackal—or dog-headed death-god. Ilja has brought it with him from his honeymoon. The ancient Egyptians believed that Anubis accompanied the deceased as a guide into the underworld.

The demigod takes charge of the departed at the gate of the beyond and leads them to the court of the dead. Anubis presents them to the celestial judges and oversees the weighing of their hearts on the "scale." If the good side of the soul is large enough and tips the scale, the soul comes into paradise. If not, the soul belongs forever to Osiris, ruler of the underworld.

Armin carefully mixes the contents of the tubes, spreads the mix onto his mother's grave, and then presses the black dog firmly down on it.

"The statue looks nice. She'll like it," says Armin to his brother, gazing at his mother's black-and-white photograph on the marble gravestone. On the stone is only the inscription: *"Waltraud Meiwes, born Vetter 6.12.1922, died 9.2.1999."*

*

Death has cut forever the umbilical cord between Waltraud Meiwes and her son. The cannibal in Armin Meiwes has been cocooned for the three decades Waltraud has ruled her son's life. Now it struggles slowly free from the narrow coils of his soul. Only one year, six months, and eight days remain before he will bring his dark fantasy to life.

BUT IF THINE EYE BE EVIL, THY WHOLE BODY SHALL BE FULL OF DARKNESS. IF THEREFORE THE LIGHT THAT IS IN THEE BE DARKNESS, HOW GREAT IS THAT DARKNESS!

(St. Matthew 6: 23)

Chapter 7

ROLE-PLAYING

T HE FIRST HALF OF ARMIN Meiwes's life has ended. Two months have passed since his mother's death on September 2, 1999, and nearly all traces of Waltraud Meiwes have been eliminated from her son's life. He has her name removed from the telephone book and replaced with "Armin Meiwes, Wüstefeld Estate," establishing himself as a lone entity. When his lady friends and acquaintances bring up the subject of his mother, Meiwes ignores them and changes the topic. He is not interested in sharing memories of bygone days. His disinterest irritates his intimates to this day. "I never saw Armin weep over his mother," his friend Nicole Agaficioaei reports to me. "I'm not even sure he was really able to grieve over her."

Another acquaintance of Meiwes from Rotenburg, Marion Reich, tells me, "I've known Armin Meiwes for seven years. I hoped, after Waltraud Meiwes died and he was freed from her pressure, that Armin would go out and circulate again. But he withdrew into the house."

Her son has not cleared out the cupboards in his mother's bedroom in the Wüstefeld estate. The white bed sheet upon which she died is the only item he has discarded. "The house is so enormous that I don't need every room," comments the prisoner, explaining his reasons for leaving her effects behind closed doors. The outward impression arises that after Waltraud's passing, he didn't want to part with her possessions, but sentimentality appears not to be the reason. He simply "didn't want to do another damned thing" for her after her death. To quote Schiller from his book, *The Conspiracy of the Fiesco in Genoa*, rather loosely, "The moor has done his duty. The moor can go."

"I had the living area and two rooms in good order," he says serenely. "If someone came to visit, it was under control. In the other rooms, I had my stuff."

"Stuff" means piles of clothing, old furniture, broken bikes, wooden toys, dozens of cardboard boxes full of books, magazines, videos, diskettes, letters, shoes and much more. The only things properly arranged are the pornographic materials and his Mickey Mouse collection: they are even methodically numbered. On the bookshelf of his former room, there are 420 notebooks, carefully organized in rows. Two life-size store mannequins guard the hallway outside his rooms in a macabre reminder of his perverse role-playing fantasy life.

Armin Meiwes lives alone in the manor house with its thirty-six rooms, except for his spotted fourteen-year-old cat "Saami." For several months after Waltraud Meiwes's death, Saami pads about the building, meowing plaintively, until he too succumbs to old age. Armin Meiwes finds him one evening after work, lifeless on the front steps. With a shovel, he digs a grave behind the house and buries him. "'Bye, Saami," says Meiwes. "Now you are with my mother."

The manor house becomes a storage box for Meiwes's fantasies. There is not a soul left to keep tabs on him—not a good thing.

At the turn of the millennium in the year 2000, Armin Meiwes is attending a party at the home of his neighbor, Nicole. "I wanted Armin, after his mother's death, to get together with people again," she explains.

Also, she reasons, her friend Martina E. and Meiwes would "make a good couple." A single mother of three children, Martina E. hits it off immediately with the Wüstefelder. A week later, they go on a first date, dancing in the Rotenburg disco "La Gondola." Martina is happy that a man is interested in her and her children, and that Meiwes treats her like a gentleman. She finds him "somehow funny," however. The expressions of tenderness don't go beyond kisses on the cheek and handholding. The Wüstefeld manor house, too, strikes her as creepy. When Meiwes reveals to her that he is also interested in men, she immediately breaks off the relationship. The episode lasts only two weeks. Today Meiwes declares, contradicting her, that he was intimate with Martina. Misrepresentation or wishful thinking?

Other than his work at the Kassel Accounting Center, Meiwes no longer has any obligations. He also seems to have no friends, save the one he talks to on the Internet.

Throughout the evening and night, he spends his time exclusively online. For hours, to the point of mental exhaustion, Meiwes surfs from one sadistic website to another. With every click, his addiction becomes more intense, ever more brutal—bloodier and bloodier—until the Wüstefelder reaches the site he has been searching for, like a dying man in the desert finally coming upon a lifesaving body of water.

It is no longer Waltraud Meiwes, but the Internet that runs his life. From his mother's lackey he mutates into a slave of the World Wide Web. His urge masters him. The electronic network pulls him magically onward into a deep black hole from which the emotionally stunted Meiwes will remain trapped for the next three years.

"Today we get down to the nitty-gritty," I say as I greet him on this, my seventh visit in the Kassel Penitentiary.

"To the nitty-gritty, that's good, yes, yes, yes," he repeats like a Master Sergeant. Otherwise, on this Thursday morning, the prisoner gives the impression of a gushing spring waiting to be tapped. Meiwes trots back and forth in the room as if he'd had five double espressos. He is as pleased as if someone had just freed him from a straitjacket. Even his voice is a couple of tones higher than usual. "Where do you want to sit? Where are the glasses? Shall I pour us some tap water? Oh yes, here's my diary."

For three hours, the cannibal and I, this time without a prison official, for we are comfortable enough with each other now, are to be cooped up in the narrow confines of the 130-square-foot conference room on the first floor of the KP. Table, two chairs, washbasin, barred window—this room is already familiar to me. The rubber tree in the unlit corner by the doorway I first saw on my third visit four weeks ago has become bent over with only three withered leaves left on its stalk. It is drying up so forlornly that before I can devote my full attention to the man-eater, I pour three glasses of water onto the dust-dry earth.

I often ask myself during my research why I'm inflicting the cannibal subject on myself. I hope its only purpose is not for me merely to save the Kassel Penitentiary's rubber tree.

"Why are you in such high spirits, Mr. Meiwes?"

The convict, seeming fidgety, pours me a glass of water and straightens his chair. "I don't know myself. It could be because we've finally closed the chapter about my mother. That was a difficult subject."

Meiwes and I sit down on two wooden chairs at the table. Almost simultaneously, we take a swallow of water. Today even, it tastes surprisingly fresh. We both settle down to the conversation. Without beating about the bush, I come straight to the point.

"Mr. Meiwes, when did you first search for cannibals and victims on the Internet?"

"Well, it was around the middle of the year 2000. After my mother passed away, I grappled very intensively with the subject of death. On the Internet, I looked at pages on death and corpses. I also downloaded many stories on this subject matter. Through a link, I happened on various cannibal pages. I saw everything there was. At first, I thought it was all fantasy, even the way the ads were formulated, so that you couldn't really believe it. There are actually people who want to let themselves be eaten and also people who are looking for others to eat."

"What was the first cannibal page called?"

"Oh, I can't remember exactly anymore."

He puts his right hand up to his mouth. "Hmm," he says, reflecting. What pushed him to take action, he expresses in numbers. "There were at the time about twenty home pages and cannibal forums, mostly in English. In German, there were then about ten. Later there were over a hundred. On a single page, there were over a thousand ads, so there were already a large number of people who had registered to be members."

In the year 2000, an estimated one hundred and ten thousand people worldwide were actively engaged on the Internet. In Germany, the number of active users at that time has been estimated at around ten thousand, mainly men, but also women. Worldwide, the number of users who want to butcher or be butchered—most of them offering themselves as victims, is put at over a million. This estimation is confirmed by the experts of the Federal Criminal Bureau. In these forums, the Internet is like cement fusing together like-minded people like bricks of an institution hidden far back off the main road.

"What exactly was in the advertisements?"

"The advertisements were designed with great care by their authors. Most were two-liners with photos of bodies or body parts attached. There were men and women. People revealed their most bizarre imaginings and told what they had already done or what they secretly dreamed about doing. Naturally, I was drawn in and answered ads at times. Wrote a couple of lines, proofread them, and 'click.'"

Armin Meiwes taps the table with his right index finger, illustrating how uncomplicated it has been up to now to make contact with "victims" and other cannibalistically inclined people. A "click" and you're in.

"Did you adopt a pseudonym?"

"At first I went in with my normal web address and only looked at the ads. The first one I answered was from a 'Luke.'" He smiles, leans his elbows on the table, reaching forward with his hands. Meiwes lulls himself in happy memory. "'Luke' offered himself on a 'gourmet chicken page' because he was only twenty years old. The heading: 'Young man, twenty, I'd like to be eaten.' Fresh meat, you see. A handsome, muscular fellow from Austria. I answered him and we chatted quite intensely with each other."

"What did you write to each other in your emails?"

"Yes, well, I thought, is this fantasy or reality? It did sound very serious, though. Luke told me he had grown up in his grandfather's house. His grandfather always angered him as a boy, with the threat that he would end up in his belly if he weren't good. His grandfather then died, and since then, Luke had imagined coming into the belly of another man. And so he was looking for someone who would do that for him."

"How did 'Luke' visualize it?"

"He wanted to be butchered. I was to stuff his abdominal cavity with lemons, season him, and then roast him like a chicken."

"A man dreams of ending up as a grilled chicken? And you believed it?"

Meiwes flutters his arms and hands as if he were himself a startled hen.

"Yes, yes, that was unbelievable for me!" he says happily. "For over thirty years I've dreamed of eating a man, and now men are offering themselves voluntarily! All my life I've been thinking I was the only one with such fantasies. But there were hundreds, no, thousands on the Internet exactly like me. I began to explore this Internet jungle systematically. Luke soon became somewhat boring in comparison to the other offers. On a torture page, I got to know 'Matteo' from Italy. Matteo wanted to be beaten to death and thought up all possible ways of dying: with an iron bar, a hammer, a shovel. We chatted daily and exchanged our fantasies. He wanted photos of how I would eat him. Luke and Matteo were my first Internet acquaintances. They both knew my private email address, too."

*

On a day in early June 2000, Meiwes enters the "Toom" property market in the Bebra-South commercial zone. He heads for the garden furniture section. On a red cardboard sign is a special sale: wooden bench for only twenty-three dollars. Meiwes feels the bench, tries the hinges, and then lies down on it. He wants to test its stability. After his careful examination, he decides to buy it. Along with it, he buys a small table, four feet long and two feet wide, with green folding legs. He piles the boxes with the furniture packed inside onto the shopping cart, pushes it to the checkout counter, and pays in cash.

In the parking lot, he puts the two heavy boxes onto the back seat of his golden Mercedes. On the way home, our lord of the manor stops in the short-term parking lot in front of the Beate Uhse shop. Meiwes passes the shelves offering various sex toys and humorous gifts—stuffed bears with sex organs, dildos in all sizes, inflatable rubber dolls with blond, red, and black hair. He also passes by the bargain counter filled with sex magazines. His destination is the remotest corner of the sex shop, the sadomasochist section. He looks purposefully for a couple of dozen hooks, a whip, cords, and handcuffs. He takes the handcuffs, packed in hard plastic, off the hanging shelf.

"Will they hold up?" he asks the well-over-fifty saleslady, who clearly has seen a lot in her in life.

"With them you can even hang someone on the wall," she quips.

"Great, just what I need."

The saleslady gives him a quizzical look. She then packs up the dozen large S-shaped iron hooks, the modern handcuffs with a toothed "rattle" and lock, and the sadomasochist whip. The whip, with a leather grip and thirty rubber knots fastened to it, comes with a printed promise to produce acute stabbing pain. Meiwes pays about eighty-seven dollars and carries the purchases out of the store in a brown bag devoid of any wording on its sides.

In Kassel, he purchases four stainless steel butcher knives with blades three, four, six and ten inches long for twelve dollars. In a market on the edge of town, he acquires several colored plastic buckets with a gallon capacity, a black plastic garbage pail with a cover, and eight silver serving platters. Later he adds to his collection a stainless steel meat grinder and a rubber hammer, which he surmises, will be "useful in stunning my victims."

After another half-hour, Armin Meiwes is back at the Wüstefeld manor house. He parks his Mercedes at the front door. It begins to drizzle. With effort, he hauls the heavy furniture pieces and the utensils up into the smoke room, which is located on the top floor of the building as is usual in old farmhouses and manors.

The 200-square-foot room was formerly utilized by the seven or eight families who lived in the house over the last hundred years as a smoke room for meat and fish. Its walls are black and sooty.

Here stands, since as far back as Meiwes can remember, an oil stove. To the right is an old bed with iron springs and no mattress. He unpacks the disassembled bench and wooden table from their boxes.

Carefully he screws together, part to part, the bench and table and places them in the center of the room. On a small sideboard in the adjoining room, Armin Meiwes arranges, like a surgeon laying out his instruments, the four razor-sharp butcher knives, an old cleaver belonging to his deceased grandmother, and three packets of "Melitta-Toppits" freezer bags on one of the silver platters he bought. With equal deliberation, he rigs the block and tackle he has used normally for renovations to the manor house. He screws five butcher hooks into the wooden beams of the ceiling. In the following days and weeks, Armin Meiwes fits out the smoke room with more accessories, such as two 100-foot ropes, "hand-woven, four-stranded, specially tear-proof," which he has had cut in a store specializing in sailing equipment.

He knots two rope-ends fast to the new table. From wooden boards, he puts together a simply shaped "X" on the back wall, a seven-by-seven-foot "St. Andrew's Cross." A St. Andrew's cross is a torture instrument with two diagonally fixed beams crossing each other. The name refers to the traditional story of the apostle Andrew, who was executed on such a cross. Meiwes plasters over the broken places in the wall with quick-drying cement and lacquers them in black, in keeping with the room's color scheme.

Out of an old umbrella and a piece of TV cable, he puts together his own whip. Later, Meiwes acquires a "cat o' nine tails," a real whip, on another visit to the Beate Uhse shop in Kassel. The term whip, incidentally, is one of the few "Polishisms" in German and is derived from the Polish word "bicz" which has become "peitsche" in the German language. A "cat o' nine tails" is a whip with nine rope-ends woven of leather. The "cat" served in past ages for torture or the disciplining of slaves on ocean voyages. Nowadays, it is used by the Dominatrix, belonging among the symbols of the sadomasochist scene. Meiwes places a dozen old mattresses against the outer wall of the sloping roof, so that the screams of potential victims cannot penetrate to the outside. After weeks of intensive work, the former smoke room is transformed into a torture chamber—or to put it more accurately—into a slaughter room.

Armin Meiwes is now a one-man commando, fully deployed. He photographs himself in the severe pose of a butcher, proud of his newly assembled torture chamber, naked—arms and legs spread out in front of the St. Andrews cross. For the next Polaroid and videotaping, he hammers ten four-inch nails next to his penis into the little wooden board on which he has laid it. Afterward, he presents the butcher knives laid out in a row on the table. Then he offers himself, without a shred of clothing, in handcuffs, chained to the new wooden bench.

*

In the conference room of the Kassel Penitentiary, smoking is forbidden. A sign with a cigarette crossed through is clearly visible on the wall. "Shall we have a smoke?" asks Armin Meiwes. "I'll take the butts with me and we'll open the window. No one will find out."

Armin Meiwes takes pleasure in the forbidden. Admittedly, in this vice of smoking, I am also weak.

"Okay." I agree to a breach of the rules.

The convict offers me a cigarette and lights it. Then he puts a Marlboro between his lips, puts a flame to the tip, and draws firmly on the filter.

"Aaah," he groans. "I need this to relax."

"I need it for my nerves. This project with you is no picnic," I reply.

"That I can understand," he answers tolerantly. Puffing on my cigarette at the open window, I resume the interview with the cannibal.

"Why did you rig up the slaughter room?"

"It was because of Matteo."

"Because of whom?"

"Well, Matteo, the Italian. Before being beaten to death with a hammer, a shovel, or the like, he wanted to be singed and browned with a flamethrower."

The smoke remains stuck in my throat. I cough loudly. Undeterred, Meiwes continues.

"The photos I made of myself were all made for him. At first, I sent him photomontages, but he saw through it right away. 'Send me real photos so that I can believe you,' he wrote. So I complied with his wishes. Matteo also wanted his penis nailed to the board, and wanted me to make cuts on his sex organ. Then he wrote asking me to put an electric oven under the scaffolding. It was his wish to be roasted alive."

"You seem to do anything other people want."

"Well then, I wanted it too. Matteo wanted a painful death. He didn't care what happened to his body. And I wanted to take pictures of somebody. It was like when you court a beloved person. You give it your all."

"And you obediently transferred Matteo's instructions into pictures and emailed them to him?"

"Yes, that's how it was. Sometimes I even improved on his suggestions. That gave Matteo real pleasure. For example, I showed in one photo how I would cut along his penis. Then I dribbled a little ketchup on my penis so that it looked like blood. Matteo was enthusiastic over my work. Also, I sent him the pictures taken in front of the St. Andrews cross, so that he could see how I would torment him and tie him up."

"Matteo was your idol, wasn't he?

"No, no. Besides Matteo, I sent these photos later, on request, also to my other chat contacts and complied with their wishes.

"Why?"

"I was in search of someone who was fit to be my brother, whom I could take into myself. And it had to be someone I especially liked."

"And with Matteo you weren't sure?

He looks sadly disappointed and pouts. "No."

"Why not, then?"

"Matteo wanted me to pick him up in person in Naples, but the Alitalia flight was much too expensive for me. Then he wrote that he had met a woman. It was too bad."

*

In its judgment on May 9, 2006, the Provincial Court of Frankfurt, under File No. 5/21 Ks 220983/05 (or/2005), comments:

> For the planned gruesome killing and then butchering of "Mattheo" [Author's comment: Thus the court calls him erroneously] he [Armin Meiwes] rigged up on the top floor of the Wüstefeld estate a "slaughter room," and fashioned in according to "Mattheo's" wishes a cross, acquired a whip and installed a steel bed, and under it a stove intended for roasting "Mattheo." He sent photos of the slaughter room to "Mattheo" by email to persuade him to come to Wüstefeld and have himself be killed and butchered. Despite these efforts, "Mattheo" broke off contact with the accused, without a meeting ever having taken place. The accused then, in the middle of the year 2000, inserted several contact ads in Internet forums for the purpose of finding a "slaughter victim." This should be a "handsome young man" between 18 and 25 years old, pleasant, and physically appealing, not too heavy, but also not too muscular. When not a single person in the specified age group replied, the accused changed his age specifications and raised the maximum age to thirty, and in addition opened, in August 2000, his own Yahoo Newsgroup, naming it "Cannibals," with himself as moderator. He also entered more soliciting ads and answered ads of others…. The accused also had lengthy, in part also personal contacts with a number of Internet partners, and he traveled often to keep agreed appointments, at which his contact partners failed to appear. In one case, the accused even went to Holland.

*

Every evening after work, the computer technician takes photos of himself as if on an assembly line. In most of them, Armin Meiwes is naked or dressed only in a rubber apron, a knitted cap, or leather boots. In some of his hundreds of photos, he is holding, like a macho-butcher, his grandmother's cleaver, or a butcher's knife. In others, legs sawn off store mannequins hang from the ceiling of the slaughter room, or a head made of painted paper maché lies on a silver tray.

"Many chat partners wanted photos showing me as a butcher," recounts the cannibal. "That worked better with fantasy names. I couldn't just write to them, 'Hello, I'm Armin Meiwes, your master butcher, I want to eat you.'"

His ironic, complacent smile is not infectious.

My conversations with Meiwes make me more and more aware of the magnitude of the butcher's perverted Internet community. Umpteen thousands of people are taken in by the swindle of the Internet anarchy and let themselves be lured into a life that promises them "happiness" and "sexual highs." It is a delusional world preying on the emotionally fragile, blurring the lines between reality and fantasy.

Yesterday's news looms in my thoughts. After the strange disappearance of a "slender youth," Focus TV reports that in Germany, every year, one hundred thousand people are reported missing to the police. Of these cases, two thirds are resolved within twenty-four hours. The other third are divided among victims of abuse, dropouts, accidental deaths, persons having problems with partners or parents, or those who have run away from home. Ninety percent of these missing reports, therefore, can be eventually cleared up.

But what about the other ten thousand missing? They vanish as if they had been swallowed up by the earth. There is no apparent reason for their disappearance, as will turn out to be the case of Meiwes's victim, Bernd Brandes. The explanation given by the police is that many people assume a different name on the Internet, making it almost impossible to trace them.

"Mr. Meiwes, how did you hide your true identity?"

"For Luke and Matteo, as I already mentioned, I used an email address with my name, ameiwes@tiscalinet.de. Then I adopted a special address. At hotmail.de I called myself, 'Antrophagus.' That means man-eater, and, as a pseudonym, I chose Franky, for the schoolmate of mine, Frank D., whom as a boy I wanted so very much to have as a younger brother and to have consumed."

Between April and June of 2000, Armin Meiwes uses a number of different Internet names and addresses, "Antrophagus" and "Metzgerin" [female butcher], among others:

antrophagus@hotmail.de
USER: ANTROPHAGUS
PASSWORD: LUKAS123

and

Metzgerin@gmx.de
USER: Martina
PASSWORD: Ameiwes

With all the care of a professional bookkeeper, he keeps a complete record of his Internet names, the individual access codes, and all of his researches on the World Wide Web. For this purpose, Meiwes sets up a red file folder and writes on the label, the code word, "Household." It sits ready at hand in his study, directly under the desk with the computer.

*

The extent of his Internet addiction can be ascertained from court records.

In its subsequent search of the house, the police discover in Armin Meiwes's three computers (PC, laptop from his company, and laptop in his car) fifty-two documents and file folders with hundreds of contact addresses, and tens of thousands of photos and videos. In the court records, under Proceedings No. ST/0353947/2002, all documents are listed in detail, for example: "The Slaughter Courtyard" (11/20/1999), "Human Meat" (4/19/2000), "The Penis" (12/6/1999), "Burger Boy" (11/28/2000) and "Cannibalism and the Culinary Life" (7/3/2001). On his computer memory disks, Meiwes saves photos of killed persons, butchering instructions, cannibal stories, and pornographic male pictures, torsos of naked men, hand-drawn sketches, and "carved-up examples" of the male body. He doesn't only save them; he even prints them all out! Altogether, the police find twenty thousand pages arranged in file folders or lying about in piles on the floor of his study. Up until the time of his arrest, according to police records, Meiwes has been in touch with four hundred persons. About sixty persons offer themselves as "slaughter victims," seven want to take part "actively or passively" in a butchering, another ten persons write him of having carried out a butchering themselves or of planning one.

There is also a printout of an article on the "Choice of the Right Youth," which Meiwes found on the Internet. It is an English-language instruction for the butchering of the male body, which, with the aid of translation software available on the Internet, he has translated into German and reformulated:

> *"Should it be permitted in the future to slaughter boys or young men, or not—I have been asking myself this question for a long time. And for me the answer is yes. For me this is an ethical question as well as a question of human nourishment in the future. I am of course well aware that an overwhelming majority of people would utter a storm of outrage if someone today were to butcher a man and prepare him for human consumption. Because for most societies cannibalism is something highly immoral. But is not the meatpacking industry today highly immoral? When might one butcher a boy, what*

regulations should there be, what can one produce from the fleshy parts? I would like to answer this question, and thereby render the necessary assistance to all those who eventually would like to slaughter a boy and may perhaps in future be permitted to do so.... Surely, it will become possible for many people to obtain half of a boy, and would then like to carve it up and process it. But perhaps it would be possible simply to buy boy's flesh only for a certain kind of sausage and make sausages. For this, no sausage kitchen with professional equipment has been needed for a long time; a few instruments would suffice.... Introduction: For the native peoples of New Guinea, human flesh was always a delicacy.... If their own son is to be slaughtered, his parents must sign a slaughter contract and give their consent....

The text goes on to discuss in detail the regulations for slaughtering, the layout of the rooms, and inspection of the flesh:

"The slaughter boys are divided into classes, for example, Class 1a: best formation of value-determining body parts, fat content— small to medium. Up to Class 4: poor formation of value-determining body parts. Boys/men assigned to Class 4 may not be slaughtered."

At another place, we read, *"More than 50% of a man's flesh comes from the legs, which consist of three parts: 1. Ham, 2. Thigh, 3. Calf."*

The slaughter instructions in this report, I need not, and will not, quote any further. We shall soon encounter their implementation in practice by Armin Meiwes in exactly those gruesome details set forth in the report.

*

A cloudburst suddenly drums heavily and loudly on the barred window of the Kassel Penitentiary. The heavy drops collect quickly on the projecting windowpane and fall down in a wall of water. Armin Meiwes shuts the window and sits down again.

In seconds, it is dark and gloomy in our conference room. In this oppressive atmosphere, Meiwes turns his head toward the window and remains in that position. Five, ten seconds pass. Nothing happens.

"I'll just turn on the light," I say, breaking the silence.

The prisoner reacts with a startled, "Yes, of course," as if I had wrenched him together with all his thoughts out of another world. I switch on the light and at the same time, on my way back to my chair, lead him back to his emotional life.

"Mr. Meiwes, your actions on the computer, the photos, the videos, and the essays, all of these were one thing. But on the Internet, you met real people who wanted to be eaten and you found that merely "exciting." All my efforts to understand you have failed. Shouldn't you have realized that you urgently needed psychiatric help?"

"If I had felt that way at the time, I probably would have spoken with a psychiatrist. But I didn't see it that way. For me, it was normal."

Normal? Even though Armin Meiwes so describes his feelings at the time, I expect, when I look into his eyes, I would perceive something like shame or at least insight. But there is only emptiness.

"Has your perverted euphoria deadened and blinded you?"

"Yes. It has to be compared to an addiction. I was addicted to cannibal-chats. There you are in a dream world you've created yourself. You work yourself farther and farther into it. And that was the problem. I couldn't find my way out. At first, I'd hoped to find someone I could talk with. But it turned out that we mutually worked each other up and completely lost a sense of reality. That is exactly the danger of the Internet. You talk about it and work yourself into it, so that it becomes normality. Then you don't think you need a psychiatrist...."

"Or a priest?"

"Pastor, priest or even an attorney. Even though those people have similar obligations to remain silent in consultations, at the time, I certainly never would have gone to see any of those. And on my own, the idea never occurred to me."

"How would it have been, then, if in the real world someone had asked you, 'May I eat you?'"

"I would have reacted exactly like anyone else. 'You're out of your mind' or 'Get lost!' That's how it is in the real world. But not on the Internet! The men I knew and liked in regular life, I never would have approached. Besides, I naturally didn't want to risk having it all come out."

*

Armin Meiwes has lasting and intensive contact with a few Internet acquaintances: among others, Jörg B. On July 1, 2001, Jörg answers one of the ads of the accused and offers himself for apparent slaughter. Jörg's internet name is "Meatboy."

"Well then, Jörg," says Meiwes, beginning a new chapter in his recollections. He tugs nervously with his right hand at the blue shirt of his prison uniform. "I conversed with him daily on the Internet. We met twice before Bernd Brandes. Well, it was a bit embarrassing because I sent him all the details about me, and he then confessed that he didn't at all want to be eaten. He offered first himself and then his two office colleagues to be eaten."

"I beg your pardon? I think I heard wrong! He wanted to offer you his office colleagues to be eaten?"

Meiwes looks bored and shrugs. "Jörg was a cook and apparently jealous of his colleague, this man named Michael. They had begun working at the same time in a hotel and Michael became a sous chef. Jörg also wanted the job but he didn't get it. The other, this Oliver, was Jörg's former apprentice and took Michael's side. That was why he wanted to eat them both with me, and afterward, let himself be butchered by me."

I still cannot believe what Armin Meiwes is telling me. I must ask him again and emphasize each syllable with exaggerated clarity, as if I were speaking with a hearing-impaired person.

"He wanted to eat up his office colleagues with you and then be butchered himself?"

My interlocutor remains very apathetic. "He said it was his fantasy. In any case, we were to butcher his colleagues, and later, I was maybe to consume him. That was the way we visualized it. But it was seriously meant."

*

Under File No. BY7403-008909-02/0, Jörg, who in his spare time is a competitive swimmer and has a passion for Alpine skiing, states the following on 12/17/2002:

> *Regarding my personal relationships, I can say that I have had a few brief relationships with female persons. But I have not yet found my dream woman. In the last two years [Author's comment: that is, since his meeting with Armin Meiwes], I have had no intimate relationship with any woman. ...I have had, however, thoughts about checking out something like that [homosexual contacts], because I wanted to know myself if I am inclined that way. I have already had intimate relationships with men, but have never gone to bed with a "man." ...About May/June 2000, I didn't feel emotionally good about it. At the time, I had fallen in love with a woman, but she wouldn't have anything to do with me. ...Also, there were problems at work. I was employed at the time as a temporary head cook. My boss then had me demoted to regular cook. Then, on my own, I quit and returned to the Black Forest. ... At that time, things were so bad I even thought of suicide.*

On the Internet, Jörg rummages about, with help from Google, searching for the term "suicide." In the process, he happens accidentally on the "eaten" forum. And here, first off, he makes contact with a certain person, Armin Meiwes. He, too, reads the ads the Wüstefelder has published as "Antrophagus:" "Hi, I'm Franky from Germany. I'm looking for young men between eighteen and thirty years to slaughter. If you have a normally built body, then come to me. I'll butcher you and eat your delectable flesh."

Later, Jörg states for the record that Meiwes described to him in his emails how he would kill him. Jörg, however, considers it rubbish. He tells Meiwes, nevertheless, that he is willing to let himself be butchered. Later, Jörg has contact also with another "operator" from the forum and two "victims." All of them, except for Meiwes, were interested only in role-playing.

When Meiwes opens his Yahoo-Newsgroup "Cannibals" in August 2000, Jörg is one of the first members. At that time, there are about thirty interested persons in the forum; at the time of his interrogation by the investigators in 2002, there were already 800! Again, 800 German men and women were dreaming of "butchering" and "being eaten" and wanting to translate it into action.

*

After several emails and a telephone conversation, Armin Meiwes and Jörg B. agree to meet on October 17, 2000. They exchange portrait photos. The rendezvous is to take place at the autobahn service area, "Tank and Rest" at the A7 in Kassel. Jörg is on his way from North Germany to Bavaria. He is coming from his family in Bad Segeberg and intending to go to his work place in the Black Forest. At the A7, he makes the planned stop.

The two meet at the entrance to the service area. They recognize each other immediately from the photos previously exchanged. "Hello, Jörg," Meiwes calls out, waving cheerily to his Internet acquaintance. He's as excited as a bashful schoolboy on his first date with a girl.

"Hello, Armin, glad to meet you," Jörg answers. The man from the Cannibal-Chat has a long face, a wide mouth, and big, bushy eyebrows. The cook, born in 1969, is six-feet-tall, has greenish brown eyes and short brown hair, and is slender and well proportioned. He works in a hotel in the Black Forest, where he also lives.

The two shake hands and enter the service area right behind the Esso gas station. Relieved over the friendly greeting, Meiwes gets from the self-service restaurant two mugs of coffee, a cream puff, and a doughnut. Jörg and the Wüstefelder take seats on two chairs at an unoccupied table in front of the window.

They talk for nearly half an hour. To begin with, they chat innocently about work and the trip. Then Jörg indicates that he is "completely heterosexual," and they talk about slaughter. For Jörg, slaughtering is "not sexual pleasure," but a "humiliation" which he needs as a "kick." He would like to take a "slaughter-fitness exam" to see if his "flesh is fit for enjoyment" and if he is suitable as a "victim." "Both colleagues are slaughter-fit," he says, raising Meiwes's hopes. During their conversation about collegial slaughter plans, a vacationing family with three kids sits down at a neighboring table.

Seeing them, Meiwes and Jörg are careful to speak softly. Like detectives in a Frederick Forsyth crime novel, they discuss the details of their plan and reach an understanding: Jörg will "chat" with Meiwes. Next follows the rehearsal for the slaughters. He delivers his colleagues. "I offer you Michael and Oliver for your menu." Jörg, "for the time being," doesn't want to take part in their actual butchering. "I have to get to know you better," he says to Meiwes at the conclusion of the discussion. "But let's make a date, anyway."

They decide on November 12, 2000, for the "role-playing" agreed upon. Meiwes takes his engagement book from his jacket and with a pencil carefully enters the date.

*

They agree to meet at the Hotel "Treff," near the Kassel-Wilhelmshöhe train station. Jörg, an employee of this chain of hotels, books a single room by phone at a reduced price.

At six p.m., the two meet in the parking lot. Jörg arrives in his old green BMW. This time their greeting is much more familiar than on the previous occasion.

They take the elevator to the second floor. Jörg opens the door with his card. They enter the three-star room. It consists of two single beds, two closets, a blue-upholstered couch, a round side-table for drinks, and a cherry-wood desk with a wooden chair. A TV sits on the mini bar cabinet.

Jörg immediately takes off his black gym shoes, pulls off his white shirt, jeans, underwear, and socks. Meiwes sizes up the fully naked man standing before him. "Shall I undress?" asks Meiwes, aroused. "It's not necessary," replies Jörg. Meiwes gives his "Okay," and so, clothed in his dark trousers and black sweater, he concludes his "flesh inspection." "Good. A little fat, but suitable for butchering. Lie down on the bed."

Jörg pulls the two blankets off the bed and tosses them next to the wooden bedstead. Then the thirty-one-year-old lies down on the bed sheet and spreads his arms and legs apart.

He lies before Meiwes like the "Vitruvian Man," the famous drawing by Leonardo Da Vinci, presumably from the period around 1485-90 of a young man with extremities outstretched. The study shows how much interested the genius Da Vinci was in the proportions of man. In contrast, the butcher Armin Meiwes is interested only in the fleshy parts. "The areas around your shoulders and neck really are something," he remarks appreciatively.

"Yes, there's no fat here, only muscles. There's good flesh on my buttocks, too, even if there's more fat," says Jörg eagerly.

"And how is it with your office colleague Michael?" demands Meiwes, impatient for an answer.

"His belly's a bit bigger, but not an awful lot. He weighs only about 140 pounds. Oliver is slender, too."

"A 140 pounds...I could cut off a nice piece of bacon from that," Meiwes reckons. "Michael is a hundred percent ripe for slaughter."

Meiwes massages Jörg's half-flaccid penis with his right hand and remarks appreciatively, "From your good piece, I can make up a nice snack."

"How will you cut me up, then?" asks the "heterosexual" Jörg, with erect organ now.

Meiwes runs his right index finger down Jörg's body. He assumes the dominant role in the game.

His voice is stronger than usual.

"Here, on your cock, my dear boy, I'll start in. I'll cut it off your body. Next comes the throat. I'll stick the knife into your larynx and push upward. Then the knife will come out on the other side of the throat."

Meiwes explains to Jörg that he would cut off his colleague's penis exactly the same way. At Jörg's request, the cannibal shows him how, after the penis has been severed, the outflow of blood can be furthered by lifting the legs. Jörg raises his legs straight up.

"That's it," says Meiwes.

"If the throat-cutting doesn't work out, I'll take a small cleaver to help me. Then I'll tie a rope around your ankles and pull you up, so that any blood left in the body can flow out."

Jörg works his fingers around his organ.

"Get the colored pencil, please," begs the subservient Jörg. "It's in the pocket of my blue jacket. Felt-tipped pens don't wash off easily from the skin. Draw it! Color me," he implores.

Meiwes sees the jacket hanging over the chair and pulls out the dark red-colored pencil.

"I brought something, too," says Meiwes, grinning without separating his teeth. He squints and his eyes become slits.

Meiwes takes his video camera out of a bag. "I want to film this." He places the camera on a shelf of the wall cupboard and adjusts the lens to focus it on the area around the bed. Then he presses the "record" button.

He goes back to the bed, kneels at the edge, and begins to rub Jörg with olive oil. On Jörg's lower left leg, he discovers an extensive burn scar and another on the left foot about two inches long.

"This flesh isn't suitable for roasting," pronounces Meiwes severely.

"That was an accident at work. I burned myself with hot pan grease while I was cooking," explains the devoted cook apologetically.

Meiwes slides the pencil point over Jörg's body. On the chest, he draws a dark red line that looks like a bleeding incision. Speaking like an experienced butcher, Meiwes announces, "From this part, I'll make a juicy cutlet."

Then he moves the pencil over the upper thigh to the genital area. "That will make a fine ham. I'll roast this piece in the oven 'til it's crisp."

"Turn over," Meiwes orders his "slaughter victim." He draws a circle around Jörg's buttocks. "And I'll make a roast ham out of your beautiful plump ass. It'll really taste great."

Now with the colored pencil, he draws a line showing how he'll carve up the belly and the area around the anus. In so doing, he touches Jörg's penis with the pencil, and says, "At this point, it's not there anymore, of course, but already in the frying pan."

Meiwes explains to Jörg how he'll remove the liver, the stomach, the heart and the lungs. "I already emailed you how I'll cut the bronchial tubes. It's a bit more complicated."

"When it's all done," Meiwes continues, "I'll wash your body. Then with a sharp knife or a saw, I'll cut through the chest bone and the spinal column in back. Then you'll be hanging in two parts. One part of the body will stay hanging, and I'll put the other part back on the slaughter bench. That half I will cut in quarters and I will cut off one leg and hang it on a hook."

Meiwes explains to Jörg where the filet in the back is located. "Is that like in a pig?" queries Jörg.

"Yes, exactly," Meiwes explains to his "slaughter victim" in the rehearsal. I cut the roasting pieces out of your buttocks and upper thighs. Anyway, you're ripe for slaughter, you've got meat on you, unlike the boy downstairs at the reception desk," he says with a smile. "That's nice."

"After all that, I'll be all prepared, and you can easily eat from me for a month," Jörg says happily.

Despite vigorous arousal in the "flesh inspection," neither of the two has an orgasm. "Thanks a lot, that'll do for today," announces "Master" Armin Meiwes, ending the rehearsal.

Jörg obeys and gets dressed without a word. Meiwes turns off the video camera and packs it back into the bag. The two leave the room. "You'll have to pay the bill, Jörg," demands Meiwes.

At the reception desk, Jörg pays the bill in cash and they take leave of each other in the parking lot with a firm handshake.

"It was fun," says Jörg.

"Yes, I thought so too," his counterpart agrees. "I still have the video. I'll enjoy it in the evening."

When Meiwes returns to the Wüstefeld manor house, he does indeed insert the videocassette into the recorder. He seats himself in the beige-colored armchair in the living room. In total quiet, he watches the "flesh inspection," while masturbating.

*

In the Kassel Penitentiary, too, quiet has returned after the cloudburst. The first rays of the sun throw the shadows of the window bars onto the floor. I turn off the light and hope that, eventually, I will succeed in shedding some light of my own on the dark inner world of Armin Meiwes.

"You made a date with a man completely unknown to you for 'slaughter role-playing.' Weren't you afraid the stranger would freak out?"

"Well, I was aware of the risk. But we had 'chatted' for at least half a year, so we already knew each other quite well. What I found most interesting was that he offered me his two office colleagues for my menu."

Since then, the word "menu" has had a different meaning for me. Every time I dine in a restaurant and the waiter politely says to me, "Here's your menu," I wince instinctively. I have to think of Armin Meiwes, who would have liked to find "Michael" or "Oliver" on it.

"For years you studied slaughter instructions. Do you think, seriously, that one can slaughter a man like a pig?"

"Yes, in principle, as only the form is different. The arrangement of the muscles is almost identical. The pig is more closely related to man than any other form of life."

"Can you show me exactly where you carve up something in a man?" I ask him challengingly.

The cannibal stands up as if on command, places himself stiff as a rod in front of me and points his right index finger to his carotid artery. "Jörg's idea was to be stabbed in the throat. Later he testified in court, stating that having his throat cut would be the pinnacle of excitement for him. I learned from him that his father is a veterinarian and that he has watched slaughtering. He always saw himself in animal form. He wanted to have his throat cut and his testicles severed, then to bleed to death. Then his belly was to be slit open and the innards removed. Next his body was to be cut in half."

"Cut in half...how?"

"Well, the head cut off, the chest bone and pelvis separated, the spinal column cut through. And then I divide the individual fleshy parts. The breast is a breast steak, from the upper arm you can make roasts and the like, and then the markings are drawn accordingly."

"Aside from the fact that you wanted a brother to 'assimilate,' was that enjoyable?"

"Yes, it was also enjoyable."

"Did you later have sexual contact?"

"No, no, not with each other, never. Jörg was completely heterosexual. He simply wouldn't have allowed it. I had asked everyone on the Internet before how he would like it, and for most of them, there was a sexual motive. But with Jörg, it wasn't important."

"Did the next meeting take place in a hotel again?"

"No. On November 19, 2000, Jörg came to me. I showed him my slaughter room on the top floor. He said, 'Look, I don't have time. I'm just passing through.' I suppose it was for him a bit weird and he left."

"Didn't you have a guilty conscience?"

"Nah, not about that. It wasn't anything unpleasant or out of the ordinary. On the contrary. We had put ourselves into this world. It was nice."

For Jörg, it was "nice" too, but exclusively in his fantasy. "And that is damned well enough," I would like to say with index finger raised.

*

Only in his second interrogation on January 24, 2003, in Kempten (Proceedings No. 34144/2003) does Jörg confess that he performed the role-playing as an act of despair and to give his sexual urge an outlet. The substance of the interrogation has been summarized by the author as follows:

> *I never had an intimate relationship with a woman. I kept quiet about it from fear of being discriminated against because at my age I didn't have a girlfriend. I answered Armin Meiwes mainly out of curiosity. I was suicidal. In my opinion, Armin wanted a contact to exchange fantasies with. I didn't assume he would do it literally. I myself really wanted to be slaughtered in the beginning, however.... He put pressure on me and asked about me when I hadn't been in touch with him.*

And on the origin of his "victim" fantasies, Jörg testifies:

> *At school, we once made an outing to a slaughterhouse. ...It was somehow satisfying. If I hung from a hook, I'd be relieved. These were my feelings. It wasn't the slaughter itself. It was*

*the moment of the killing. At the moment that I
thought about the slaughtering, I masturbated.*

When his office colleagues, Michael and Oliver, are
later confronted by the police with the fact that they were to
have been slaughtered, they are stunned, and are unable and
unwilling to believe it. They assume it is a TV prank by
"Hidden Camera." Only after twenty minutes, after reading
through the police findings, do Jörg's two colleagues grasp
the truth of the testimony. They are completely distraught
and shocked.

Jörg writes to each of them on January 26, 2003, a
letter of apology with the same text:

> *Hello Michael. Since you understandably
> don't want to speak with me, I'm writing you this
> letter on the advice of my psychologist.... I most
> sincerely apologize for having offered you to this
> Armin M. for slaughtering.... I don't know
> exactly what was wrong with me. He...tried to
> persuade me that first another, and then I,
> should be slaughtered. Sick, right? Anyway, I
> find it so sick that I'm not only getting
> ambulatory psychological help, but also I want
> to get stationary treatment in the psychiatric
> clinic. ...So it's not a simple "I apologize," but an
> "I apologize and I'll see to it that at least such a
> thing never happens again".... because I'm sick,
> such fantasies aren't normal.*

Michael and Oliver leave Jörg's letter unanswered.
Jörg has been under psychological treatment for years. He
was charged with representation of violence (the proceedings
were suspended after a six-month suspended sentence on
probation and a modest fine was imposed).

*

In the Kassel Penitentiary, the allowed conference
time of three hours nears its end. Before I go, I would like to
catch a certain reaction from Armin Meiwes.

"After the role-playing, this man came into your life."

I pull an enlarged portrait photo from my briefcase. Meiwes gazes at it, takes it in both hands. After looking at it for a few seconds, he says the name in a soft voice, "Bernd Brandes." His gaze remains fixed on the brown eyes hidden behind the eyeglasses of the man in the photograph.

"In mid-February 2002, I answered an ad he had inserted under the name, 'Cator,' in the Cannibal Newsgroup. The ad was headed with the words, 'Your Dinner.' The text by Bernd Brandes, word for word was, 'I offer to let myself be eaten alive. No slaughter, but eating. Therefore, whoever really wants to do it needs a genuine victim.'"

...BUT I AM CARNAL, SOLD UNDER SIN. I DO NOT UNDERSTAND MY OWN ACTIONS. FOR I DO NOT DO WHAT I WANT, BUT I DO THE VERY THING I HATE. NOW IF DO NOT DO WHAT I WANT, I AGREE THAT THE LAW IS GOOD, SO THEN IT IS NO LONGER I THAT DO IT, BUT SIN THAT DWELLETH WITHIN ME.

(Romans 7: 14-17)

Chapter 8

CATOR, BORN AS MEAT

Two hundred and fifty miles from the Wüstefeld estate, on Monday, February 5, 2001, Bernd Brandes is sitting in front of his computer in the study of his apartment in Berlin-Tempelhof.

To be precise, his full name is Bernd Jürgen Brandes. This man is in his forty-fourth year, five-feet-seven inches tall, and slender. He wears round, silver-rimmed glasses and has gray-green eyes. His black hair, lightly streaked with gray, is crew cut, an inch long. His forehead seems too high. Because of stress, he is gradually growing bald in spots about the size of a two-Euro coin. Embarrassed by these blemishes, he combs his hair so that they can't be seen at first glance. Bernd Brandes has even considered flying to London to visit a specialized clinic to have artificial hair planted at the top of his forehead and on the other bare spots. He had read that world star, Sir Elton John, acquired his toupee from there. Brandes had to give up the plan, however, on account of the cost, and jokes about it with his office colleagues. "If I lose any more hair," he laughs, "it will all go. That'll look sexy, too."

Since 1990, the year he finally came out to the world and embraced his homosexuality, Brandes has set greater store in his external appearance. He is almost ridiculously vain. He has shaved off his moustache, lost twenty-two pounds in the space of one year, and conditioned his body by exercising with dumbbells in the sport studio, "Fit on Rosenthaler Platz," at 125 Torstrasse. He also wears more modern and casual clothes than he did before. He favors light blue Levi 501 jeans, size 30-30, white long-sleeved shirts, and dark blue Nike gym shoes, size 8. During the day, he goes around in "boss" suits or in loud jackets. One of these jackets, a glaring ocher yellow, exemplifies his desire to be seen.

Bernd Brandes is a division chief in the internationally known Siemens, Inc., in Berlin-Spandau, in the "telephonic development" area. In "Siemens City," built in 1899, he heads a team with eight associates. His annual gross income is around 70,000 Euros, which, at the time, is a quite hefty salary of 105,000 dollars, and he owns a portfolio of Siemens shares, which he has deposited in the Berlin Savings Bank. He is regarded as somewhat self-willed, obstinate, and computer-obsessed.

In his study, fifteen PCs are humming, among them his high-performance eight hundred-megahertz "Pentium III" computer, which he now boots up on the desk in his thirteen hundred-square-foot apartment. He is in direct contact with his employer through a network and can even work from home. Through the network, he can get onto the Internet considerably faster than an average user in the year 2001.

While Bernd Brandes surfs, his friend René is already in bed at seven p.m. He is a blonde baker with a bit of a paunch. He has to be up and out at two a.m., since his bus leaves at two-twenty-eight. Twenty-five years old, René is almost exactly eighteen years younger than Brandes. The exchange of words between the life-partners often went like this:

"When are you coming? Everything okay with you?" asks the blonde René from the bedroom.

"Sure, right away, my pet. I'll just quickly check my emails," Brandes calls out, pulling deeply on his Camel cigarette, now the fortieth the chain-smoker has lit today.

The Siemens manager logs in to the Cannibal Newsgroup, "Nullo." In this forum, the members exchange their fantasies on the subject of "Emasculation." His pseudonym here, too, is "Cator." "Cator, born as meat." He sees the sealed yellow envelope icon. Brandes has just received a message.

The email comes from a certain "Antrophagus." It bears the heading, "Re: Your dinner." With a click on his mouse, Brandes opens it and reads the text. In haste, he scans every word written by the sender. "Hello, Cator, I read your ad. I'll slaughter you, but only if you really want me to. Let me hear from you. Your master butcher, Franky."

"Franky" is the Internet name of Armin Meiwes. Brandes taps out his reply on the keys. Instinctively, he senses that this unknown man is meant for him.

*

As the old saying goes, "For every pot, there's a cover." Bernd Brandes has found Armin Meiwes.

Like the Wüstefelder, Brandes leads a bizarre double-life, and for almost the last twenty years, he has been at risk of giving himself away: a password forgotten in a drawer, a scrap of paper with a telephone number in his jacket, a slip of the tongue to a friend. Just one careless moment could destroy his lifestyle and lay bare his sickly side. To the outer world, Brandes lives life as a normal sort of man, but hidden inside is the completely incomprehensible truth; the certified engineer is plagued by the desperate longing to have his penis bitten off by a man, and then be torn apart, butchered, and eaten alive.

The coincidence of two people like Armin Meiwes and Bernd Brandes meeting in the universe of the Internet is possible only because they are connected by a common passion: cannibalism in complementing roles. One is tempted to say, carelessly, "The two have found each other." What Meiwes lacks, Brandes has, and vice versa. Bernd Jürgen Brandes is born on January 19, 1958 in Berlin-Schöneberg, the only son of a prosperous physician and his wife. When he is five years old, in 1963, the boy loses his mother in a single moment. During a family vacation on the North Sea island of Sylt, Mrs. Brandes becomes a victim of a mysterious traffic accident. It is determined by the police actually to be a suicide staged to look like happenstance. Her husband, the elder Brandes, later testifies in court that his wife, who was an anesthetist, committed a serious technical error during an operation. The patient died, and Mrs. Brandes could never forgive herself. Finally, when the emotional burden became too much, she took her own life.

The father tells his son that his mother has died without giving the boy any details or offering him any comfort. What results is an anxious, deeply disturbed child, who is never to get over his mother's puzzling disappearance from his life. He isn't even allowed to ask his father, "Where is Mommy now?"

The subject is forever banned. It also remains unclear whether Bernd Brandes has ever learned that his mother may have died by her own hand or whether he has been told of his mother's professional error.

An only child, he is left to cope alone with this tragedy, a trauma from which Brandes will never recover. In the father's overwhelming silence, the child finds himself abandoned.

*

In the forensic-medical opinion delivered during the criminal proceedings against Armin Meiwes, Prof. Dr. Beier offers the following diagnosis:

> *His mother's premature death may have been a decisive moment for him, falling as it did in a vulnerable (according to general psychological development concepts) phase of his life. That is, it affected the five-year-old boy, who thereafter grew up alone with his father (and was cared for mostly by au pair girls), until, three years after his mother's death, a second wife entered his father's life. Bernd Brandes seems not to have gotten along well with this stepmother, but was inconspicuous and adaptable in his subsequent development. His psychosexual development, however, may have been highly unusual: the available information leaves...not the slightest doubt that in Bernd Brandes, an authentic desire for his penis to be cut off existed along with a sensation of (considerable) pain in the buildup of sexual arousal.*

*

Ten-year-old Bernd Brandes is a fine, conscientious schoolboy with "very good behavior." He has a reserved personality, but regarded by intimate friends at school as "high-spirited" and "generous." He is a student in the special mathematics and fine arts courses. At ten, he passes his fifteen-minute swimming test, and, at eleven, the advanced swimming test. The physician's son is proud of his cloth insignia with the two waves, won for the 400-meter long distance swim, the dive from the twelve-foot board, and the diving drills. At fourteen, he voluntarily takes part "with gratifyingly eager attention" in religious teaching by the church's Education Committee.

Brandes passes his graduation exam at the Erich Hoepner High School in Berlin-Charlottenburg with an average grade of two-point-three. Next, he completes his studies in electrical engineering at the Berlin Technical University. He finishes the main examination in electrical engineering on November 3, 1986 with a rating of "good," and the course in control engineering with "very good." Immediately after completing his studies, he finds permanent employment in the "Telephonic Development" area with the Siemens Company in Berlin, where in 1981 and 1982, he does his practical training. In 1992, the thirty-four-year-old Bernd Brandes advances to Division Chief with executive pay and works in a responsible position. He becomes progressively more estranged from his father, who moves away with his second wife, a former employee from his practice. To his professional colleagues, Brandes gives the impression of a man who seems to stand on the sunny side of life.

His intimates report unanimously that Brandes feels himself to be rejected by his dominant, almost tyrannical father, who views his son as a piteous weakling. The son can never win the praise, love, or understanding of his father. Bernd's professional accomplishments do not impress the man. When finally Bernd bares his soul to his father and confesses his homosexuality, the elder Brandes rejects him and breaks off forever with his son. For Bernd, it is as painful as if a sword had been plunged into his heart.

This tragedy looms over Bernd, growing into a surge of hatred for his father, but, even worse, a hatred of himself. Bernd Brandes becomes a masochist.

*

What is a masochist? In the foreign language dictionary of the Bertelsmann Publishing Group, the definition is "A person who finds sexual satisfaction in suffering mistreatment." The term "masochist is named after the Austrian writer, Leopold von Sacher-Masoch, who wrote intensely of such desires during his lifetime (1836-95).

Masochism arises from morbid personality disturbances. In most cases, the causes of masochism can be traced to disturbances in the affected person's family history or to traumatic experiences. A masochist only reaches sexual pleasure when he is debased, humiliated, or bodily mistreated, or when pain is inflicted on him. Symptoms include need for punishment, obsequiousness, and toleration of pain and humiliation, to which no healthy person would ever voluntarily submit. The AOK Health Insurance group writes about its effects: "Masochism is a malady which can lead to serious bodily harm. Since pain is the body's alarm signal, there arises in extreme enjoyment of pain, the risk of no longer being aware of dangerous situations. In severe cases, this may lead to self-destruction or mutilation." To identify the causes, psychologists and behavior therapists analyze the family history of the person concerned.

*

In the subsequent court proceedings, Bernd's father avails himself of a witness's right to remain silent. He does not want to testify. The physician only states the following in a telephone conversation with the expert on May 10, 2003:

> ...That inwardly, he has totally distanced himself from his son because he simply cannot understand the circumstances of

his death. He has long enough pondered, without reaching a reasonable conclusion, why his son could have evinced inclinations of this kind, and then decided to end this inner debate because he fears he would otherwise "go mad." His son has in a certain way died as far as he is concerned, and outwardly, he would—for self-protection—deny the relationship, since in his present place of residence he would have to expect damage to his reputation. He does however, confirm important biographical dates, and testifies that Bernd's mother died in an automobile accident in 1963 on vacation on the island of Sylt. This was a heavy blow to him, and obviously to the boy, whom he did not inform of the circumstances of her death. In his opinion, it had been suicide, for which she "sought out" the traffic accident. …He never revealed these background details to his son, and for the next three years took care of him alone or employed au pair girls for the purpose. His second marriage took place in 1966. The overall development of his son in childhood and youth he can describe nevertheless as uneventful. His son later found good professional connections and "always had lady friends."

*

The relationships that Bernd Brandes maintains, both publicly and in secret, can be reconstructed and sketched based on the available facts and research, as follows:

Brandes, who later admits to being gay, at first establishes a heterosexual identity. For seven years, from 1987 to '94, he is in a relationship with Anja B. [Name changed, correct name known to the author] with whom he lives. Their love collapses—according to the testimony of his stepmother and his father— "because Bernd Brandes seldom left the house, and took no part in cultural activities or sports, and thus lived a very introverted life." Further details, according to the court records, are not known, and testimony by Anja B. is not available. It is very possible, however, that his initial homosexual contacts may be responsible for the break. During a business trip to the United States in 1994, it seems he had sexual contact with a foreigner, for after his return, he has himself tested for HIV by his personal physician. Results: "negative."

*

It is snowing on this December day before Christmas in 2005. Large snowflakes are blanketing the Brandenburg Gate, making the capital, for a few hours, a "winter wonderland." The capital is as brightly lit by the Christmas decorations at five p.m. as an airport's runway at night. "Let's hope the pilots coming in from the GUS countries and Kazakhstan won't mistake our Kurfürstendamm for a landing strip," I say to cheer myself up in the damp cold before my next difficult conversation.

On the snow-covered sidewalk, I skid in my gym shoes walking toward the Friedrichstrasse subway station. I am on my way to my meeting with Anja B. After some research, I have tracked down Bernd Brandes's first love, and she agreed to a personal meeting.

Her two-room apartment is located in a dark gray building dating back to the 19th century in Berlin-Tempelhof, in the former eastern part of the capital, ten stops from my origination point of the Kaiserin-Augusta-Strasse station.

After I've rung the bell, the forty-five-year-old secretary of a tax adviser opens her door on the third floor. Anja B. is a delicate woman, about five-feet-five inches tall, the type one trusts immediately: short brown hair, modern eyeglass frames, green eyes, and a kindly aura. "Hello, nice to meet you," she says, greeting me in her distinctive Berlin accent.

The rental apartment, about five hundred square feet in size, smells of Christmas cookies and vanilla. A cat scurries through the vestibule. "She's visiting from my neighbor's," explains Anja B., "but she likes it better here with me than over there with her."

In her living room, she has set up three vanilla-scented candles in glass, like those sold in drugstores. We sit down on a beige-colored couch with simple cloth upholstery. She brings fresh coffee in a glass pitcher along with two porcelain cups from the large kitchen. Then she offers freshly baked cinnamon stars and vanilla croissants. "Thank you so much. It's very considerate of you," I say. "Oh, gosh, Bernd was also one of the few men who appreciated things like this," she answers.

"Well, it's natural," I say, rashly.

Suddenly, tears are running down her cheeks! She plucks a paper handkerchief from her pants pocket. "It always gets to me," she says apologetically, "that my ex-boyfriend was eaten. Won't you have more croissants? I baked them fresh."

"Yes, please," I answer. "And thank you also for being willing to talk to me about Bernd Brandes."

Anja B. sighs deeply, wipes away the tears, and begins to tell me about him. "You know, I met Bernd through an ad in the magazine, 'Tip.' Bernd was a Capricorn and I was a Virgo. We fit perfectly together as we were both rather rational types. I wrote him. For seven and a half years, we were a couple! We lived together from 1987 to 1994."

Her eyes become moist again. "Bernd, heavens! It was only after I'd moved in with him that he confessed he had published three differently worded advertisements. Then he got replies from three different types of women. Bernd said, 'So what? I decided on you anyway.' I was so mad!"

Her hearty laughter works on me like a libation and allows me to connect to the happiness and romantic love she had enjoyed. "The special thing about Bernd was the inner calm he radiated. I was only twenty-six years old. He gave me security, as he was a genuine native. Neither of us wanted very much to have children. Bernd said, 'Let's just the two of us enjoy the time we have.' He was absolutely right. Bernd was educated and always up to date. He liked 'Star Wars' and horror films—he got such a charge watching them—but he also read bestsellers. Bernd instilled in me, as his partner, the feeling, 'I know everything, I can do anything.' For example, he drove cars very well and he could show his feelings. In men, that's a rare combination."

She's able to laugh again. "But he could also be really stubborn and he was easily hurt. Sometimes Bernd really shocked me with his emotional outbursts. Once he cried like a child because I was happier about a birthday card than the mirror he'd given me. It was a hand-mirror—made in the prison where a friend of his worked as a locksmith. He cried over a mirror—isn't that sweet?"

"If you really loved each other so deeply, why did the relationship break up?"

"Bernd went to the US on business. This was something out of the ordinary. So, I flew to him. He arranged my trip, but I had to pay for it myself. He was different somehow. I just can't explain it. Bernd always seemed so typically manly, and that time he was, I don't know how to put it—weak.

"After my return, I was suddenly diagnosed by my doctor with multiple sclerosis, MS. When I wanted to walk straight ahead, my leg went to the right. Other men confronted with such a situation would simply take off. But Bernd was always there for me! He went to the doctor with me, to the therapist, to the specialist, to educational seminars. Bernd even called his father, a doctor, with whom he had always been on bad terms, to ask if he knew of a specialist for me. Bernd was really a big-hearted man."

Now Anja B. can no longer hold back her tears. She sobs in my arms. "It has to have been love," I think. After a minute or two, she regains control of herself and continues. "My illness changed us. For me, MS overturned everything. I had to rearrange my life. I went to bed at half-past eight and he, such a workaholic, sat in front of his computer until one o'clock in the morning. We talked less, I mean less about us, and only about other things. I sat in a golden cage, but I was alone. He sat hunched over the computer through the night, and we no longer slept together. Emotionally we'd already been apart for a long time. And then one day, I fell in love. I told him, 'Bernd, I'm going to look for another place to stay. And I won't sleep with you anymore.' He didn't understand this, and it probably frustrated him a lot. After a year I moved out."

"Did you never sense something of his homosexuality?" I query. Anja B. rests her lower arms on her knee and takes her coffee cup in both hands. "I never noticed any homosexual tendency in him. Bernd didn't behave like a queer, but rather very macho. Well, I did notice sometimes when we danced, the way he moved his wrist. My women friends said Bernd's motions were funny."

"He never told you he liked men, too?"

"No. Only after years, around the end of the nineties, he confessed to me over a glass of champagne, that for years when he sat at his computer at night and I was asleep, he had logged onto certain gay websites and had met men. He also called 0190 numbers on which young men can be heard moaning. When he told me that, I almost fell off my chair! Bernd told me that, even as a child, he had had a 'queer' experience with a schoolmate. The Internet fascinated him; he could get a 'charge' and remain anonymous. For me, Bernd Brandes was suddenly a second man whom I didn't know. With me, he was always normal. But I always hoped he would be happy."

"Would you have tolerated his bisexuality?"

Anja B. frowns, shakes her head in annoyance, and declares in a firm voice, "If I had known of his true tendencies, I would have dragged him to the doctor! I think he stumbled onto this 'men's scene' and was drawn into the wrong company. Gays get moved into sex faster and heavier. He liked young men. My hairdresser saw him at the 'Christopher Street Day' with a Filipino boy who looked like a woman. Bernd also lost a lot of weight so he could fit into this 'scene.'"

"Can you imagine why he wanted to have his sexual organ cut off?"

Anja B. reflects briefly, then speaks with deliberation. "I think Bernd Brandes was wholly prey to his homosexual urges. It caused him to lose all willpower. He must have had that wish for a long time, and then he realized Meiwes was serious. Bernd isn't the type to say, 'So, we'll try it out and do it a little.' He has always planned everything to the last detail—that is for sure."

We drink up our coffee, nibble Christmas croissants, and chat a little about Berlin and her life. Her illness has not robbed Anja, who now lives as a single woman and has only her mother, of her zest for life. Before I take my leave, she brings up the familiar subject again. "What shocks me the most are all these men who want to be eaten. They're physicians, businessmen...to me it's incomprehensible."

We wish each other "Merry Christmas," and she embraces me in farewell.

*

In contrast to Armin Meiwes, Bernd Brandes leaves no record of his two-decade double life or his sickly addictions. He leaves no farewell letter, not even a scribbled note; only a formless will. Instead of explaining himself, we hear only from those people whom Brandes knew well: friends, colleagues, loved ones, or those obsessed with sex. There are eight voices who describe not only his public, but also his hidden side—that of the "extremely perverted masochist." The women and men speak vicariously of his fragmented existence and display the facets of his character like a kaleidoscope. Reading their words, one comes upon a cascade of oppressive obsession, lies, deceits, and affairs. From the individual descriptions, one could not suppose they are discussing the same person. As in a mosaic, nevertheless, the individual reports form a composite picture that will end in gruesome self-destruction.

*

Voice One: Jimmy F.*, the ex-male prostitute [*Name changed, correct name known to the author.]

The Berlin Railroad Station at the Zoological Garden, called "Zoo" for short, is a social gathering place within the Federal capital. It is a mild July day in the year 2007. Behind the station building, on Jebenstrasse, men of all sorts— young, scarred, foreign, muscular, gaunt and mostly drug-addicted—slouch along the sidewalk like lifeless souls. Many are not even sixteen years old. "How about it?" says one of them to me, probably a Rumanian illegal immigrant, as he passes by me. "No thanks," I reply. The skinny youth nudges me on the shoulder with his right hand. "Hey, come on, let's have a little fun. Fifty Euros [about seventy-five dollars] and I'll give you a blow job without a rubber."

"Buzz off, I've got an appointment." I press a five-Euro note into the boy's hand. "Get yourself something to eat." "Thanks," he says, sounding almost relieved.

Even at a distance, I can see the six-foot-three, dark-skinned man with whom I have a one p.m. appointment. He is at the main entrance to the station. Deeply bent, he stands there like a crooked pole, as if his frail shoulders had a heavy, invisible burden to bear. I go to the black man and we shake hands. "Hello, I'm Jimmy," he introduces himself in a weak, high voice. "Glad you came," I reply. His handshake is as soft as his words. Jimmy F. is wearing black jeans and a white, ironed shirt with dirty spots on the collar. His shirt is unbuttoned, and it reveals bright spots on the skin of his chest. I gaze into his striking features. His eyes look feverish, fearful, as if a beast of prey stood behind him. His entire body trembles as he stands; traces of the past are still open wounds on his heart. Now forty-two years old, this man was the beloved friend of Bernd Brandes, that man who had his penis cut off and himself slaughtered.

"Please use a different name for me," he says, almost imploringly. "My parents and my twenty-year-old daughter have already been through enough."

"I'll be glad to do that," I promise.

We walk a few paces and sit down in front of the entrance to the Zoo, on a bench under a chestnut tree. The bench is in the shade, well protected from the noonday sun. Jimmy F. pulls a silver case from his trouser pocket, takes out a hand-rolled cigarette, lights it, and begins to talk in a rush of words.

"You know, it was over there that I first met Bernd Brandes in October, 1995." With his left hand, he points in the direction of the underpass to the station. "I didn't have a good impression of him. He was odd. If you work on the street, you get to read people's faces. Bernd Brandes was a funny, shy, reserved type. I was standing in the hall of the Zoo station, drinking a cup of coffee. He didn't come straight to me. Before our first contact on Jebenstrasse, he certainly must have observed me for half an hour from a distance. I don't usually like to deal with such people. They're unpredictable. Usually the 'steady fifi's'—that's what we call our customers—act differently. They speak to us directly, and afterwards, we go to eat together, or into bed. When Bernd didn't make a move to bring us together, I took matters into my own hands. I established contact with hand signals and eye contact. Bernd seemed satisfied with my approach, answered my look, and then I followed him on foot a couple of hundred yards in the direction of the University, out of this area."

"Bernd had glasses on and wore a leather jacket and jeans. He looked like an older student. We made small talk at first. I asked him for a cigarette. We talked about our professions, and I told him I was a student at the University. In the course of our conversation, I asked him, 'Are you interested in boys?' He said, 'Yes.' 'Are you interested in me?' Bernd said, 'Yes, colored boys like you have a special appeal for me.' Then, I told him right off about my taboos. 'I don't do anything without a condom or far-out things that could hurt me.' That was all right with him."

Jimmy—father from the Congo, mother from Tanzania—worked a while in reinforced concrete construction and then landed on the street as a prostitute. He pulls on his nearly burnt-out cigarette stub and continues in a steadier tone with the rest of his story.

"So I got into his car. We were on familiar terms right away. Bernd took me directly to his apartment in Berlin-Tempelhof, at 11 Burchardstrasse. First off, he showed me his computer room, where he had at least fifteen PCs—all working! He said, 'I'm a computer technician. It's my job.' He was a real high-tech freak, always wanted the latest electronics that came on the market. I asked him if he often brought boys home, as it would be dangerous with all the computer stuff he had. He said, 'No, but with you, I have a good feeling.'

"Bernd turned on the television and we chatted for a while on the couch. After about twenty-five minutes, he said, 'Do you want to shower?' I showered and we went into his bedroom. The room was all mirrors, every wall, and even the ceiling. Bernd asked me to suck him off. While I was doing it, he said suddenly, 'Nibble my cock a bit.' He moaned and said, 'I want to see your white teeth; that gives me a charge. Bite me! Yeah, bite harder.'"

"Wasn't that unusual for you?" I interrupt.

He lights another cigarette, inhales briefly, and starts gesticulating vigorously, as if he wants to gather his words together in the air.

"Well, with the pain thing, it's nothing unusual. It's completely normal in the sadomasochistic scene. The mirrors were placed so that Bernd could see everything in clear detail. He was really big on pain; he wanted me to hurt him physically, mostly in the genital and chest areas. It totally turned him on, my white teeth and their contrast with my dark skin. He gave me very clear instructions on what to do. And in our later appointments, I always had to bite so that he saw my teeth. So for me, it was a very harmless matter. It was all over in ten minutes and he had his orgasm. He gave me a hundred marks and drove me home. Afterward, Bernd gave me his phone number and I gave him mine."

"Did he call you right after that?" I want to know.

"Yes, the very next day. At the beginning, we met often here at the Zoo subway station. As I said, he gave me very demanding instructions. 'Bite me here on the nipple; bite me there on my cock.' Sometimes he wanted sex twice in a day. We had sex in his car, in a sex booth at the Zoo station, or in the park. We met about four times a month for five years between 1995 and 2000. Weekends, I visited him in his apartment. We watched video movies or enjoyed everyday things, without engaging in sex. And Bernd often poured out his heart to me."

"What was he unhappy about?" I ask.

"Oh, he was always telling me about his new girlfriends, and then about his friend René, and once he asked me, 'Tell me, what do you think? Am I straight or gay?' And my answer was, 'Bernd, you must know that yourself.' He said, 'I love them all,' but the truth was, he couldn't be loyal to anybody. Six weeks later, he was upset again over the situation with women. In my opinion, he couldn't sort out his double life and was completely confused in his relationships. He was always involved in several directions and always had lovers. He told me also about these other loves and went into raptures about one-night stands with men. He described it all to me, down to the last detail. His affairs with men were mostly over quickly and didn't tax him emotionally as much as the relationships with women that came to an end."

"Was he unable to make women happy?"

Jimmy reflects. He passes his right hand over his cheek and then rubs his chin. His reply does not really answer my question, but nonetheless reveals a lot.

"Judging from Bernd's accounts, I had the impression that he could have quite normal sexual intercourse with women. For myself, I was careful not to harm either Bernd or myself when we had sex. We never had anal intercourse. When I sucked him off, he alerted me promptly before the semen came out. He finished it off with his hand while I had to pinch or bite his nipples with my fingers or teeth. At the same time, I was supposed to say 'nasty things' to him. For example, I'd say I would flog his cock or his chest."

"Did that heighten Brandes's desire for pain?" I pursue.

"Yes, again and again he wanted me to say, 'I'll bite your cock off.' He was wild over it. At some point, he wanted it during intercourse, too."

Jimmy gazes at me wide-eyed and awaits the journalist's next question. When I say nothing, he continues without prompting.

"It must have been in the Advent season of 1998, when he was again, as he always was before Christmas, very depressed. He had problems with his father, who did not accept him. He never spoke of his dead mother during those ten years. I could hear from his voice on the phone that things were not going right for him. So I drove over to him. He opened the door and stood there, undressed down to his undershorts. This was very unusual. I took off my shoes. Bernd set great store by cleanliness. Then, in the living room, I suddenly noticed a knife with a ten-inch blade, lying on the table. He said, 'Come, we'll go to the bedroom. Oh, and bring the knife with you, because today you're going to cut it off.' I didn't trust myself to dispute him; anyway, I thought it was only a game. But Bernd meant it seriously. He pulled his undershorts down, lay down on the bed, and said, 'Please put the knife in position.' I did so. He watched the whole thing in the ceiling mirror, as I moved the knife over him and pressed the blade against his penis. That excited him so much that he yelled, 'Please, cut it off, go ahead, and cut it off.' For me, the knife had to serve as an instrument for heightening Bernd's sexual enjoyment. I pressed a little harder, but, of course, didn't wound him. He shouted, 'Great, fantastic!' And then he had his orgasm. That was that."

"Did you never ask why he wanted that?"

"No. He couldn't have answered that question himself. Bernd just had to have pain. The more intense the pain I inflicted on his penis, the greater his enjoyment. But if the pain got too bad, he let me know and I stopped. But he pressed me more and more to turn his fantasy into action. He offered me money: ten thousand marks [forty thousand dollars], later one hundred thousand marks, his car, his computer, anything, if I would just bite off or cut off his penis. I said, 'I wouldn't do that for all the money in the world.'"

"Were you his only sexual partner?"

"No. Bernd had to have sex several times a day. Because of his addiction to pain, he visited sadomasochistic studios. I know that his friend, René, often accompanied him there. I, myself, was never present. I did, however, see scars and wounds on his penis that could certainly have been made by biting."

"Bernd also advertised on the Internet."

"I know, I know. He looked for perverted sexual partners everywhere."

"Did you break off with him because of that?"

"No. He was my friend. We went to the movies and discotheques together. But all of a sudden, the contact was abruptly broken off. I looked for him everywhere, went to his apartment, but no one came to the door. In the bars we went to all the time, no one had seen him. He hadn't been seen in months, and then, suddenly, this newspaper article appeared."

Dead silence.

"A friend told me someone had been eaten. Before that, he had had his penis cut off. I knew immediately, 'Good God, it's Bernd.' I ran to the nearest kiosk and bought the Bild-Zeitung. When I saw the photo, I was so shocked I couldn't read the article. I only cried. It was his supreme wish, but he didn't want to die."

Jimmy sobs. Tears course down his cheeks. After regaining some degree of control over himself, he continues slowly.

"I was completely beside myself. I was, physically and emotionally, a wreck. I couldn't eat, I couldn't think clearly, I couldn't get over what had happened to Bernd. I couldn't sleep at night. Finally, a good lady friend advised me, 'Look, Jimmy, you've got to get help,' and...."

His voice fails. Jimmy breaks down. He turns away from me and has a fit of uncontrolled sobbing. His whole body doubles up and goes stiff. I put my hand on his shoulder and try to comfort him, but, in this situation, I feel powerless. How was I to help him? He weeps and weeps. I decide just to be there. After a few minutes, the man calms himself and says, "You know, for six months I've been under psychological care. But as you see, my wounds aren't yet healed. I still have to cope with them."

Suddenly, he adds, "Thank you for letting me talk with you. It was a kind of therapy for me."

Before Jimmy and I part, I must know something else. "You're suffering. But do you think Bernd died happy?"

"No." He shakes his head. "Bernd surely did not die happy, because he never knew where he belonged. He never found a home with his father. He never found a home with a friend, male or female. Perhaps he missed God. That's why he was so lonely and disoriented."

"I think that in Bernd Brandes's case, we can see what happens when the devil gets his way," I brood aloud to myself.

Jimmy nods thoughtfully. "There's something in what you say. Do you know, Bernd's awful death held some good for me? As I rode by a church on my bicycle, I saw the garden in front of it, all gone to seed. As if someone had called me, I went in to the priest and asked if I could tend his garden. Since then I've been working in the church and organizing classical music concerts. I have found God and have my feet on solid ground."

I have no further questions. We shake hands in farewell, and I leave Berlin.

*

Voice Two: Alexandra, the second love.

In the interrogation of witnesses in the Berlin District Court on April 30, 2001, Alexandra L., born in 1973, (Proceedings No. 010310/4776-1) testifies as follows:

> *We saw each other for the first time on October 9, 1996. It was on the Bayerischer Platz. We had been acquainted through an ad in the "Second Hand." As time went on, we got to know each other more intimately, went to the movies together, block parties, and the like. So in February or March of 1997, I moved in with him, but kept my apartment. In May of 1997, we flew together to Florida for three and a half*

weeks. Afterwards, I learned from other sources that Mr. Brandes had gone deep into debt for this trip. Later on, we lived together less and less. Mr. Brandes was more and more occupied with his computer and couldn't be persuaded any longer to go to the movies or do anything else that was fun. I devoted myself regularly to sports and later to my parachute jumps, and that way I was able to make other friends. So in November 1997, I moved out of his apartment and back into mine. On January 19, 1998, I congratulated Mr. Brandes on his 40th birthday. The friendship became a platonic one. Here I would like to state that Mr. Brandes informed me, some time in 1998, that through an ad he had become acquainted with an African woman and had subsidized her to the extent of paying her airfare to Germany, and apparently sent her more money (the amount was between 3000 and 5000 D-marks). I would also like to state that in September or October 1998, during a pleasant gathering in his home when we were having a heart-to-heart talk over a bottle of champagne, Mr. Brandes told me he was attracted to men. I also reminded him that I had frequently seen a male person in his car.

Under further interrogation on January 14, 2003, Alexandra L. describes her sexual relationship with Bernd Brandes:

Throughout that time, we regularly had perfectly normal sexual intercourse. Nothing happened out of the ordinary, and he never demanded of me anything I did not consider quite normal. There was no violence of any kind. We never hurt each other having sex.

*

Voice Three: Andreas Kuss, the superior.

Bernd Brandes's immediate superior in the Siemens Company, Andreas Kuss, born July 3, 1953, testifies under interrogation at Police Headquarters at Hersfeld-Rotenburg (Proceedings No. ST/0353947/2002) concerning Bernd Brandes, the following:

Mr. Brandes was very popular in his group. He was well accepted as Chief, and allowed his colleagues the necessary freedom of action. During my service with him, there were here and there problems. When we sat together in consultations, it happened once that he took a position opposed to mine. In a number of business questions, he was rather unreasonable. I discussed these problems with him, however, promptly in meetings between just the two of us. These consultations were always very calm and straightforward. He held his ground, however.... Some time around the end of the nineties, he let it be known in the company that he had a new lady friend. He never gave her name, however. From conversations, I inferred that the person might be a man. He never said this himself, however.... He complained to me that he had paid ten thousand marks to obtain a woman from Africa. As far as I can remember, the woman was to come from Nigeria. He then went to the airport at an agreed time to pick this woman up, but she did not come. It is reported that he met another man there who also wanted to fetch this woman. They fell into conversation and tried to get the money back with the aid of a lawyer. As far as I know, he got no money back. I regard these allegations by Bernd Brandes as questionable. I think there were too many coincidences in his account.

In a personal meeting in Berlin, in the "Hopfingerbräu" restaurant in the new train station, the certified mathematician, Andreas Kuss, married with four children, elaborates. "Bernd liked to experiment. I think being gay was a sort of exploration for Bernd Brandes. Not having normal sex. He wanted to know how it would be to feel like a woman. But he didn't behave queer. You could talk with him about male subjects or about women. A female colleague always took his funny talk as a shtick. She said, 'He's no queer.'"

*

Voices Four and Five: Andrea and André S., computer friends.

This married couple, in a conversation with the police (Proceeding No. ST/0353947/22002), state the following:

> Mr. and Mrs. S. stated that they had known Bernd Brandes since 1996. Bernd at that time kept the biggest mailbox in Berlin. [Author's note: The Internet community was in the name of "The Best BBS in Town," and counted one hundred and twenty members who were interested in computers. At irregular intervals, the users met to discuss hardware and software.] [Translator's note: the title is in English.] Mr. S. called him up because he wanted to have an Internet address. These conversations developed over time into friendship.... At the end of 1996, Bernd became acquainted, through the magazine, "Tip," with a certain Conni, with whom he was together for six months. As for the reason why the relationship broke up, he said, "It just didn't work any more." After this relationship, he became acquainted, again through "Tip," with Alexandra L., with whom he was together for approximately a year. The relationship was quite a good one, but Bernd said nothing about marriage....
>
> In mid-1998, Brandes told them he had a new girlfriend, but did not give her name. It was a secret. After Christmas, they say, he told them he was gay, and this alleged girlfriend was

*in reality a friend by the name of "Jero." Bernd
had even given this Jero a cell phone of his own,
so they could keep in contact. At some time, he
told them that Jero was making an incredible
number of telephone calls at his expense. He got
very upset about these high expenditures.
Moreover, he said, Jero had been unfaithful. At
that point, Bernd separated from him. At some
point during this period, he told them for the
first time that he picked up male prostitutes,
either from Nollendorfplatz or by telephone
through "Tip." As for his sexual habits, he
mentioned only that he did not practice anal
intercourse...and that he had gotten a new lease
on life when he declared his homosexuality....
Bernd, they said, had been genuinely happy.
Then at some time, he had met René. The two of
them had had a relationship similar to
marriage. René also moved in with him,
although he was not really the type of man
Bernd preferred.... On the question whether
there had ever been any mention of AIDS, S.
knew that Bernd said he had had himself tested
for HIV.... He had also mentioned that he
always used a condom for sex.... He had never
expressed suicidal intentions.*

In a telephone conversation with me, André S.
supplemented his testimony, adding the following: "Bernd
was a little unworldly. He also said that black women aroused
him more than his mistress did at the time. I might add that
once Bernd Brandes played Santa Claus for my son."

*

Voice Six: Victor P., one more prostitute among
many.

The film-setter, born March 10, 1967, in Havana,
Cuba, states to the LKA 4124 Berlin (Proceeding no.
010310/4776) on September 11, 2001, the following:

I have been living in Germany for eleven years, learned German in high school, and have a spoken and written understanding of the German language. I met him [Bernd Brandes] about two years ago. I had placed an ad in "Tip."

In his second interrogation, on January 11, 2003, he states further [Author's note: For easier reading, some passages have been summarized]:

In my ad, I said I was looking for contacts with men who wanted a massage or company. In that kind of activity, I wanted to earn a little money, because at that time I was unemployed.... You could say I prostituted myself. In the ad, I had given my cell phone number, and persons who were interested called me on it. Among other "customers," Bernd Jürgen Brandes called me at some point.... On my first visit, we talked and I then gave him a massage. This first massage was for relaxation. There was no sexual contact.... I got 50 D-marks [$12.50 US] for the first massage. In the course of time, however, we became such good friends that he no longer paid for each contact. But whenever I had financial problems, he helped me out. For example, he took over my telephone bill, or paid other bills. About a week after my first visit, I did have sexual contacts with Brandes. [Author's note: on further questioning, the witness states that he is HIV-positive and that Brandes knew it.] We exchanged caresses; we gave each other blowjobs, and played with each other's bottoms with our fingers.... Later on we inserted our penises in each other's anuses. We both used a condom.... After a while, he told me to bite his penis. I did it, and then we always thought up something new. I also licked his body and he put his toes in my mouth. I really bit him only on the penis and testicles. He liked it when I bit those places hard....

*Later he hit on the idea of having me
bite off his penis. So I bit him really hard on the
penis. It seemed as if it gave him an orgasm. He
didn't yell. We had a long discussion about the
after-effects of biting off his penis. As a human
being, I really could not do that. I couldn't
imagine how I was to bite off his penis. He would
have had to go to the hospital and wouldn't have
had a penis any more. Furthermore, I didn't
know how he would have reacted when his penis
was really off. But he assured me that nothing
would happen to me if I did that to him. He
would really want it. He offered me some money,
relatively fast, if I would bite off his penis. First,
it was 1,000 thousand D-marks, and later on, he
raised it to 5,000 marks.... He had fantasies of
some sort, which I can't really understand. He
only said it would feel "totally awesome" to have
his penis bitten off, and he really wanted to
experience it. I should just do it and he would
worry about the consequences. He had
apparently thought it all out.... At the time I had
regarded his demands as fantasy. Somehow, he
only wanted to have the feeling that his penis
had been bitten off. But I knew he was serious
about it. Whether he wanted to commit suicide, I
can't say. He never wanted it as far as I know....
There was never any talk of it. He never
mentioned wanting to have himself eaten.*

Voice Seven: Frank D., colleague and friend.

In the "Rexrodt," a restaurant in Hamburg, on
January 8, 2007, at eight in the evening, I meet Frank D.,
born in 1958 and a friend of Bernd Brandes. Here is his
account:

*"I got to know Bernd Brandes in 1977,
during my student days. At twenty, Bernd
already had a card file with his girlfriends'
telephone numbers. He was living then with his
father and stepmother in Berlin-Wannsee. I was*

in his home once. It was guarded by a huge Doberman. I didn't dare move a finger. Later he got me a job in the Development Office at Siemens. Bernd told me once, during the lunch hour, that on a business trip he had engaged a black call girl. He found it interesting. Bernd had a steady girlfriend, but also cruised the red-light district. I think he was on the lookout for something special. He always wanted to collect novel experiences and escape everyday life. He was also sociable. After his father moved away, he faithfully looked after his grandmother, who was still living in Berlin. And he always did it gladly. His grandmother passed away in the mid-nineties. She was someone with whom he had an important relationship. She may have triggered his change of heart."

On January 15, 2003, Frank D. is interrogated in Berlin on the subject "Bernd Brandes" (Proceeding No. ST/0132109/2002):

Whenever Bernd was bothered about something, he told me about it. Sometimes he even cried. On his relationships with women, I can say that they were most often terminated by the women because Bernd devoted too much of his time to his computer.... He told me that he picked up boys in a certain quarter of Berlin and brought them home with him. He didn't go into detail, but I assume that in the red-light district he invited boys into his car and brought them home. He told me he had sexual relations with these boys.... In fact, he told me of his homosexual contacts really with pride and pleasure. I have told no one here in the company about it, however....

It is possible that Bernd was able to go on the Internet and service his Yahoo mailbox from here at the Siemens Company.... Possible connections with Yahoo or similar private contacts are not saved.... He never discussed with me his private Internet contacts.... As for the Rotenburg contact, the "Antrophagus," I can't say anything at all.... I simply cannot understand Brandes's behavior prior to his death. He never really went into details with me about sexual activities with the boys from the red-light district. It happened once that he was slightly injured in the anal region and was too embarrassed to go to a doctor. That is how I learned of his sexual contacts with these prostitutes.... With his office colleagues and staff, he was very reserved. He always kept his private life separate from his work. As far as I know, he also did not have a wide circle of friends.

*

Voice Eight: René J., the last young lover.

René J. makes the following statements in his three interrogations on April 11, 2001, May 8, 2001, and January 14, 2003 [Author's note: For better readability, some passages of individual interrogations have been summarized]:

I have known Mr. Brandes since August 20, 1999. We became acquainted at a private party. Since the host was also homosexual, most of those present were gays. I assumed Bernd was also homosexual, like me. We got along well, and there was sexual attraction between us. At that time, I was living at home with my parents. I brought Bernd home with me, and we had sexual contact there that very night. As time went on, we attended film events together or went out to eat. Around the end of 1999, I moved into Mr. Brandes's apartment. We divided the living expenses by comparing our incomes and prorating the expenses accordingly. My share of the expenses was 710 marks, of which I deposited 500 marks on the first day of the month into the household cashbox—a little red box in our kitchen cupboard—and gave the balance of 210 marks directly to Bernd. We lived in an arrangement like marriage. We were relatively seldom in the gay scene, but when we were we went to the "Andreas-Kneipe," the "Pussycat," or the "Prinz Knecht." I had sexual contacts with Bernd in the manner customary among homosexuals. I had completely normal sex with him. Naturally, I would insert my penis into his anus. He never inserted his penis into me, however. Our intercourse was always protected; that is, we always used condoms.

About our intercourse, I have to say that Bernd was the passive partner and I the active one. That's the way it is in the homosexual scene, and I would regard it as quite normal. During intercourse, caresses were exchanged. There was never any violence. We were always careful never to cause each other any pain. And he never demanded that we do anything that could have hurt us. Bernd Brandes is really very reserved when he's at a party, for example. But if you know him more intimately, he is a very happy, generous, and intelligent human being.

As far as I was concerned, I can say that for me, he was my only partner. I assumed that that was just as true for him. Now I am somewhat in doubt, because from reading evidence about individual connections, I have concluded that Bernd, apparently in February, had at least telephone contact with others. He never gave the slightest indication of wanting to have his penis bitten off. Nor did I know of any suicide plans. We wanted to go on summer vacation together. When I hear now that he was in touch with the perpetrator as early as January 2001, I cannot understand why he bought a refrigerator, an expensive TV set, and a valuable stereo.

*

The last meeting between Bernd Brandes and his father takes place at Christmas, 2000. The encounter is, as always, anything but cordial. Bernd feels uncomfortable. Regarding the father, expert witness Prof. Dr. Beier states:

> *The information about the same-sex orientation had completely surprised him, and he could only say that he—his son—must know how he wanted to live. At the same time it was all for him, as a father, completely incomprehensible. Also, about the special inclinations that may have been revealed by the killing and slaughtering, he was unable to conceive, let alone have any idea, of what conflicts or confusion could have arisen in his son's mind. In any case, he had never heard anything about depressive moods or other psychic disturbances, and could say with certainty that March 9th [Author's note: the date of Bernd Brandes's death] had had for his son no significance—in any case as far as he knew— and he also had no recollection of ever having heard the name "Cator." He was convinced, however, that his son had thought through the things he had done—even though for him, the father, they were very inconceivable—and carried them out with full knowledge of what he was doing. Nothing else would fit in with his own picture of his son.*

*

"I am Cator," Bernd Brandes replies to "Antrophagus," Armin Meiwes, by email. "Yes, I really do want it. I want you to cut off my cock, tear the flesh off my bones while I'm still alive, and eat me up."

Thirty-two days are left until the slaughter.

FOR THEY THAT ARE AFTER THE FLESH DO MIND THE THINGS OF THE FLESH; BUT THEY THAT ARE AFTER THE SPIRIT, MIND THE THINGS OF THE SPIRIT. FOR TO BE CARNALLY MINDED IS DEATH (...) SO THAT THEY THAT ARE IN THE FLESH AND CANNOT PLEASE GOD.

(Romans 8: 5-8)

CHAPTER 9
CANNIBAL CHAT

A white, ten-foot long spiral electric cable hangs out of a crack in the wall and over the door to Consultation Room 4 in the Kassel Penitentiary on this 12th day of May 2007. The cable ends in a black plastic garbage pail. A white floor fan distributes the warm air flowing in through the open window like a Sahara wind. The temperature is ninety degrees.

"Tomorrow I'm to be transferred to the Weiterstadt Penitentiary. Orders from the so-called Assignment Committee. They check to see if I'm suited to this venerable institution," says Armin Meiwes with a touch of sarcasm. "Many prisoners only learn about it on the day they're transferred. Me, they informed in writing five days ago. So I'll be riding in a prison transport for two days, right across Hesse, and then it'll be decided in a five-minute discussion that I am to come back here." He shakes his head in perplexity.

"I'm being swept out of here, lock, stock, and barrel," he says, continuing the "Meiwes Move" saga. "I have to take everything along: my TV, the Sony PlayStation, the fridge, and my clothing—right down to the underwear. It must be an enormous expense. Oh well, I don't care. Tomorrow I'm just having a little outing."

*

Since this work must give an account of events in the recent past, we've undertaken to record all the details of the "cannibal chat" between Armin Meiwes and Bernd Brandes. For many people, it represents a hard-core thriller on the border, or even over the border, of the tolerable. If the contents of this book were fictitious—and I mean that quite seriously and without the slightest irony—I would have to add here a note of caution warning the readers about what they are about to encounter.

"Mr. Meiwes, will you tell me about your subsequent contact with Bernd Brandes?"

"Right. I had then told him accordingly, that as Franky, the butcher, I could fulfill his wish to have his penis removed and consumed. I can't remember the exact wording. The first emails have been lost because I was having problems at the time with my hard-drive memory. Everything else I printed out. I was very methodical."

"How did you introduce yourself to Bernd Brandes?"

"I sold myself to him basically on the grounds that I lived alone in a house and wanted to carry out slaughters. Right away he asked me, 'How do you visualize it? What's the scenario?' I sent him photos of the slaughter room and the slaughter preparations. I also photographed my front teeth, which Bernd absolutely insisted on seeing. He always replied immediately. It was quite important to him that his genitals be cut off and that he himself eat them raw. That was his main concern."

I show the prisoner again the photo portrait of Bernd Brandes.

"What are your feelings when you look into his face?"

He turns his head slightly to the side and sighs, "Yes, I see a friend. A friend, a nice human being, even if he wasn't exactly the way I'd hoped and wished. I think for him, it also wasn't the way he'd hoped. But it's a nice memory."

"Why? Wasn't he the 'perfect brother' for you?"

"Well, it would be best if I read to you how it all began." Meiwes pulls his nickel-colored glasses out of his left shirt pocket, puts them on his nose, and leafs through a red notebook he has brought to the interview.

"I have here the records of chats between Bernd and me," he intones like a high school principal. "I'd like to read to you now what Bernd Brandes wrote me and what I wrote him. As I said, my first replies have been lost because my hard-drive memory was damaged. Anyhow, I answered right away his first email of February 5, 2001. Until our first meeting, we sent emails back and forth every single day."

"Cator" Bernd Brandes writes to "Antrophagus" Armin Meiwes on February 5, 2001:

> *Hi Franky, here I am…. You already have my photos from the profile. Hmm, what else is there to say?... I'm 36, 5'7", weigh 158 pounds. The pictures are a year old, so not much has changed. I hope you're really serious about it, because I really want it and have already met enough cyber-cannibals…. You first have to bite off my cock and my balls, one after another. But you don't absolutely have to begin there; I'd like to feel and see your teeth in other fleshy parts. But my cock and balls must absolutely be bitten off. Then I'll be ready for slaughter, if you'd like. I'm certainly at your disposal for sex first (and during it, of course), if you want, for you to play with your food. Let me hear from you and tell me something about yourself. Regards, Cator.*

"Antrophagus," alias Armin Meiwes, writes "Cator" Bernd Brandes on February 8, 2001:

> *You are not very old. Of course, the younger the nicer, but even the younger ones don't bite into me the way I'd like. If all goes well, another slaughter boy said he's coming over who is 25 years old. Once a guy called me, he was 59 years old, it was really far out, such an old guy; he'd have been a bit too tough. Anyone under the age of 40 can be considered perfectly suitable for slaughter. Franky.*

Meiwes lowers his eyes and gazes at me over his glasses. "We made a date right away for slaughter on February 23rd and 24th. Bernd had to cancel it because of a business deadline, so we agreed on March 9, 2001. I suggested that he come and live with me, so we could get to know each other better."

"Antrophagus" goes on reading aloud the correspondence with Bernd Brandes.

"Antrophagus" writes to "Cator" on February 14, 2001:

> *Hi Cator, was up to my ears in work the last few days, that's why I haven't answered yet; besides I wasn't home over the weekend. Haven't heard from the 25-year-old in several days. Guess he got chickenshit....*

"Antrophagus: to "Cator" on February 18, 2001:

> *Of course, I'll allow time. Live flesh is surely a bit harder to cut up than roasted flesh. I'll be sure to have something to chew on, and, besides, I want to enjoy it. If you don't back out, and I hope you won't, I can also bite your tongue off. By that time, I'll have the scent of blood in my nostrils, so I'll certainly bite you all over and tear your flesh off the bones. Anyway, I won't slaughter you until you're dead; as long as you're still alive, you'll experience true "hell on earth." My little pecker is looking forward to you. He's 7 inches long erect; I hope that's enough for you.... I discovered my secret feeling when I was very young, already wanted to make a meal of my schoolmates, some of them were juicy boys. Always imagined how I'd rape them, and then cut them up and eat them. Or with boys I really liked, I imagined how I'd seduce them, then drug them, slowly undress them and really enjoy their bodies before eating them. Even with boys I hadn't slept with, I would feel their muscles, and imagine what delicious morsels could be made from them. And now I know it's especially delicious. Franky.*

"Cator" answers "Antrophagus" on February 19, 2001:

> *It was the same with me as with you. Since puberty, I've wanted to be bitten and eaten. This desire has lasted a long time, and will last*

until it finally comes true. I'm looking forward even more to our first and only encounter...Cator.

"Antrophagus" writes later on:

Hi Cator, today I took pictures with my video camera. Now we can see something in the pictures. I hope you like it. I'm feeling really horny, wanting to bore into you, and then I'll bite into your shoulder or your calves. Going to Berlin first sounds tempting, but unfortunately, I'm short of time; anyway, it won't be long now. In my thoughts, I'm fucking the daylights out of you every day and already tasting your blood between my teeth. Franky.

"Cator" reports on February 20, 2001:

It won't be hell, but heaven on earth when we meet. And I'm sure I won't want to hold out a week until you rip out my vitals with your teeth. I'm looking forward to having your cock in my body. Fuck all my orifices, the more there are, the more possibilities you'll have... Too bad, you can't come to Berlin first, but you're right, it won't be long. How will I recognize you on March 9th? You can hardly stand around with your mouth open or your pants open. What do you do professionally, that you can have a company car as well? All best, Cator.

"Antrophagus" replies to "Cator" directly by return email:

I'm horny for the sight of you. Can you, before you come, send me a picture of yourself and I'll send you one of me? Standing with my pants open in the train station would surely be dumb. Professionally, I'm a computer technician and repair PCs and ATMs in banks. That's why I'm so often traveling here in the Hessian region. Franky.

"Cator" to "Antrophagus," also on February 20, 2001:

I hope you'll also bite some muscle-flesh off me, for example from my arm or pieces of my hand. Like to see how the blood trickles from the corners of your mouth and simultaneously feel your orgasm in my ass. Your juice spurts into my openings while my (blood) juice flows out of me. I won't need my hands any more, anyway, because every orgasm of mine (comes anyway without help from my hands) would make my balls smaller for you. Best, Cator. P.S. Steady on. I hope 3/9 comes soon and you mean it really seriously...

"Cator" writes on February 21, 2001, to "Antrophagus:"

Here's a picture of my face. It's a bit older (taken Dec. 31, '99) and my hair isn't the same, since I now have it cut to five inches long, and I've gained a little weight since then. I hope you've kept your horniness and your appetite for me when you look at the photo. I have photos of myself, full length and naked, from in front and behind. Unfortunately, not with me here, but if you'd like to see them too, I can send them to you. Cator.

"Antrophagus" answers directly:

Hi Cator, you look pretty raunchy. I can really imagine my teeth ripping you open. Naked shots are naturally more arousing, but this way I can imagine how your body is shaped, and that makes things much more exciting. Franky.

"Cator" write on February 22, 2001:

To keep you from bursting, here are the two nude photos of me. How and where do we meet on March 9th? As I wrote, I'll take a train at 7 or 8 a.m. and so will be there before noon. I hope you won't have had breakfast, because I'll be bringing enough flesh with me ...Cator.

Cator writes again:

Then I only hope you won't stand me up, can really go through with it, and don't have a problem about doing away with me. Shouldn't be a nightmare for you after realizing your dream. Nobody will know what's become of me. I'm not at all nervous, just madly excited about finally achieving my life's goal. You should also let the video camera run so that you can enjoy it again. As for the Ulrike matter—she was a girl who vanished suddenly—you can see how a person can disappear without a trace. We could invite somebody else, even if it contradicts your principle of only him who wants it.

"Cator" writes in a later email:

I have no problem at all with AIDS, because I've been tested. And I don't run around. Want to be a good meat deliverer, compared with the usual meat delivery services (BSE and hoof-and-mouth disease). Won't leave you anyway, at least not totally. I think, if you like it the way you imagine it, I won't be alone for long in the freezer because a part of me will stay with you as food in your cells, when you invite the next one.

"Antrophagus" to "Cator," February 26, 2001:

Hi Cator, what's the expression with Paulchen Panther: today isn't every day, I'll come back, no question.... We'll get there somehow.

Friday March 2, 2001, "Cator" writes at 7:28 a.m.:

Hi Frank.... Everything okay with you for a week from Friday? Today I completely shaved the hair off my genital area so you can bite easier. You can remove the rest yourself. In the breast area, you can bite the place where you shaved it. Then it couldn't be fresher.... My nipples are already looking forward to visiting your stomach. Greetings Cator.

At 9:51 a.m., he adds:

I simply have to see how your teeth slowly go down lower and lower on my cock (behind the head or into it), and my cock tries to avoid the pressure and then, when that won't work any more, the blood vessels burst and the blood trickles from your lips. I'll watch while you chew the first piece and swallow it, then turn to the throbbing, bleeding remainder. You can use it as a straw to suck up more blood until your teeth resume their work on the next piece. When the cock's off, I hope you'll pass on to the hairless balls. Since there won't be a cock anymore to block the view, I can watch as you happily pull one ball after the other out of the sack and ingest it. Cator, your meat! That's what I was born for, and on the 9th, I'll have reached my life's goal.

Armin Meiwes pauses briefly. He takes a sip of water. A drop runs slowly down the glass. He wipes it off the table with the middle finger of his left hand and turns to the next email from Cator.

What happens to my remains? All right, I don't want to bug you beforehand, but these days it's important to get rid of trash, especially in this case. And it's funny, since we made our date I've been besieged with inquiries. ...But whatever the case, the main thing is that it will now be real.

*

On Monday, March 5, 2001, Bernd Jürgen Brandes applies to his employer for leave on Friday, March 9th. His supervisor, Andreas Kuss, under interrogation states for the record on February 11, 2003:

> *Prior to his disappearance, Bernd told me on Monday he wanted to take a day's flextime leave the following Friday. He had enough flextime hours, so I approved it. Previously he had always told me in good time whenever he wanted a day off. There were never any problems with it. He wanted this day off for personal reasons because there was something he wanted to take care of. He gave me no details.*

*

On Wednesday, March 7, 2001, at 10:22 a.m., Bernd Brandes sends another email to Armin Meiwes:

> *I've deleted from my computer all private matters that refer to my "hobby"…Since I'm leaving early tomorrow morning (as if to work), there's no problem there. I explained that I have to go on a business trip for several days, which happens often anyway. In case it doesn't work out for us, contrary to expectations, I'll have finished my business trip early. Now a thought occurs to me about that. At work, I'll take several days leave, no problem there either. In case our plans don't work out, I'll go in on Monday and won't take the rest of my leave. I'll pay for my train ticket in cash, so there's no indication of how I left Berlin. I'll have simply gone and disappeared. Who would expect me to be already in the region of Kassel? And no one who knows me personally knows my pseudonym "Cator." All entries mentioning "Cator" and the clubs we'll delete together on Friday, or you*

alone after the main course, thus no references at all (you could also do it Friday evening from an Internet café. You'll get the password of course from me). As you see, I'm well prepared. My purpose is not to throw you into the frying pan, but to be eaten. Hope you'll be in the Chat soon. Hope Friday comes soon, and with your teeth in me. ...Cator.

*

Most of the emails are written by Bernd Brandes during work hours. The last three days before the agreed meeting, Meiwes and Brandes communicate not by telephone, but almost exclusively through "Yahoo Messenger," which they have both downloaded and installed in their computers. "Yahoo Messenger" is an immediate chat session with text, broadcast worldwide. As with telephone conversations, the dialogues—in contrast to emails—are transmitted directly and practically without time delay. Yahoo Messenger is free and can be downloaded, installed, and used with a valid Yahoo password. According to the Nielsen Net Rating, the service has around 4.65 million users worldwide.

Armin Meiwes printed out and painstakingly filed the text between him and Bernd Brandes, as he did all other "cannibal" documents. The record contains further bloody details of the planned slaughter and the last-known arrangements between Brandes and Meiwes. The latter are recorded in full detail. For better readability, only the typographical errors have been corrected; nothing of substance has been changed. The simultaneous written exchange may cause answers to be delayed. From the journalistic and judicial viewpoints, these records are indispensable as evidence into the minds and motives of Armin Meiwes and Bernd Brandes. Among the copies retained, a "Willingness Agreement" can be identified, in which Brandes expressed his willingness to be slaughtered.

Armin Meiwes, age 10, in 1972, riding his pony, "Polly." Armin looked happy, but in reality he felt lonesome and abandoned. Armin Meiwes longed for a younger brother who would never leave him.

By 1971, the Meiwes family had split apart; the father and two half-brothers left the home in Essen, and the secondary residence in Wüstefeld as well, and moved away. Armin Meiwes was 9 years old and spent his vacations on the estate, but, from 1980 on, he lived in Wüstefeld with his embittered mother alone in the large, 36-room frame house.

Armin Meiwes was a reasonably good student and loved animals. During one of his stays at the Wüstefeld estate he observed the slaughtering of a hog by a farmer. Little Armin, however, was not shocked, instead he was fascinated.

Armin Meiwes at the age of 9. Proudly he posed in front of the Wüstefeld estate in the blue Citroen owned by his elder half-brother Werner (at that time 25 years old) in July 1971.

Armin Meiwes—the vacationer—on the charter yacht "Seespiel." Together with three friends and a woman, he spent his vacation at the Baltic Sea from May 26-June 8, 1990.

Armin Meiwes at age 23 in June 1984 during his Staff Sergeant course in Bremen. Meiwes joined the German Army ("Bundeswehr") on January 1, 1981, and enlisted for 12 years. His dream was to become a professional soldier.

The dining room in the Wüstefeld estate. Here Armin Meiwes sat at the feast table arranged with two candleholders, cut glass and the finest chinaware and ate the flesh of Bernd Brandes as filet steak with Princess potatoes and brussel sprouts. In addition, he enjoyed a good bottle of red wine.

Within this tub victim Bernd Brandes had a bath in his own blood after Armin Meiwes cut off his penis with a butcher knife by request. The computer engineer from Berlin enjoyed the blood gushing from his wound and coloring the water red.

The estate in Wüstefeld. Since Armin Meiwes' arrest December 10, 2002, the frame house with its 36 rooms has been vacant. The attic is a playground for martens and the basement is flooded. In front of the house Armin Meiwes' golden Mercedes sits decaying.

This was most likely Armin Meiwes' study .

The slaughter room on the second floor of the Wüstefeld estate. Here was where it happened. Armin Meiwes reconstructd the former smoke room into a slaughter room in the summer of the year 2000. The bed with the stoves placed beneath it was designed to work as a barbecue grill for an Internet acquaintance from the cannibal bulletin board.

The victim: Bernd Brandes, degreed engineer from Berlin, born on January 19, 1958, died in the morning on March 10, 2001. The computer technician wanted to be erased and destroyed, "to be zeroed" as it is known among experts. Right before his death he tried to eat his own severed genital.

Armin Meiwes during one of his many conversations with author Günter Stampf inside the high-security prison Kassel 1.

TUESDAY, MARCH 6, 2001
THREE DAYS UNTIL THE MEETING

Documented Messenger record from original communications between Brandes (Cator99) and Meiwes (Antrophagus):

Cator99:	Hellooooo????
Antrophagus:	Hi, Cator.
Cator99:	Hi, again.
Cator99:	Problems?
Antrophagus:	What do you do professionally that makes you stay up so late?
Cator99:	Only sometimes on the weekend. Can't sleep properly anyway because of our meeting.
Antrophagus:	That's a reason, naturally.
Antrophagus:	Yesterday I was bone-tired—it was a strenuous day.
Cator99:	I work with computers, too, in telecommunications.
Antrophagus:	Oh yes, sounds interesting.
Cator99:	I believe you.
Cator99:	Tell me more after your first bite....
Antrophagus:	Yesterday the snowfall tied us up, 'til noon you could hardly move.
Cator99:	It was that way in Berlin, too. But the main streets were well plowed by noon.
Antrophagus:	Tonight we can chat, if I don't fall asleep.
Antrophagus:	Already looking forward to our meeting, will surely be super-raunchy.
Cator99:	I'll be there! Probably around 4:00. I hope it'll be super-raunchy, have no other opportunity.
Cator99:	Set your alarm clock?????
Antrophagus:	Still a couple of days to March 9th
Antrophagus:	I'll do it.
Cator99:	Still far too many. I'd rather have met yesterday and felt it.
Antrophagus:	Can't have everything. It'll be a while before you feel my teeth.

Cator99:	Just can't wait anymore. Have you already slaughtered a person?
Antrophagus:	Only in my dreams, sad to say, but in my thoughts I do it every evening.
Cator99:	So I'm the first? You didn't have human flesh before—or did you?
Antrophagus:	No, you can't get it in the supermarket.
Cator99:	Your emails sounded different. How do you know then that it'll taste good and you won't feel sick just from drinking blood?
Antrophagus:	But I've set up a slaughter room in my attic because it's my dearest wish to slaughter someone and fresh blood tastes good. Once I was so horny, I took a syringe and drew out some blood to drink it.
Cator99:	Yes, I saw the picture of the slaughter room. So I'll be the one to consecrate it. And your blood tasted good, I guess.
Antrophagus:	It was very tasty. Once when I used the syringe, it slipped and pierced my hand. That was delightful. Blood is the juice of giving, anyway. I mean living. Contains everything needed for nourishment.
Cator99:	Then I just hope you don't back out and can really go through with it, and won't have a problem about doing me in...
Cator99:	(That's the way it's supposed to be with vampires, if they exist.)
Antrophagus	Cutting off your cock is not going to be very easy, because living flesh is more resistant than when it's roasted, but I'll manage it.
Antrophagus:	One thing is sure: our dreams will be fulfilled.
Cator99:	There isn't as much in it as with muscle-flesh.
Antrophagus:	The penis is mainly a spongy tissue filled with blood.
Cator99:	I hope so for us both. I hope you've already thought about what to do with the leftovers. Shouldn't be a nightmare for you after your dream is fulfilled. Nobody will know what became of me.

Antrophagus: Well, when you're dead I'll take you out and slice you up expertly.
              Other than a few bones and bits of flesh (skin, cartilage, tendons), there won't be much left of you.
Cator99:   Oh yes, there'll be a lot left, like bones—I hope you have a good place to hide it (don't want to know, it's your problem).
Antrophagus: The bones will be dried and ground up.
              I'll take care of it.
Cator99:   Okay, good, as fertilizer, heard of it. OK, I see you've given it some thought. Good! Sounds like I'm the first, very good.
Antrophagus: And you won't be the last, I hope.
              Was already about to get myself a boy from the street, but I want to kill only someone who wants it too.
Cator99:   Doesn't sound bad. Yes, if this isn't legal in our country, it's better in my eyes than grabbing someone right off the street...
Cator99:   Okay, let's chat or phone some more tonight, in case you want to call me, (the other way around would be foolish because of the proof of the number in my phone bill).
Antrophagus: Exactly, would be nice if it were legal, everything's fine; have to do a little shopping.
              All right then, until tonight!
Cator99:   OK then, until tonight, I hope you'll be there ...have fun
Antrophagus: I'll set my alarm.
Antrophagus: 'Til then.

WEDNESDAY, MARCH 7, 2001
TWO DAYS UNTIL THE MEETING

Cator99:   Hello.
Antrophagus: Hi.
Cator99:   Nice seeing you online...
Cator99:   Everything ready?

Antrophagus: Yesterday I didn't have time.

Yes, everything's ready.

Cator99: Yes, I read it. Sorry if I bugged you, but I can hardly wait.

Antrophagus: Same here.

Cator99: I'm not at all nervous, just wild to reach my life's goal at last.

How does it look?

Antrophagus: I'm nervous, but we'll get on top of it.

Cator99: Have you read my last email? Sent it beforehand when you were online only briefly ...Why are you nervous?

Antrophagus: Isn't done every day.

Cator99: All right, but there's no reason to be nervous, seems to me. Would you like to live the month over several times, or not?

Antrophagus: I do that every day in my thoughts.

Cator99: No, I meant in real life would you want to.... You should run the video camera so you can enjoy it again.

Antrophagus: I'll do that anyway.

Cator99: Good. I'd love to see a replay of how you bit off my cock (before it's my balls' turn, so I can maybe come again)...let's see if that'll work...

Antrophagus: That will certainly be possible, if you don't collapse first.

Cator99: I just hope I don't collapse when we're handling my cock. It would be too early.

Antrophagus: So, now I have more time. Just spoke to my sister-in-law on the phone.

I hope you don't collapse. It would really be too soon. When I've bitten off the head of your penis, I can also tie up your cock.

Antrophagus: Are you still there?

Cator99: Still here!

Antrophagus: When the head is off, you surely won't bleed to death right away.

Cator99: Bandaging a little wouldn't be a bad idea, but not until only a small part of my cock is left.

A couple of centimeters should be enough.

Antrophagus: Certainly. I can't wait to see if you can still "come."

[Author's comment: The ensuing text passage from the Messenger recording will not be reproduced here. At other places as well, individual passages have been omitted, and this will be indicated. The record in these text passages is beyond all power of imagination.]

Antrophagus: It will get raunchy; can imagine again and again how I'll bite into your calves, shoulders and chest.
And then at the end it's your cock's turn as the high point.
And then I'll consume it.

Cator99: You'd have to shave my chest and legs, anyway (would be conspicuous if I did it beforehand). But please don't just bite into it. I'd like to see and feel how you bite pieces off my chest (I'll see your teeth best when they're working).

[Text passage deleted]

Antrophagus: Yes, but not all at once. I want to have something of you a bit longer.

Cator99: In case I survive my balls, then cut or bite open my cheeks so that you can open my mouth wide, and then chew up my tongue right down to the root.

Antrophagus: And several climaxes, too.

Cator99: Do you have my entire flesh, or what do you mean by that?

Antrophagus: I mean orgasms as long as you're still alive.

Cator99: Nothing wrong with pauses. You can't keep on coming indefinitely. But then get some bandages. Don't want to bleed to death

	without something happening. But my flesh should be enough for your breakfast, lunch, and supper.
Antrophagus:	Yes, I assume so.
	I have enough bandages.
Cator99:	Maybe we can cook or roast part of me for dinner.
	Would like to dine off something of myself.
Antrophagus:	Yes, let's see—a piece of the thigh or the ham.
Cator99:	Yes, I'll leave that to you. One doesn't usually discuss these things with animals to be slaughtered.
Antrophagus:	Quite right, but it's raunchier this way.
Cator99:	Lord, I'd like to come right now, but it would stop too soon. Shit...
Antrophagus:	Only two days left.
Cator99:	Have you any idea how to bandage properly? Shouldn't bite off the nipples first because many blood vessels end there. Better a part above or below.

[Text passage deleted]

Antrophagus:	Raunchy, the nipples of course, although it will surely be easier to bandage them than the truncated penis.
Cator99:	(Think about it: chew 20 times before swallowing.)
Antrophagus:	Will do.
Cator99:	Try to keep me alive as long as possible. That would be good. You could also tie off the testicles beforehand.

[Text passage deleted]

| Cator99: | How will you tie off a nipple? The cock offers a tie-off possibility because of its form, like the balls, too. But not the male nipples. Should tie off small points and not large |

	areas. Serves no purpose for me to be completely wrapped in gauze.
Antrophagus:	Would have done that anyway. The balls can be tied off perfectly, and there it wouldn't bleed so much as the penis.
Cator99:	We can put a bandage on my chest, or just a big sticking plaster, with plenty of gauze.
Antrophagus:	Balls should also be a good area soaked in blood.

[Text passage deleted]

Cator99:	In case you don't want to eat any of that (cock or balls) raw, you'll have in my mouth a greedy customer, if you want to feed me with flesh.
Antrophagus:	But not so bloody as a penis full to bursting. Am already horny to have your balls in my mouth.
Cator99:	Right, but the penis has reserve sluices, not the scrotum.
Antrophagus:	You're right.
Cator99:	*[Text passage deleted]*
Antrophagus:	*[Text passage deleted]* then I'll show it to you again before it goes into my mouth.
Cator99:	Besides, they're very sensitive and there's a strong probability that I'll topple over. On top of that, without the cock, the opening for pulling it out is near there. Leave it on the tissues connecting it to the body while you're eating it—don't swallow right away, chew it thoroughly first and bite it off before you cut the connecting tissue. (Think about it: chew 20 times before swallowing.)
Antrophagus:	Will do.
Cator99:	The Ulrike case shows how someone can disappear without a trace. With me, there'll be two suitcases.

(Only with adults, it's not so interesting for the press and the cops.)

Antrophagus: That's right. Every year thousands disappear in Germany, as I've heard on TV.

Or the famous husband who just goes to get cigarettes.

Cator99: It doesn't matter much (to me). Are there prostitutes where you live?

Antrophagus: Yes, sure.

Cator99: Well, Kassel isn't as big.... One could invite someone, even if it goes against your principle of only him who wants it. Then it would come to my cock and balls before it's their turn....

Antrophagus: But with prostitutes, there's also a high risk of being infected with AIDS.

Cator99: True, unfortunately. Now with me that's no problem, because I've been tested and I don't "run around." Want to be a good meat deliverer, contrary to other meat deliverers (BSE and MKS).

Antrophagus: Yes, I very much hope so. Human flesh may be the only kind that can be eaten without hesitation because it's more regularly and thoroughly inspected than "normal" slaughter animals.

Cator99: That's the way I see it. It's time it was legalized...

Antrophagus: In big cities like in South America or India there surely must be some people who'd be glad if it were.

Cator99: I hope you won't draw out too much blood, because of our meeting day after tomorrow (less than 48 hours now).

[Text passage deleted]

Antrophagus: For a lubricant, I apply olive oil. It's healthier than synthetic liquids. I have enough juice in me that I can inject into you. Don't worry.

Cator99: It's also good for roasting, and why not begin

	to fatten me up? It's to be roasted anyway.
Antrophagus:	Exactly.
Cator99:	I'd be glad to pleasure you orally as long as my tongue is still there.
	[Text passage deleted]
	I can also bite into yours, as hard as you want, or not yet....
	I'm said to give a good blowjob, or so I'm told, without boasting.
	But that depends on you. Look for the holes you'd like to fuck.
Antrophagus:	Yes, we'll look into that when you're here. Of course, I'll wash it first...hygiene is really important.
Cator99:	Really wild that we don't need condoms.
Antrophagus:	But only because right after that I'm going to consume you whole. Otherwise, it would be something different.
Cator99:	*[Text passage deleted]*
	Right. Condoms won't prevent you from making a meal of me, so we can do without them. And I'm hardly at risk of getting HIV.
Antrophagus:	Oh yeah. It'll be a riot when you're over here, inside me.
	At least not from me. And the incubation period for AIDS, I think, is six months.
Cator99:	HIV from someone other than you, after I've been with you? Really, shouldn't go, or should I? I don't care whether you have HIV or not. Still won't leave you (at least not completely).
Antrophagus:	True words.
Cator99:	Well, in six months' time you probably won't be nibbling at me. You probably won't be able to keep me alive that long. I'd bet rather on a period of 1 – 3 days.
Antrophagus:	Right, in six months there may still be part of you in the freezer, unless by that time I've completely consumed you—and maybe many other lads after you.

Cator99: I rather think not, or part of my flesh won't be in there alone. I think, if you like it the way you imagine it, I won't be long in the freezer. Since part of me will stay with you anyway (as food in your cells), I'll be there, so to speak, when you invite the next one.

Antrophagus: Exactly right.

Cator99: Incidentally, I hope you can keep your lips open as long as possible when you bite into me, so I can see your teeth, too. You have a large, handsome mouth, which exposes your teeth all the way to the side, if I saw correctly in the photos. Really raunchy, if I can see your teeth working, until the pain stops suddenly because a piece of flesh is still hanging between your teeth.

Antrophagus: It's when I bite hard that the teeth are bared. Raw flesh is much more solid than roasted flesh. You'll really be able to admire my teeth.

Cator99: Wild, sink them nice and slow, over and over, into my flesh and bite or tear off the chunks.... I think that if you get hornier and hornier, during your orgasm you won't be able to control it any longer, maybe happen sooner. And after your orgasm, being able to eat the piece calmly I imagine is very sexy for you.

Antrophagus: I'm already horny as a goat.

Cator99: *[Text passage deleted]*

Antrophagus: Yes, let's both enjoy it as long as possible.

Cator99: It's only the first piece that can pose problems when you bite it. If you stay in that area, the main effort is over and not so much natural resistance is to be expected. From me, you won't get any resistance at all. I hope that's all right.

Antrophagus: I hope so, too. Otherwise, I'll have to tie you up, but we'll see when the time comes. It will certainly be painful.

Cator99:	I'll be sure to scream, but you live in the country, you said, so there's no problem.
Antrophagus:	I'll soundproof the room where we'll do it.
Cator99:	Of course, it'll be painful. I take that for granted. That's why my balls mustn't be eaten first—I'm very sensitive there.
Antrophagus:	I'm eager to know how you'll taste.
Cator99:	*[Text passage deleted]*
Antrophagus:	Yes, I know. I'm already familiar with the anatomy. Especially with boys.
Cator99:	Good. Then you can continue your studies with a living subject....
Antrophagus:	Raunchy.
Cator99:	First for me, I think I probably won't survive that long. You'll be in a frenzy.
Antrophagus:	I value that, too. Anyway, it'll be fascinating to see how much a person can bear before the body gives out.
Cator99:	It might differ from one person to another, in loss of blood, how tight you tie me. There are quite a few places where I'm not so sensitive, and others where I'm very sensitive....
Antrophagus:	Right. Those factors can play an important role. It's not only the loss of blood that matters, but also the trauma, which happens to anyone.
Cator99:	Other than my testicles, which are especially sensitive to pain, my upper thighs/calves (not so much), arms and chest (except the nipples themselves) are also not so pain-sensitive. My penis is well trained as far as biting goes.
Cator99:	It bled 24 hours ago because a blood vessel inside it had burst. Had no problems with it. On the contrary, would have liked to see more. Only my counterpart shrank back.
Antrophagus:	Then we'll just hope for the best.
Cator99:	And if I go downhill faster than hoped, it's still okay; I know what's going to happen to my flesh....

Antrophagus: Yes, under normal conditions certainly not a pleasant sight.

It can be seen only when you're here or have already been bitten off.

Cator99: I'd most like to offer you my flesh this evening.

Antrophagus: Patience, it won't be much longer.

Cator99: Incidentally, I spent a little time under the sunlamp so my skin wouldn't look quite so pale. Couldn't get much tan, though.

Antrophagus: You'll taste good, though, believe me.

Cator99: Patience? You just don't know how I've longed for it.... I've been looking around so hard since autumn of 1999. Not all my other attempts before (without the Internet) had worked out

Antrophagus: Same for me—could hardly tell someone I'd like to have him to eat.

Cator99: I've already told several people they should eat me (at least my genitals), but that inhibition threshold ruined everything.

Antrophagus Right, the Internet was a fantastic discovery; since I've been connected to it, I've been able to spread my wings for the first time. Before that, it was a problem.

Cator99: Yes, same here.

Antrophagus: Better stop now, let's have a littl intermission, want to go into town a short while.

Cator99: A larger group can be reached, shouldn't have happened in Germany. I'd also be prepared to go to the US, for example. Had a super offer there, too, but it fell through....

Cator99: Okay, I'll be online until 4 p.m. Have fun

Antrophagus: All's well—'til then

Cator99: 'Til later....

THURSDAY, MARCH 8, 2001
28 HOURS UNTIL THE MEETING

Antrophagus:	Hi, so, here I am again. Helloooo.
Cator99:	Am still here, too (at work, where else?)
Antrophagus:	At work I can't surf so long—you have it made.
Cator99:	Yes, but not always, (now the phone's ringing …)
Antrophagus:	Oh, cooked something to eat just now, that's why it took a little longer.
Cator99:	What do you have?
Antrophagus:	Nothing sensational, Spaghetti Carbonara and mixed salad.
Cator99:	For Spaghetti Carbonara, you may not have to buy anything anymore; there'll be enough flesh for the various possible preparations. What are you going to do with the unprocessed fleshy parts?
Antrophagus:	Well, whatever tendons, skin, intestines, and so forth are left over will be buried. I'll put the so-called separation flesh through the meat grinder for sausage.
Cator99:	In this desk job in front of my new computer, one can always be online in Messenger. What will you do with the brain?
Antrophagus:	I'll leave it where it is. I didn't want to split your skull.
Cator99:	And some of the glands like the gallbladder, et cetera?
Antrophagus:	Bury them.
Cator99:	Down into the soil? Still there?
Antrophagus:	Yes, as for the skull, I'll have to think it over again, but it will be safe to bury it. Yes. Best place would be the cemetery. That's where it would attract the least notice if a skull were found there.
Cator99:	Well now, the skull (=bone)—maybe you should grind it up in case it turns out like

bones: that's medically the most important part.

Antrophagus: We have a nice little cemetery here.

Cator99: I think it's problematic. With that part, something can be proved.

Antrophagus: Let's see. I'll dispose of it properly.

Antrophagus: Would be a good idea surely, to make use of some of it some other way, not only as food.

Cator99: So grinding it up would be best. Moreover, a lot could be proved from the teeth. Yes, the skull as an ashtray.

Antrophagus: I'll do it. You don't have to wrack your brains over it anymore.

Cator99: An important thing in disposing of the remains is that no conclusions be drawn about my (ex-) person and you. And DNA-scans and teeth are important clues.

Antrophagus: I'll get on top of it. It's only important that I get your flesh. Then I'll get rid of the rest.

Cator99: Okay, didn't want to bug you, but nowadays it's important to plan ahead for getting rid of the refuse, especially in this case.

Antrophagus: Right. Anyway, I'm not so stupid as to dump your remains on an autobahn parking lot or something like that.

Cator99: I thought so.

Antrophagus: I've pulled my thoughts together, and if all goes according to plan, nobody will get wind of it.

Cator99: Good ...By the way, it's really funny—since we made our deal, inquiries have been raining down on me, but as I said, the very best inquiry materialized out of nothing from the US (=no further reaction). And they absolutely had to have me....

Antrophagus: You'll be completely inside me.
Yes, unfortunately, it was the same with the victims I've had up to now.
First, they drive one crazy, they're really wild

	about it, and at the last moment they chicken out.
Cator99:	Yes, with the offers from the US I'd have been divided into three.... The real turn-on in the offer was that the one who wanted to "take care of my genitals" was black (and for me it would have been the optimum: white teeth in black skin). But what the hell—main thing is that it's finally going to be real. Then a couple of days before we were to meet I heard nothing more from him.
	Yes, it all depends on that.
Antrophagus:	I got one also from the States, and I stupidly even bought him a ticket, only he didn't come. There you are. Once you're here, there's no backing out.
Cator99:	He probably sold the ticket and got a good laugh out of it....
Antrophagus:	Nah, I got my money back, but not all of it.
Cator99:	It's shit with the cybers who pretend to take it seriously. If they just said right out that it's to remain fantasy, then O.K. Even then, one could exchange ideas.
Antrophagus:	He hadn't even gone to the airport.
	Exactly. With my cyber friend, I chat almost every evening. He was honest enough to tell me he didn't mean it very seriously, only in fantasy.
Cator99:	As long as you don't shrink from me, on FR [Friday is apparently meant] there'll be absolutely no way back, only forward between your teeth and deeper in.
Antrophagus:	Yes. The only way to leave the house is through the drainpipe.
Cator99:	Drainpipe? Well, I don't regard your mouth that way. And my remains, well, it's all the same to me, just as it's all the same to me that my life will trickle out through your mouth.
Antrophagus:	No, I didn't mean that either. You'll get into

	the drainpipe only through my body. Are you still there?
Cator99:	So in that manner, if it's best, we have to leave it there. And sexually on Friday, it's the best way, and otherwise I've achieved what I wanted to. So also O.K. Makes sense, what I learned as a child.
Antrophagus:	What did you learn as a child?
Cator99:	And on that path are only the usable remains of me, and I don't care. It's time for me to serve you as meaningful use of flesh and for your orgasm.
Antrophagus:	That we should stop when it's at its best?
Cator99:	How was that? I didn't get that part before.
Antrophagus:	That's a good attitude. You'll surely taste good.
Cator99:	Yes. To stop when it's at its best goes for my life and for sex, this will be best with you (being eaten is for me the sexual maximum).
Antrophagus:	I think for me, it's half the other way around—for me the eating is the maximum.
Cator99:	That's why it's so suitable. If it weren't sexy for you, too, it wouldn't be half as good for me. It's just too bad that my molars (lower right very well shaped) can't be sunk before then into male flesh. But I haven't had the same opportunities you've had. Never mind: the most important part of all comes on Friday.
Antrophagus:	I can hardly wait to sink my teeth into you.
Cator99:	(Would have been a nice experience.) But perhaps YOU will give me something more of your flesh to savor...
Antrophagus:	Let's see, we can see it Friday.
Cator99:	It's sexy, too, that the pain will increase until it's unbearable, and then stop suddenly when the piece of flesh is off.
Antrophagus:	I don't know. I think the pain will still be there when a piece is gone.
Cator99:	That's different from the pain caused by the

pressure of the teeth. The exposed nerves will rebel afterward, but you can bite the same place again and finish off those nerves...
Are you a smoker or nonsmoker?

Antrophagus: It'll show when I have my teeth there. I'm a smoker. I hope you don't mind.

Cator99: Not at all. I smoke, too...
Hope you don't mind...

Antrophagus: Then its O.K., smoked meat stays fresh longer.

Cator99: Right.

Antrophagus: So let's call it a day, otherwise it'll get too expensive.

Cator99: Your teeth/tongue looked like a smoker in the picture.

Antrophagus: I wouldn't have thought it would show. I brush my teeth regularly.

Cator99: Don't you have a flat rate? You dog you. O.K., I must go and get my ticket... 'Til Friday at the latest. If you want, we can chat again or you can just call me during the day.

Antrophagus: All's well. So long until tomorrow.

Cator99: That's O.K., but light discolorations from the nicotine can't be completely removed (or it was only the light and you have radiantly white teeth).

Antrophagus: They don't shine like in the ads, but they're O.K., and above all firm.

Cator99: I'll bring myself as breakfast.

Antrophagus: I'll have an appetite—rely on it.

Cator99: Until tomorrow, latest Friday.

Antrophagus: Yes, 'til tomorrow.

Cator99: Bye.

Antrophagus: Bye.

*

It is Thursday, March 8, 2001. Bernd Brandes excuses himself to his living partner René, offering a pretext for being out of touch the following day. In his interrogation on April 11, 2001, René's recollection is the following: *[Comment: summarized by the author for better readability]:*

> *I was on leave that week. There were no arguments. In February, the Siemens Company paid him a sort of bonus—around 10,000 to 15,000 marks—out of which he made substantial purchases (refrigerator, television set, printer). For that year, a vacation trip was also planned. We talked about it, but didn't decide on a place to go. When he came home on Thursday evening, he explained that he had a lot to do the next day, and that he could not be reached on his cell phone or at work. The evening passed quite normally, we went to bed at about 20:30. When I went to the toilet at 5:30, he was still asleep. Then I went back to sleep. About 9:00, I got up, and he had already left the apartment. He had taken with him as usual his door key, wallet, and cell phone. I assumed that he had gone to work. At that time, it was not known to me that he had that day off.*

*

As already agreed with Armin Meiwes, and before leaving for the Zoo train station on the morning of March 9, 2001, Bernd Brandes expertly deletes from his computer for the last time all those dates that could indicate his plans. He withdraws 300 marks from an automatic teller machine.

At 7:41, at the Zoo station, Bernd Brandes boards the ICE 793 train from Berlin to Kassel. Duration of the trip: two hours, thirty-three minutes. Arrival time in Kassel: 10:14 a.m. He does not buy a return ticket.

AND GOD SAW THAT THE WICKEDNESS OF MAN WAS GREAT IN THE EARTH, AND THAT EVERY IMAGINATION OF THE THOUGHTS OF HIS HEART WAS ONLY EVIL CONTINUALLY. AND THE LORD WAS SORRY THAT HE HAD MADE MAN ON THE EARTH, AND IT GRIEVED HIM AT HIS HEART.

(Genesis 6: 5-6)

CHAPTER 10

APPOINTMENT WITH DEATH

FROM THE FRANKFURT AM Main Airport, a thirty-three-minute taxi ride takes me to the Weiterstadt Penitentiary, to which the prisoner Armin Meiwes has been transferred by the "Assignment Committee" for a hearing. Here it will be decided, in a discussion with executive officials and the prison psychologist, whether the prisoner is to continue serving his life sentence in the Kassel Penitentiary or in another Hessian facility.

Armin Meiwes has reported to me in our last discussion the preparations for the contract agreed on with Bernd Brandes. The descriptions in the emails and the copy of the Messenger exchanges are, for the most part, beyond repulsive. Meiwes's recollections and the minutiae of the email exchanges and chats with Bernd Brandes sharpen one's perception of every gruesome detail. The motivating force of both men was lust. The more often they repeated their fantasies, the more strongly their wish became to translate them into reality. Armin Meiwes and Bernd Brandes became slaves of their desires. At some moment in time, they could no longer think of anything else, and only could fix their focus on that one special day.

The confessions of Meiwes echo in my head like screams of prisoners under torture. I am overwhelmed by disgust. Work on the book becomes ever more of a burden. Sometimes I feel as if I had been put through a meat grinder of Meiwes's: shredded, reduced to mush, and no longer myself. Added to the psychic pressure, the long-term stress of the project has produced physical effects. Unexpectedly, during an automobile trip, I break out in a cold sweat. The abysses of the human souls I am exploring become like an ulcer in my intestines. My pulse is racing so fast that I have to stop the car at the curb, open the door, and vomit into the gutter. I don't know what I fear more: the next discussions with the outwardly "nice, pleasant" Meiwes, or the critics who will reproach me for writing the unvarnished truth and protest, "How can one go so far? Must we wallow in this filth?"

It is too late, however, to worry about the critics, because I'm stuck, if you will, in the "filth," not to drown in it or pull others down with me, but rather to shine a spotlight into the dark side of the Internet. It is the slime that oozes everywhere around us all. We cannot pretend such baseness does not exist, and we must understand the consequences. According to jurists and prosecuting attorneys, action alone does not make a person guilty, but the intent behind the deed—the motive—coupled with it, does. Like conspirators, Meiwes and Brandes could converse on the Internet about their abnormal fantasies without fear of being found out. Both immersed themselves in this parallel world and became quickly accustomed to its existence while the natural world around them began to fade. This is the great danger by which we, and our children, can be drawn in and destroyed, and which goes ignored by politicians and the majority of society. This peril must be nipped in the bud.

In the more than one hundred existing cannibal-pages, there is no obligation to identify one's self. Any child, any adolescent, any suicidal person can log in. Thousands of these users are truly in need of immediate psychological help, but receiving none, they may turn their fascination into action.

Gradually, it is becoming ever clearer to me why I am writing this book. One cannot forever just turn away in disgust and give the excuse, "Cannibalism does exist, but it has nothing to do with us." It does indeed have something to do with us, all of us in our society. To solve a problem, we have to come to terms with it, just as a pedophile hunter must delve into the world of molesters and rapists, probing their minds, or an undercover policeman must blend into the haunts of drug dealers to identify these sellers of poison and save lives.

*

In the taxi on the way to Weiterstadt, for a "diversion," I dip into a few technical books on "Cannibalism."

The "Dictionary of Derivations" defines the term "cannibal" as follows: "Man-eater, primitive, uncivilized person; from 'canibal,' corrupted by erroneous spelling during the age of the conquistadores, inhabitant of the Caribees."

The word "cannibal," therefore, was itself already *corrupted.* The "Great Bertelsmann Lexikon" (2000 edition) states, "The custom, originating in sorcery practices and now nearly eradicated, of eating human body parts. Cannibalism is attributed to individual areas or tribes in Africa and South America, Southeast Asia, Australia and Oceania." To elaborate, one could add today, "Since 2001, this practice has spread into Germany in particular localities."

Meiwes asserted a number of times during the interviews that he believed "his younger brother lived on in him through being consumed." This would be his "Mana." "Mana," according to Bertelsmann, comes from Polynesian and means "effective." The Lexikon further explains, "In the lore of the South Seas people, a supernatural, extraordinarily effective, impersonal power inherent in leading persons (chiefs, valiant warriors, priests, physicians), animals, plants, spirits and things, and said to be transferable." In millennia-old beliefs of many peoples, the Aztecs for example, this was the case through the sacrifice and consumption of human flesh. Cannibalism is as old as humanity itself.

In reading "On Being Human and Being Eaten—an Illustrated History of Cannibalism," I discover by accident on page 162 the feature film Armin Meiwes had told me about, "The Cook, the Thief, His Wife, & Her Lover," by Peter Greenaway. The French classic was shown on the ARD or the ZDF, when Armin Meiwes was eleven years old, and "inspired" him, according to his statements. Its plot can be summarized thus: In the high-class restaurant, "Le Hollandais," Mafia boss, Albert Spica, is dining with his frustrated wife and an anxious group of friends. Madame gets involved with the book collector, Michael, who is thereupon murdered by Spica. Madame Spica serves her husband the roasted corpse of Michael at a banquet. As a special delicacy, she offers him the dead man's penis. Ha, there it is again, the "roasted cock." (Black humor, says a psychologist friend, is supposed to help relieve my stress.)

The destination of my trip today, the Weiterstadt Penitentiary, is a facility run by the Justice Administration of the State of Hesse. The home page of the prison reads like an advertisement brochure for a three-star wellness hotel on the Baltic Sea. "The premises are bright and welcoming. Light falls onto the 400-yard-long access road, along which, on both sides, are seven lodging houses, the administrative center and the dispensary. The L-shaped lodging quarters consist of three buildings with wide corridors, which can accommodate forty inmates each. These buildings are separated from one another by glass building-stones.... Each lodging house has a free-time courtyard fitted out with trees and rocks, a small basketball court, and semicircular benches of stone and wood. This modern facility commenced operation in May 1997, after a construction period of twelve years. Bars and high walls have remained, but otherwise the architecture of the Penitentiary resembles a postmodern industrial facility."

For ten days, Armin Meiwes, the cannibal, has been serving his sentence here. "Nice for him," I mumble to myself. "You have reached your destination," says the voice of the navigation system to the taxi driver and me.

*

Friday, March 9, 2001: day of the slaughter
Berlin, Zoo train station, about 7:30 a.m.

In a light drizzle on this late winter day, Bernd Brandes boards the train at the Berlin Zoo station bound for Kassel. The express, with a top speed of 250 kilometers [155 miles] an hour, has two locomotives and a dining car with a restaurant. The neatly dressed graduate engineer takes a seat in the smoking section of a second-class car, presumably one of the window seats.

Brandes looks fresh and youthful, although he is already forty-three years old. For his one-way journey, the native Berliner is wearing a gray-green summer jacket, a green Nike baseball cap, a blue-gray shirt, light blue jeans, blue socks, dark-blue gym shoes, and a silver Junghans wristwatch with a metal wristband.

In a white plastic bag, he has a "Lift" drinking bottle (.5 liter, plastic), his silver Siemens SL 45 cell phone, a key ring, his wallet with the three hundred marks from the ATM, and his personal identity card.

No witnesses are to be found who know of his trip or any of the details of the journey. As planned in advance, it is determined that Brandes leave on the ICE train punctually at 7:41 a.m. and be transported on to the somber gloom of his own yearned-for death.

The timetable calls for the arrival of the Intercity Express in Kassel after two hours and thirty-three minutes.

Kassel-Wilhelmshöhe train station, 10:14 a.m.

The Kassel-Wilhelmshöhe train station is a depot of very modern design with two through-tracks and four platforms. It was opened on November 13, 1991. The wide platforms, because of the high ceilings and the rows of supporting pillars on either side, are dark and drafty, which earned the station the nickname "palace of a thousand winds." There are no elevators or escalators, which draws complaints from passengers even today.

In one of his last emails to "Cator" Bernd Brandes, "Antrophagus" Armin Meiwes described their meeting place as follows: "In the middle of the platform, a wide ramp leads up to the station building. Go up this ramp and you will see a dark-blue statue, some fifteen-feet tall. To the left of the statue is the information desk, and to the right, a bistro. We'll meet at this statue. In case something happens to prevent or delay our meeting, please give me your cell phone number so I can inform you. I'll have on black pants, a black jacket and, around my neck, a red checked scarf. I'm looking forward to it. Franky."

Bernd Brandes emails him his cell phone number: "Hi Franky, my cell phone number is 0179-290XXXX. Can hardly wait. Cator."

*

For today's interview with Armin Meiwes, I enter through the main door to the Weiterstadt Penitentiary.

After the compulsory and much stricter security checks than in the Kassel Penitentiary (I am not allowed to bring in a camera or a ballpoint pen; only a single pencil and three sheets of blank paper are permitted), the prison official leads me from the entrance to a room in the basement. "In here," directs the official in a bored voice. With a minimum of explanatory words, he leads me through the door.

Visitors' Room 5 is a sterile box, about 300 square feet in size with whitewashed walls, the result resembling a dentist's waiting room. At a long narrow table, two chairs are lined up on each side, facing each other. Hardly have I entered the room when the main actor steps onto the stage. A security official accompanies Meiwes. The prisoner looks as self-confident and friendly as before.

"Hello, how are things going?" he asks cheerfully.

"Thanks, badly," I reply honestly. "Since our last meeting, I've been having stomach trouble. It was probably the chat exchanges."

Meiwes laughs. I don't laugh with him. I don't think it is so funny. We shake hands politely.

His handshake is much firmer than at the beginning of our talks four months ago. This time, Meiwes really squeezes my hand. Presumably, it's intentional, because I once told Meiwes, he had an unusually soft handshake. He does everything possible to avoid any mannerism that could be considered not "manly." Thus, he adjusts himself to fit the role he wants to inhabit.

We sit down on the chairs. The official remains standing in the room, the closed door behind him, sullenly observing the meeting. In the presence of the guard and other prisoners and their visitors, I resume the interview with the cannibal.

"What was your first impression when you picked up Bernd Brandes at the station?

"Well, we'd exchanged portrait photos, so we were able to recognize each other immediately."

Meiwes likes the subject we're discussing. "I had mailed him, at his request, photos of my teeth and genitals. So we already knew each other well. We'd also agreed exactly where to meet in case we lost each other in the station. His train arrived on time at 10:14 in the morning. I was already waiting on the platform and was on pins and needles wondering if he'd really come. Bernd Brandes was one of the first passengers to get off and I saw him from a distance. He had on a baseball cap, dark shirt, jacket, blue jeans, and he was holding a plastic bag in his hand. He came directly up to me and said, 'Hello, nice to see you. Let's get off the platform. There are too many people around.' 'Sure,' I answered. 'The exit's just up there.' Without saying much to each other, we walked into the station hall and to the parking lot. I had my car there, a green Lancia Kappa Kombi diesel. The car's tag number was HEF-TW 11 and it drove very smoothly at high speed."

Meiwes ends his monologue with a theatrical pause. He gazes at me and seems to sense my eagerness to get on with it.

"Mr. Meiwes, what happened then?"

"We got into the car and drove out of Kassel. Bernd seemed very nice. He hadn't eaten for a while to make sure his intestines were empty. In the car, he started groping me. Naturally, I stopped him, but went on driving. During the trip, I wanted to concentrate on driving and not get into an accident."

"What did Brandes do then?"

"He put his hand on my crotch, rubbed it, and tried to open my pants. Kisses and caresses exchanged and so on. He was really in a stew of desire. I told Bernd flatly, 'Stop it. Wait until we're in my home. It's only sixty kilometers.' He answered, 'Yes, but I absolutely want to go through with it

213

today.' I said, 'If it's still your deepest wish as much now as before, then we'll do it. I've been looking forward to it for weeks.'"

Wüstefeld estate, 11:30 a.m.

After the hour's drive from Kassel, the two men arrive at the estate in Wüstefeld. "I parked the Lancia in the courtyard," says Armin Meiwes, "and we went into the house. We then went right to the living room with the adjoining greenhouse."

Meiwes goes excitedly into the kitchen to make coffee. "When I came back, Bernd Brandes was standing there, without my having asked him to do anything, stark naked in the room."

Armin Meiwes observes Bernd Brandes's body with the sober gaze of a physician. He is attentive and concentrates on the essentials. To his happy surprise, Brandes stands up to his stern test. Meiwes senses that the moment he has awaited for three decades has at last arrived. He feels as if he had prepared himself throughout his life for this guest. For this day, he has carried on through long stretches of time with great patience. Although he dreamed of his desire coming true, he has never believed that he would ever really reach his final goal.

"I want you to be able to admire your food," says Brandes.

"He wasn't visibly aroused," recalls Meiwes. "But as far as I was concerned, he looked very delicious.

But Meiwes is quick to realize that neighbors passing by could easily see into the glass greenhouse, and that naked Bernd Brandes, standing in the middle of the room, was all too clearly visible. "It was embarrassing to me because it was possible for someone to observe what was going on. I said to him, 'Get away from there! Come into the dining room before someone sees you.'"

"What did you feel when you looked at his naked body?"

Meiwes turns his head to the left and looks up at me with a knowing smile. "Bernd presented himself to me as thirty-six years old. Actually, he was forty-three. At that age, one can't tell the difference. He looked great. A good, trim figure. He wasn't muscular. He looked just as I'd imagined. I mean, a nice, pleasant man. He was about five-feet-seven inches tall, so a bit shorter than I was. I asked him to get dressed. But he insisted on staying as he was and only put on a shirt as a concession to me, and we sat down together at the coffee table in the winter garden."

"What did you and he talk about?"

"We had already decided beforehand on the Internet, the details of how we'd go about it. We drank coffee first and he pressed me. 'Come on, show me the room.' He meant the slaughter room."

The Wüstefeld estate, 12 noon

Armin Meiwes yields to Brandes's vehement urging. He leads his guest, naked down to his dark blue socks, into the hallway and up to the second floor.

"We stood in front of the room. I opened the door slowly and switched on the light. Bernd went in and turned all the way around looking very attentively at the room. The slaughter room appealed to him and he wanted right away to have sex with me."

*

The sexual activities in the "slaughter room" last exactly fourteen minutes, thirty seconds. The duration of the act is so precisely known because directly before they began the activity, Meiwes turns on his Medion video camera and the scenes are accordingly documented. He records the first of three Hi-8 cassettes with the heading "Cator," retroactively dated by Meiwes as March 10, 2001, at 4:15 p.m., and numbered 1/3, 2/3, 3/3. The video of the act is held by the State Prosecutor's Office under lock and key. I, therefore, have Meiwes relate the episode to me as he remembers it. In the following account, I shall leave out the most revolting details.

*

Armin Meiwes and Bernd Brandes are in the slaughter room on the second floor of the Wüstefeld estate. Brandes lies on his back on the bed, which is covered with a white sheet. Meiwes kneels over him, at the level of his upper thighs. Both men are naked to their socks. They stroke and caress each other. They do not have sexual intercourse, however, since Meiwes does not get an erection. When Brandes shoves his hand into Meiwes's mouth, the latter bites it hard. "Does it turn you on?" asks Brandes. Meiwes answers, "Slaughtering and biting are two different things." Brandes challenges Meiwes to bite the head of his penis, and then complains, "You didn't really bite!" Thereupon Meiwes bites Brandes so hard on the upper right thigh that Brandes sits bolt upright in pain. Brandes ends the sexual activities with the words, "Let's have a smoke." Both leave the bed, go downstairs, and smoke a cigarette. Meiwes stops the video recording.

*

In the Weiterstadt Penitentiary, it is customary for things to take their course in an emphatically easygoing manner. The official in the room seems to get nervous and shifts from one foot to another.

Armin Meiwes looks innocuous. He asks, "I don't shock you, do I—or do I?" I don't want to be lured into such game playing and counter with a question.

"Weren't you shocked?"

"Well, Brandes went right to the point and wanted matters to get brutal. We lay down on the iron bedstead. I had put a mattress and bedclothes on it ahead of time for Bernd. But his idea was for me to tear the raw flesh from his bones while we were having sex. He said, 'Tear the flesh from my body! Bite me everywhere. Yes, bite me harder, harder!'"

Meiwes is thoroughly keyed up as he goes on with his account. He speaks louder, faster, and more excitedly. "I had to bite his chest muscles and the balls of his hands. I bit as hard as I could, but not as hard as he had hoped. I wanted to get to know him for a week or so and not bite him to death right away."

"Was he really in such a rage because you didn't bite him hard enough?"

"Yes. He got nasty and said, 'You just don't know how. You're too soft. You can't inflict pain the way I'd like it.' As I said, Bernd's idea was for the raw flesh to be torn from his bones. Although the marks of my teeth could be seen on his skin, he was annoyed and complained, 'Nah, you don't know how.'"

"Did you ask him why you had to tear the flesh off his body?"

"No, I didn't, no. He wanted it that way and I wanted to respect his wishes and carry them out."

"Were you able to carry out his wish later on?"

"No. A person shouldn't do what he wouldn't want for himself," he explains like an instructor in a class on sexual behavior. "To bite someone during sex, to bite off chucks of flesh, is certainly not what I would like having done to me. But if somebody bites me, without biting off chunks of flesh, I would have no objection. It was simply his desperate wish and what he felt he must have."

"How did you end the sexual intercourse?"

"Bernd had an orgasm. It hadn't gone as he'd wanted. Not even the biting business. Then we stopped and had a cigarette. He said repeatedly, 'You just don't know how. It isn't working.' Armin Meiwes makes a derisive gesture with his hand, puts on a condescending expression, and imitates Bernd Brandes. 'You can't bite off my cock,' Bernd said. ' You can't slaughter me at all.'"

"What was his motive?"

"Bernd Brandes wanted to experience his high point. He said, 'When you consume me alive, I'll experience the ultimate ecstasy. That is my life's goal.'"

*

Forty-three-year-old Bernd Brandes, in the opinion of the expert, was prey to a strong, masochistic death urge. Brandes can find his "fulfillment" and "security" only when his life is snuffed out in agonizing pain. What a tragic, awful inclination.

The wish for extinguishment of the body derives from a large number of possible motives, such as the "medical theory" (sickness), the "learning theory" (psychic disturbance from observation of behavior types), or the "sociological theory" (disorientation). In 1909, Sigmund Freud described the human death urge, which contradicts the life urge. In Brandes's case, the expert opinion felt the explanation most applicable to Brandes was the "aggression theory" as well as the "narcissus theory."

The Vienna psychoanalyst Wilhelm Stekel asserted in 1910, "No one kills himself who does not wish to kill someone else, or least wishes for someone else's death." The wish for release from the body is seen as the opposite of aggression and is directed against one's self. Negative feelings arising in early childhood, due to rejection or withdrawal of love, are experienced as self-hate. One's own death is felt as just punishment, for the patient feels himself guilty because of his hate, and has a need, therefore, to do away with himself.

Many of these individuals have had difficult childhoods and have known the so-called "broken home" situation (death or loss of a parent or inadequate care). When a person inflicts pain on his body, he cannot tolerate his bodily shell and cannot tolerate himself. Auto aggression, for the sick person, is a kind of self-defense mechanism constructed to avoid dealing with the "inner pain," the emotional wound.

In his psychological assessment, Prof. Dr. Beier observes:

> *In reference to Bernd Brandes this means: Through his masochistic inclination, he can achieve a relief from, or at least an abatement of, guilt feelings, in which it cannot*

*be accidental that the focus of the greatest pain
infliction is transferred...to his own male
genitals.... Much more likely is the assumption
of such strong guilt feelings in the emotional life
of Brandes that he had the feeling of being able
to achieve real relief from guilt only through
great suffering—inflicted by another man—even
to the sacrifice of his own sexuality. Bernd
Brandes felt himself—despite his success and
his competence in the technical field—as an
absolute nullity, and he wished to give
expression to this feeling and end as an absolute
nullity (to be nullified).*

Whether Brandes was aware of these theories, or
embraced the spiritual yearning for "dissolution"—to live on
in some form in another body—cannot be ascertained in
retrospect. It is highly likely, however, that he was obsessed
with a masochistic urge for the "ultimate sexual climax" that
simultaneously signified his own death.

"Mr. Meiwes, you have always stated that you
wanted to consume a younger brother for love. Was Bernd
Brandes searching, in your opinion, for a similar relationship
or only the ultimate, masochistic climax?"

"I think that for him, it was a sexual thing, but he did
want to enter this relationship, and, in that way, live on. He
had also written previously in his emails, 'I'll become a part
of you anyway, at least as food in your cells.' I wanted to
enter this relationship with him, too. That's why I wanted to
know him more intimately. Only Bernd pressed the matter—
endlessly."

"Was Bernd Brandes interested in knowing why you
wanted the 'consumption'?"

"I told him how I imagined it. Bernd was to become
part of me. Today the way I see it is that he pushed for the
destruction of as much of him as possible. There should be
nothing left of him. Not a piece of flesh, not a bone, nothing.
That was exactly the way I saw it then, that he wanted to
enter this connection mentally, as well."

"And then he wanted to go back?"

"No. He changed his mind and said, 'You can't slaughter me until I'm unconscious. Otherwise, you can't bring it off. If I get tired now, then maybe you can do it.' I suggested, 'You can drink a tranquilizing liquid and then I'll stab you. I'll go and see if I have anything. I think when a girlfriend of mine was here, she left something.'"

Meiwes goes from the slaughter room into the kitchen and takes out of the medicine cabinet a half-full bottle labeled "Wick-MediNait," a strong cold medicine to be taken at night.

"I gave it to Bernd and he drank it all down. He really wanted to be stabbed fully conscious, but Bernd said to me, 'When you see me getting sleepy, you can castrate me. You cut off my penis and then cut my throat.' We went from the slaughter room down into the living room. Bernd got dressed there. We drank coffee again and waited for him finally to get tired."

For thirty or forty minutes the two sit there, talking about computers and telephone equipment, and finally, after a full hour, Armin Meiwes steers the conversation cautiously back to "slaughter details."

Bernd says, "Nah, that won't happen with us—drive me back to the station. If I get tired on the way, you can turn around."

"I answered, jokingly, 'Well, turning around on the autobahn isn't easy. I'd rather take the next exit.'"

"Were you disappointed?"

"Yes, of course I was disappointed because my life's dream wasn't fulfilled. But I couldn't be mad at him. I'd written him before that I only wanted to consume someone who also really wanted it of his own accord."

*

Kassel-Wilhelmshöhe train station, about 2 p.m.

Armin Meiwes and Bernd Brandes arrive back at the Kassel-Wilhelmshöhe intercity train station. They have hardly spoken during the trip. Shortly before getting out, Meiwes says again how sorry he is that it didn't work out. He says to his traveling companion, "All my life I have wished for someone I could take into myself and who would remain with me always. Shame it came to nothing with us. I thought you were really nice." Brandes reflects again for a moment, but then decides to go back to Berlin.

They get out of the Lancia and enter the station hall together. They go to look up the departure time of the next express train for Berlin. On the schedule board, they find the ICE to Berlin, 2:44 p.m. "I'll take that one," Brandes decides, and buys his return ticket to Berlin for one hundred sixty-three D-marks from the automatic ticket machine. About half an hour remains until departure time.

What then happens is based only on the testimony of Armin Meiwes. It is entirely unclear and not provable what triggers Brandes's ensuing change of mind. Although he already has the return ticket to Berlin in his pocket, he does a surprising about-face. It's a decision on life and death, between returning home and slaughter, between reason and madness.

This is how Meiwes recalls those moments:

"Bernd went to the station restroom and when he came back, he said suddenly, 'If I go back to Berlin now, I'll be facing a showdown.'"

"With whom would he be having a showdown?"

"At that time, I didn't understand what he was talking about because he had told me he lived alone. He completely hid from me the fact that he had a living companion. Bernd had this idea. 'If I drink more of the cold medicine and take a couple of sleeping pills on top of it, then I'll surely get tired and you can do it.'"

"Why would a man who was planning to die, do as Bernd Brandes did, buy a hi-fi set and a TV? And plan a vacation with his friend, René? It doesn't fit with your account."

"Yes, it does! Bernd made a will in January 2001, two months ahead of our meeting. It's in the hands of the police, too. Many months before that, he was already in touch with three cannibals, including one from the United States who wanted to sever his penis and slaughter him. Bernd completely hid his personal relationships from me. He said he lived alone and that no one would miss him. He would take time off from work and therefore no one would know what had become of him."

In his interrogation (Proceeding No. ST/0132109/2002), Armin Meiwes testifies as follows for the record:

He said his parents had died quite young. He had told me he worked as a manager in the Siemens Company and had a friend.

I confront him with this testimony.

"So you did know that he had a living companion."

"I knew he had a friend. But he did not tell me he lived with him or that it was real love."

"Why didn't you let him go at the station and say, 'Let's let our fantasies remain fantasies'?"

Meiwes flinches at the question, but quickly collects himself. "Well, I confess I was glad Bernd thought it over and didn't want to leave me. You could see it almost as a spontaneous decision. I gave Bernd the car key so he could sit in the vehicle. In the meantime, I went to the Landgraf Karl Pharmacy, opposite the station, and bought another bottle of 'Wick-MediNait' liquid cold medicine and a packet of 'Vivinox' sleeping pills. It was ten of three. The pharmacist told me expressly that the liquid and the sleeping pills must never be taken together. I told her my girlfriend had a cold and needed the liquid and that I couldn't sleep because of her cold and needed the pills. I paid the bill for thirty-five-ten marks in cash—on the sales slip appeared the warning 'impairment of reaction ability'—and returned to the car. Bernd was already sitting in the front passenger seat. He immediately swallowed ten sleeping pills and drank down the 'Wick-MediNait' liquid. I started the engine and we drove back to Wüstefeld. We hardly said a word to each other because he wanted to fall asleep."

The truth of what transpired between Meiwes and Brandes to cause Brandes to change his mind yet again and return to the Meiwes's slaughter room cannot be ascertained in retrospect. It is also possibly not relevant.

With the half-drugged Brandes in the passenger seat of his "really fast" 136-HP Lancia, top speed of two hundred and ten kilometers per hour, Meiwes races back to Wüstefeld before his "slaughter victim" changes his mind again.

THUS SAITH THE LORD OF HOSTS: TURN YE NOW
FROM YOUR EVIL WAYS, AND FROM YOUR EVIL DOINGS:
BUT THEY DID NOT HEAR, NOR HEARKEN UNTO ME.

(Zechariah 1: 4)

CHAPTER 11

THE KILLING

The Wüstefeld estate, 4:30 p.m.

The drive to Wüstefeld Manor is the last automobile drive Bernd Brandes will ever take. At four-thirty in the afternoon, Armin Meiwes stops his Lancia in front of his residence. Next to him sits Bernd Brandes. After swallowing ten sleeping pills along with the liquid cold medicine, he is already slightly dazed.

*

In the Weiterstadt Penitentiary, the prisoner Armin Meiwes folds his hands as if in prayer. He is intensely concentrated, straightforward, and ready to answer me in utter clarity.

"Mr. Brandes had consumed ten, full-strength Vivinox and a bottle of Wick-MediNait. Was he at all responsive on the trip back?"

"Well, as I told you, on the drive home we didn't speak too much because Bernd Brandes wanted to go to sleep. But he was still conscious. We talked of ordinary things, such as work. Because we were on the autobahn, we passed by my company. Bernd said that with Siemens, he was in charge of telephone facilities, and I answered that I had exactly the same type of Siemens equipment in my home. At the end of the sixty-minute drive, he told me he had sold his car a while back, for one symbolic D-mark. Time flew by during the trip."

"What was the situation when you got back to the manor house?"

"Yes, well, I was keyed up because now I was so close to realizing my dream. Bernd was able to get out of the car and enter the house by himself. We then went upstairs again to the slaughter room on the second floor. Bernd undressed again and lay down naked on the bed so he could go to sleep. I lay down next to him, but still dressed. Bernd looked up at the soot marks on the ceiling of the former smoke-room. He said, 'Look, those are cows or flowers.' It was like when children lie on their backs in a field of flowers or on the sand at the beach gazing at the clouds and seeing the shapes as animals...that kind of thing."

"So Bernd Brandes was 'high'?"

"Bernd was full of meds and still quite awake. He was outright euphoric. He didn't seem tired, nor was he sleepy or dazed, but he kept on trying to go to sleep. Later, when I wasn't in the room, he drank half a bottle of schnapps."

Bernd Brandes's blood alcohol level, as later determined at the Institute for Forensic Medicine, is 1.4 per thousand maximum at the time of the act, 0.8 minimum. He was, therefore, at least in a "tipsy condition."

Armin Meiwes describes the dramatic moments. "Around quarter past six in the evening, he says, 'I can't stand it any longer! Do it! Now!' I answered, 'All right, if you want, then we'll do it.' I had already set up the video camera on a tripod in the slaughter room, as agreed upon in the Internet chat. I turned on the camera. Bernd wanted to see right afterwards how the cutting off of his organ had been done."

It is incomprehensible. Meiwes described the act of mutilation to me in a manner as dry and matter-of-fact as if he were explaining the recipe for making apple strudel.

"He actually wanted to see it again?"

"Yes, he wanted to watch the removal of his penis in the video right afterward. The thought excited him. I went and got a knife with about a six-inch blade that was lying ready on the silver tray in the next room. I returned to the slaughter room with it and at his request pushed the record key of the video camera."

*

The Wüstefeld manor house, slaughter room, about 6:30 p.m.

The video camera records the ensuing events on the Hi-8-cassette under No. 2/3, later labeled "Cator, March 10, 2001," in exact chronological sequence. In the subsequent court proceedings, the tape is admitted as evidence and played. In the first trial it is shown to two jurors, one of them Rosemarie L., fifty-seven years of age. At points where it becomes especially disgusting, the commercial employee covers her face with her hands. When she leaves, the court reporter for a Berlin newspaper notes, "She looks as if she were about to vomit."

*

Armin Meiwes next places a wooden platter on the table in the slaughter room. Bernd Brandes walks up to the table and puts his penis on the platter. Meiwes holds the penis and the platter steady with his hands. Brandes stands still; he is not bound and wanted to feel "free."

"I got a wooden platter from the kitchen and put it on the table. Bernd went up to it and laid his penis on it. I then tried to cut off the penis with a small slaughter knife."

*

Meiwes grasps Bernd Brandes's penis in his right hand, while the left holds the slaughter knife. He puts the knife on the base of the penis. Brandes says, "I'll scream." As Meiwes presses the knife downward, Brandes screams in pain and jumps five feet back from the table.

"Bernd laid his erected organ on the platter and I started to cut off his penis at the base. It didn't work, however. The knife was too blunt. I only scratched the skin."

*

In the slaughter room, the two men are arguing about the knife Meiwes had chosen. "That knife isn't sharp, get another," Brandes demands of Meiwes. He answers, "It is, too, sharp." Brandes retorts, "But you saw that it doesn't cut." Meiwes says, "Think I'm nuts? All right, then, I didn't cut right through," then, "It's bleeding for sure." Brandes, through his pain, complains, "The anesthetic isn't working and the knife doesn't cut."

"I checked the knife. It was new and should have cut. From the next room, I got the large slaughter knife and Bernd laid his penis on the wooden platter again."

Meiwes puts the larger knife on the base of Brandes's penis again. The knife penetrates the skin of the penis. Brandes screams repeatedly. Meiwes moves the knife several times, saying, "One, and two."

"Bernd demanded that I try again with the new knife. It worked much better. On the first cut, I nearly severed the penis, but had to finish the work with two more slashes. Bernd screamed and jumped back from the table, but then was glad to see how freely his wound bled. He found it thrilling."

*

The severed penis lies on the wooden platter. Blood flows from the line of the cut. Bernd Brandes is bleeding profusely and says, "Does it ever hurt! I'm passing out. How you sawed around." Armin Meiwes answers, "That's the way you wanted it." Then Meiwes bandages the wound.

"A minute or two after I had cut off his penis, Bernd said, 'I have no pain at all.' He was astonished and found it amazing. Bernd was sure he'd fall unconscious in a short time from the heavy loss of blood. So I put a bandage on him."

*

Armin Meiwes tries to cut the severed penis in half. "It's really tough," he says. Bernd Brandes sits down on the bed.

"Bernd was happy his penis was off and that he was bleeding so profusely. Since he hadn't fainted, he wanted to eat a penis half himself. On the spot, I put half of his sexual organ in his hand. Bernd said how weird the line of the cut looked. Then he sank his teeth into the raw flesh and tried to bite off a piece. It didn't work, however. So I suggested that we prepare the penis for boiling or roasting."

*

Armin Meiwes gets up from his chair in the conference room of the Weiterstadt Penitentiary. "I have to stretch. The chairs are a bit uncomfortable," he comments in a strained tone of voice. After Meiwes's account, I also have a queasy feeling in the stomach. The prison official doesn't stir when Meiwes stands and walks away from the table. Meiwes goes toward the barred window and I follow him. We look at the recreation courtyard with its trees and rocks, the little basketball court, and the semicircular benches of stone and wood. I grant him thirty seconds of time off and then resume my questioning.

"Did you not have a spark of doubt? Did you ever say to yourself, 'I can't do this'?"

"I had doubts that day because everything had gone wrong. First, he wouldn't get tired. Then the business with the blunt knife...well, yes." Armin Meiwes gazes into the distance.

"Why, for heaven's sake, didn't you say, 'Let's end this lunacy.'?"

The prisoner slowly turns to face me. After a painfully long pause, he says slowly and deliberately, "After what had happened with the cutting off of the organ, we couldn't go back. We didn't want to, either."

"Didn't you feel any disgust?"

"For me, it was unpleasant. Yes, disgusting, too."

"And for Bernd Brandes?"

"For him, it was beautiful. For him, it was the very best that he had imagined. On the second try, it went fast, cut once properly, cut a couple of times afterward. It was only two, three seconds. And then he yelled terribly, but briefly, maybe twenty, thirty seconds. 'Ouch! Ouch! Now I'm passing out. I've got to sit down first.' Just a few seconds later he said, 'Oh, now it doesn't hurt at all anymore.' He was very surprised himself because he had hoped it would give him more pain."

"Hoped?"

"Yes, he'd hoped for more pain."

When he screamed, didn't the banal thought occur to you that the neighbors might hear something?"

"Nobody could hear us. The room was completely soundproofed with mattresses. Even if the radio had been turned up at high volume, it couldn't have been heard on the street."

"Had you turned music on?"

"There was dead silence after I had put the makeshift bandage on Bernd's wound. He wanted to eat his entire sex organ himself. Bernd was fascinated by the sight and said, 'It looks like in medical treatises.' I cut the penis right through and he bit into the penis half, but it was too tough. It made him so sad. He had imagined it all quite differently."

"Was it seriously his wish?"

"Yes, it was his wish," Meiwes repeats firmly. "Well, I said to him, 'It'll probably be better roasted.' So he gave me back his piece. I laid it next to the other half-penis on the wooden platter and went down to the kitchen. He stayed upstairs in bed in the slaughter room and said, 'Don't get any ideas about calling an emergency medic.'"

Wüstefeld manor house, kitchen, ground floor, about 7 p.m.

"I rinsed off both halves under the tap and laid them on a wooden carving board. Then I took a Polaroid photo of them, but it was blurred. I put water on the stove and when it came to a boil, I put both halves into it to blanch them. They swelled out of shape quickly, so I removed them from the pot and rinsed them in cold water. Then I seasoned the penis halves with salt, pepper, and garlic, and broiled them in a pan with cooking oil. The fresh flesh shrank fast and then became hard as rock. I arranged both halves on a plate with fresh tomatoes and took them with utensils upstairs to Bernd. I hurried because I was afraid Bernd would soon faint."

"Was it Bernd Brandes's last wish that you fulfilled?"

"It was his highest wish to be able to eat part of his penis, not his last. But, more on that later. When I reached the upstairs room, Bernd was still lying in bed. The mattress on it was soaked in blood. I served him the roasted penis on a china platter with a red border. Bernd straightened up. He took the roasted penis off the platter with his right hand and bit into the rock-hard part and complained, 'It's not edible, either raw or roasted.'"

"Did you eat some of it, too?"

"Yes, I tried it. But the other half was just as tough and had shrunk meanwhile by a centimeter. We couldn't even stick a fork into it. Then I took away the portions and the utensils. The shrunken penis halves I threw into the black plastic bucket for slaughter waste. I had previously put the bucket there for this purpose."

"What happened then?"

"Bernd said to me, 'If I hold out until tomorrow, we can eat my balls for breakfast. One for you and one for me.'"

"To judge from your account, Bernd Brandes had a very black sense of humor."

Armin Meiwes becomes almost heated. "No, he meant it seriously." Then he goes back to his story.

"Bernd lay down in bed again as he didn't want to soak the whole place in blood. I stroked his face and calmed him. He hoped he would go to sleep—in spite of his disappointment. He wanted to go to sleep with music playing. I turned on the radio that was standing upstairs in the slaughter room. He wanted to hear an ordinary broadcast. I looked for FFH because it always plays the biggest hits. I turned on a floor lamp and turned off the ceiling light, so he could go to sleep. We also told each other our real names. Until then he had addressed me as Franky and I'd addressed him as Cator. He said his name was Bernd, and I said, 'I'm Armin.'"

*

Wüstefeld manor house, 1st floor, around 8 p.m.

"Then, about every quarter-hour, I checked to see if Bernd had dozed off because he had told me very clearly, 'As soon as I'm asleep, cut my throat.' But he didn't go to sleep. It must have been about an hour and a half after the amputation that Bernd called me to the room. He said, 'Armin, I'm so cold. Can you run some hot water for me? Then the blood can flow out of my body better.' I answered, 'Yeah, sure, Bernd.' I went down to the first floor and turned on the bath water. And then he went down to the bathroom by himself. I explained the faucet handles and told him it would take the boiler twenty minutes to heat the water. I took off the bandage I had put on him before and Bernd climbed into the tub. Then he sat down in the warm water. He was happy to see how the blood spurted out of the open wound. 'Look,' he said, 'it's like a spring.'"

"He wanted to bleed to death while still alive?"

"Yes. That's how he wanted it. Bernd told me he had often cut his penis himself and that once the wound had even bled for twenty-four hours. The friend who was living with him at the time was disgusted by it. I felt the same way. Bernd was having a good time bathing in his own blood. Then he wanted to go to sleep in the bathtub."

"What did you do during that time?"

"I went to my room, which was next to the bathroom, and read a 'Star Trek' novel. I turned the radio up louder; he wanted to hear music even in the bathroom. Then, as before, I checked on him every quarter-hour. He ran the hot water repeatedly. He'd closed his eyes. After about two and a half hours, I heard him call to me. I went to the bathroom immediately. At that moment, he climbed out of the tub himself and then collapsed unconscious."

"How did you react?"

"I patted him and got him awake again. I lifted him up, but then he fell unconscious again. Then I tried to carry him up to the slaughter room. Halfway up the stairs, he woke up again. At the top of the stairs, he tried to walk by himself. Bernd suddenly felt fit and lively again and said, 'Yes, if I walk now, the circulation will start again, then the blood will flow out better. I'll pass out faster and then you can finally do it.' But because he was taking so long to pass out, he reminded me, 'If I'm still alive tomorrow morning, then we'll have my balls for breakfast. And don't even think of calling an emergency medic!'"

"Why shouldn't you have gone for help?"

"It was Bernd's greatest fear that he would be referred to a psychiatrist. Anyway, I somehow got him into bed. He was shivering because his skin had been soaked by the water, so I brought him a second blanket, and then I checked on him again, as before, every quarter to half-hour. I wanted to know if he was unconscious, had fallen asleep, or had died."

Wüstefeld manor house, slaughter room, March 10, 2001, 3:30 a.m.

"Then, toward three-thirty at night, I heard a rumbling about upstairs. Bernd had gotten up. To one side of the room stood a couple of boards from a clothes cupboard that had been taken apart and, in the darkness, he had stumbled over them. Bernd lay unconscious by the bed. I brought him to. He said, 'Armin, I've got to piss.' I answered, 'Then piss into the bed, it's full of blood! If you stand up now, you'll be dead. You have no blood left in you.' He said again, 'Nah, I have to piss.' He stood up again and then collapsed for good. I couldn't bring him to again."

"What were the last words of Bernd Brandes?"

"His last words were, "I have to piss.""

*

⸳ house, about 4:15 a.m.

iwes lays the unconscious Bernd Brandes
ɛn table in the slaughter room. He puts on
ɪughter apron. "The apron was made from a
ɛt of the kind used by elderly people. I
fastened it to an ordinary kitchen apron with safety pins. To
make it stay on better, I put on an Army belt." He turns on
the video camera again.

*In the slaughter room, Armin Meiwes lays Bernd
Brandes naked on the table and ties his arms and legs with
rope.*

"Bernd Brandes at this point was unconscious. I laid
Bernd on the table and tied his hands and feet tight so he
wouldn't fall off in case he regained consciousness. I had
already prepared the ropes. Then I got the video camera and
the slaughter tools from the next room. I labeled a
videocassette and inserted it. The camera was on a tripod
and I adjusted it to frame Bernd's upper body. I spoke to
Bernd, but he didn't respond. He was already in a coma.

"I assumed at that moment that Bernd was already
dead. I couldn't detect any breathing. I kissed him on the
mouth and said a brief prayer, something like 'Lord, forgive
him and forgive me.' Only when I later watched the video, did
I notice that Bernd's chest was still rising and falling and
that his head and lips were still moving slightly."

*

*In the slaughter room, Armin Meiwes grasps Bernd
Brandes's neck with his right hand. He says, "My pulse is
racing, yours isn't at all." Then he picks up the knife in the
other hand. Meiwes takes a long breath and suddenly puts it
down. After a moment, he grasps the knife again, turns Bernd*

Brandes's head slightly to the right, and lowers the knife to his throat.

"It was an indescribable feeling. I felt anger and joy at the same time. I hated myself for wanting to do it and I hated Bernd because he had come to me. On the other hand, I had an unbelievable feeling of happiness. It all went the way Bernd wanted."

*

Armin Meiwes puts the knife to the upper part of Bernd Brandes's throat and presses it in. The knife comes out on the opposite side of the throat. Meiwes pulls out the knife, turns it around, and inserts it again into the path of the cut. Finally, he cuts open the neck area.

"Blood trickled out, but didn't spurt. I stuck him in the left side of the throat, until the knife came out on the other side. Next, I slit the throat open from above, almost down to the bone. I was surprised that a little blood flowed out. I assumed he was already dead. Then I wanted to cut off his head, so I cut downward as far as the spinal column."

*

Armin Meiwes widens the opening in Bernd Brandes's neck and throat area. Then he sets up the video camera again. He tries to hang Brandes on the hook sunk into the ceiling. He draws the rope knotted to Brandes's bonds through the hook and prepares for the hanging. Meanwhile, a pool of blood has formed on the table. Meiwes puts out bowls to catch the blood that runs over the table edges. Meiwes says, "Now, how am I going to get you up there?"

"I couldn't cut off the head because of the spinal column. I pushed the table closer under the ceiling hooks and untied the rope. I knotted one end to one foot, drew the rope through the hook, and tied the other end to the other foot.

Then with the block and tackle, I pulled Bernd upward, with his feet to the ceiling. His head was still lying on the table."

*

Meiwes tries again to cut off Bernd Brandes's head. He cuts from all sides of the neck and throat area and tries to pull the head loose by turning it all around, but this does not succeed. Meiwes pushes the table to the side, so that the head juts halfway down into the bucket.

He circles the hanging body and says, "You've got a fat behind, fatter than I thought."

YE CANNOT DRINK THE CUP OF THE LORD, AND THE CUP OF DEMONS: YE CANNOT BE PARTAKERS OF THE LORD'S TABLE, AND OF THE TABLE OF DEMONS. DO WE PROVOKE THE LORD TO JEALOUSY? ARE WE STRONGER THAN HE?

(1 Corinthians 10: 21, 22)

Chapter 12
THE SLAUGHTERING

A CONVENTIONAL SLAUGHTERING IN Germany is regulated in detail by the March 3, 1997 "Ordinance for Protection of Animals in Connection with Slaughtering or Killing." The term "slaughtering," as defined in textbooks, means the killing of working animals to obtain their meat for human consumption and to supply by-products such as skin and bones for further processing. Slaughtering may be carried out only by trained butchers. The butcher, according to the Animal Protection and Slaughtering Ordinance, must demonstrate basic familiarity with topics such as animal anatomy and physiology, as well as animal behavior. He must be adequately informed about the orderly carrying out of anesthetization and slaughtering of the animal. The butcher must also prove that he knows how to use the tools and equipment necessary for slaughtering and that he properly maintains them.

*

The "man-eater," Armin Meiwes, has prepared himself for years through the study of medical textbooks and on the Internet for the successful enactment of his own human butchering. On this point, Prof. Dr. Beier, in his forensic-sexual-medical opinion, states:

> Here it should be noted that the lowering of the "pathology threshold" through the various Internet connections must have had great relevance for the performance of the acts under discussion (creation of new group norms: slaughtering is "all right" if the victim wants it). This also becomes clear from reading an article accessible on the Internet (and in Armin Meiwes's possession) entitled "Instructions for

*the Slaughtering of Humans for use as Food."
There, with frightening disdain, is stated that
the human being is at an ideal age between "13
and early 20's" ("this animal is as good as fully
grown, but still tender enough and offers such
meat variety that one can do anything with
it…"). We are instructed how to obtain "animals
for slaughter" ("imports" from the "rural areas of
the Caucasus, Tibet, India, Islamic countries or
the Andes, to minimize the risk of illness"). Even
small children can be considered. "In general,
children before puberty are considerably easier
to overpower, to make compliant, to handle and
to process because of their lower weight, lesser
strength and size, as well as their childish
naiveté, and their flesh is in every case healthier
than that of a full-grown animal." The highly
detailed killing and slaughtering instructions,
recommending "vacation places" (less risk of
discovery) from time to time, best of all river
banks (for cleaning of the slaughter victim),
assign to slaughter victims the character of mere
objects, which even in instructions for
slaughtering animals would sound "cold-
blooded." This is to be emphasized, for this is a
breach of a taboo, which has been since the dawn
of time, a feature of the great majority of
cultures. To put it differently, it is to be
presumed there is no stronger taboo than the
taboo that attaches to cannibalistic behavior….*

Armin Meiwes reads the slaughtering instruction
twice before acting, and then deletes it. He explains, "This
instruction is intended for the slaughtering of innocent
children." Meiwes seeks and finds on the Internet dozens of
other slaughtering instructions which form the basis of the
macabre and dreadful carving up of Bernd Brandes. He
breaks through the barrier of the last taboo, the slaughtering
of a person and absolute fusion with him by eating the
human flesh. For most of us, there is a vague perception of

the concept ("I'd love to eat you," "Love goes through the stomach"), but overall, such thoughts are alien and incomprehensible. Through the cyber-community of the Internet, the impermissible has become permissible. Armin Meiwes has crossed the boundaries of fantasy. He has turned the horrible, the forbidden, into reality.

*

Wüstefeld manor house, slaughter room, 2nd floor, Saturday, March 10, 2001, about 5 a.m.

The three Hi-8 cassettes continue to videotape the slaughter of Bernd Brandes by Armin Meiwes, documenting the procedure in full objectivity. The slaughtering video is seen in the first session by the jurors—the lay judges.

*

Armin Meiwes now cuts open the body in the genital area. For this, he uses a cleaver of the kind to be found in many households. Next, he turns to the innards. He reaches with both hands into Brandes's abdominal cavity and removes the innards, now and again cutting off individual pieces of flesh. Finally, Meiwes removes the heart, holds it in front of the camera, and says, "One boy's heart."

"First I pulled out the innards. I didn't want to eat the liver because of possible toxic substances. Then I removed the heart and lungs. I was surprised that the heart was so small."

Meiwes tries to twist off Bernd Brandes's head, succeeding only after several attempts. The head falls to the floor. Meiwes grabs it, holds it up to the camera, and then sets it on the table.

"I had to twist the head around three hundred and sixty degrees to get it off. Then I put it upright in a bowl and put the bowl on the table. His eyes were shut of course, but he was supposed to watch despite that."

After Armin Meiwes has taken out the lungs, he pulls the chest apart and removes the windpipe and the hyoid bone. He speaks several times to Bernd Brandes as if he were still alive. He says for example, "Shall I cut you in half now, my darling?"

"To cut the pelvis apart, I used the cleaver. After bisecting the trunk, I brought these body parts down to the bathroom and rinsed them in hot water. I shaved off the hair with a razor. Then I brought the halves back upstairs to the slaughter room and hung them on a butcher's hook from the ceiling. One by one, I took down the halves and carved them up expertly. I pulled off the skin, worked the bones loose, and divided the flesh into portions. While doing this, I thought about how to prepare the individual parts, for example as roasts, goulash, or schnitzels."

Armin Meiwes carves up the first body half as far as the hips. Zooming in with the distance setting, he holds up a severed arm to the camera.

"I separated the skin and muscles from the arm and carved it up."

*

It is shortly before sunrise on Saturday, March 10, 2001. At the manor, the birds are already chirping. Meiwes has spent a whole hour hacking up the body of Bernd Brandes, cutting it into pieces and disemboweling it. Now he is exhausted. At five-fifteen a.m., Meiwes turns off the video camera. At the switch to the right of the front door, he turns off the light in the slaughter room. He leaves Bernd Brandes's body halves hanging from the two ceiling hooks. He doesn't close the door to the room. He goes downstairs from the second to the first floor and into his bedroom. Meiwes washes his hands and puts on his fresh blue cotton pajamas. He lies down in bed and goes right to sleep.

*

I feel unwell. These events are becoming ever more dreadful, revolting, and unacceptable to me. Hearing the description of the emasculation and death of Bernd Brandes was deeply depressing to me. But it is the awful truth and not for me to judge. In these depths of disgust, I have only a sense of oppression.

The night's sleep before my next visit to Armin Meiwes in the Kassel Penitentiary was brief and restless. I dreamed once again of Armin Meiwes and the Internet. I invite him to my home and am afraid of him as I hear him mounting the steps. In my dream, I was about to introduce him to my wife. Suddenly I realized who this visitor was and I found no escape. I heard his steps coming closer and closer and I woke up bathed in sweat. After two hours spent pacing back and forth in my apartment, I finally went back to bed. In my second dream, I wanted to send an email. As I was typing at my computer keyboard, the keys suddenly became as sharp as kitchen knives. I looked at my fingers and they were covered with blood.

In contrast, Armin Meiwes's mood seems to improve with each of my visits. On this day, he looks downright happy. "Hellloooo," he gushes in greeting, "wonderful to see you!"

"Great to see you in such a good mood," I reply dryly. "We're going to talk again about the slaughtering of Bernd Brandes," I say, trying as hard as I can to frame my words with journalistic impassivity, but it doesn't work. So I confess, "The subject has become for me an absolute nightmare." Meiwes doesn't change his expression. "Oh well, there are worse things."

I stare at him motionless. At this moment, I can think that nothing could be worse than to emasculate a man, kill him with a knife, and afterwards behead and disembowel him.

We sit down at the table and breathe in each other's faces.

"Were you able to sleep after the slaughter?"

"Well then, under the circumstances, I was at the moment completely done in. Bernd and I had previously chatted with each other for two whole nights. With all this excitement and the carving up of his body, I fell into bed, more or less dead. It was all over at last."

"And on the floor above you, the body halves were hanging?"

"Yes. I'd left them to hang from the ceiling. Bernd Brandes's innards I put in the bucket. I just didn't care then. I only wanted to go to bed."

"How was your first sleep after the deed?"

He seems to be pleased with the question and slides back and forth on his chair. "I didn't have any nightmares, if that's what you want to know. I slept from sheer exhaustion."

Meiwes doesn't sugarcoat the descriptions of his butchering activities in flowery words. He calls things by their names and continues his report in a tone too cheerful for me.

"While you were carving up the body, did you think about anything in particular?"

"While I was pulling apart Bernd Brandes's body, I did think about something...logical," he says, his tone derisive and mocking. His gaze is defiant.

"What did you think about?"

"Well, at that moment, I knew that Bernd was dead and that I couldn't add any more to his pain. By then it was no longer as dramatic as it had been with the first stab."

"You mean the stab in the killing?"

"Yes, sure. I hesitated for a long time. At that moment, I assumed he had already died. It can be seen in the video. I prayed, I kissed him on the lips, picked up the knife, put the knife down again. Then I took the knife in my hand and then put it aside yet again. I prayed one more time. At that moment, I didn't know myself what to do. I thought it over. Shall I pray to the devil or to God, or whatever? And then I prayed God for forgiveness. I found the courage to pick up the knife again, and after hesitating several times, pushed it in. That stab was unbearably hard for me."

"Did you have the feeling that the devil was present?"

Armin Meiwes stretches his upper body, draws himself up and remains in that posture. "No, not really, certainly not. If so, then perhaps there were guardian angels that looked away. There was no devil."

"But this act was surely not God-willed. Do you agree with me there?"

"I don't know what God will do with me, and since I believe that God directs what happens in this world, I also think He allowed it—permitted it. He could maybe have prevented it. Perhaps He even tried."

What a concept! The Christian view would be that God is everywhere, even where there is evil. Only man decides what he does. Under no circumstances, in my belief, can this deed have been God-willed. My head swims in the presence of this fatuous complacency.

"Did you feel nothing at all?"

"Yes, I had the feeling that Bernd himself was still in the slaughter chamber after his death. Even later, hours later, he was present during the carving up of his body. It was his wish to be able to share the experience, and I have it in my thoughts. The cutting with the knife in my memory is quite different from what I see in the video. Whether that was conscious or subconscious, I can't say. I hated myself, hated the fact that I am the one who stands there with the knife. And I feel rage toward Bernd for doing that to me. At the same time, I was happy that it was how it was."

"This seems odd, doesn't it? Or does it?"

The prisoner looks aside, tugs nervously at the left sleeve of his shirt and evades a quick answer.

"What do you mean by that, Mr. Meiwes?"

"Fact is, I did it," he confesses honestly. "I stabbed Bernd Brandes in the throat with the knife. If someone else had come, someone who hadn't pressed so, hadn't fired me up and directed me, I probably couldn't have done it at all."

It sounds as if Armin Meiwes wanted to find excuses for himself and shift much of the blame to Bernd Brandes, as if he had made a contract with Meiwes to die. Those familiar with the sadomasochistic scene explain the inconsistency with this line of reasoning: the one we call a masochist (in this case, Bernd Brandes) is actually the one who is exhibiting sadism. He gives orders in violent words and commanding tones ("Hurt me! Hit me!" or the way Bernd sternly ordered, "Tear my flesh off the bones!"). In the opposite position, is the so-called sadist, the one who inflicts the torture (in this case Armin Meiwes). He is actually the one who must bow humbly to these commands. Regardless, this argument is no reason for a judge—or me for that matter—to jump to defend Armin Meiwes. He has broken the highest taboo of humanity.

"How had you imagined the act with Bernd Brandes?"

"The idea was that it should all be nice, perhaps even romantic. It was really only awful and atrocious. It was over too soon, in the middle of the night. I had thought that because Bernd felt so strong, he would last until the next morning. But no, he just had to die the same day. Without the pressure and without the desperate wish to carry it out the same day, it probably would not have come to that."

"Do you think Bernd Brandes died happy?"

"That is exactly it!" Meiwes pounds the table with both fists to lend special emphasis to his next sentences. "Bernd wanted to have the flesh torn from his bones while he was alive. I couldn't do it. In that, I failed to fulfill his wishes. But at the end, he was happy. He enjoyed the time after his amputation until his death. Bernd experienced ten absolutely happy hours. For two and a half hours, he sat in the bathtub and enjoyed seeing the blood spurt from the wound in his genital area. So he sat there in his own blood. That sight was not a nice one for me. The actual moment of death, for which Bernd longed, he stretched out as far as it would go. It is incomprehensible that the happiest moment of his life was also his last."

"What did you do during the time Bernd Brandes lay dying? That was over ten hours."

"I waited. It seemed like an eternity. I thought there'd be no end to it."

"I notice one detail. In the video during the carving up, you placed the severed head of Bernd Brandes in such a way that it faced in the direction of his torso. What was the purpose of that?"

"As far as I was concerned, as I already mentioned, Bernd was not yet dead. He was still in the room, even if only in my mind. I wanted him to see for himself what happened to him. That was his wish."

"Killing was a problem for you, but not slaughtering?"

"No. It was like cutting up a pig. Meat is meat. It worked out well with the knife, the cleaver, and the circular saw, but took a lot of effort."

"How did you proceed then?"

"On Saturday, March 10, 2001, after four and a half hours of sleep, I got up at around ten a.m. I went up immediately to the slaughter room without even having coffee," he says proudly. "I wanted to see if rigor mortis had completely set in. But I found that it hadn't. So I went down and had coffee in peace and quiet. Toward noon, I went upstairs again to continue dissecting Bernd's body."

For criminologists, the post-criminal phase of Armin Meiwes's deed is not unusual. Such perpetrators act quite normal, unconcerned, and ordinary, even directly after committing such a heinous act. They devote themselves quite calmly to everyday matters, such as taking nourishment or ordinary marital affairs. They are able to distance themselves from the act as if they themselves were only observers and not participants.

*

Armin Meiwes changes the videocassette and inserts a new tape in the camera. He zooms to the chest area of Bernd Brandes's left body half. Deftly, he separates pieces of flesh from the fat and puts them in a waiting bowl.

"I collected small pieces of flesh, and later, without fat and tendons, put them through the meat grinder. I packed the ground meat and froze it."

*

Meiwes fiddles about with the left body half and tries to carve up the shoulder. Then he gets to work on the left arm. He is surprised by the dark color of the flesh.

"I had seen photos in which bright-colored human flesh was to be seen. So I was surprised at the dark color. It was probably because Bernd was so old."

*

Meiwes waves Bernd Brandes's forearm back and forth in front of the camera. Then he lays the upper arm on the table and pulls off the skin. Next, he lays the left leg on the table and changes the size of the camera's focus. With the cleaver, he chops off the foot and then removes the skin from the leg.

"I put the leg on the table and severed the foot. Before that, I had placed a carving board under it. I was surprised at the amount of fat on the leg. I then separated the upper and lower thighs and collected the flesh on prepared trays."

*

Meiwes skins the buttocks and cuts from them, and from the upper thigh, large chunks of flesh. He comments on his activities, for example, saying, "That's the thigh," or "a really beautiful piece." He then removes the flesh from the chest bones. Repeatedly, he talks to the previous owner of the body, Bernd Brandes.

He then turns to the right body half, which is still hanging from the ceiling.

"I cut off the right arm and, afterward, skinned the remaining body half. The procedure with the second half went more smoothly than with the first. I carved the flesh into portions and packed them into freezer bags. These I labeled 'Cator.'"

*

Meiwes zooms the camera in on the table again, so that the viewer can get a good close-up of how he skins the body. He pats it repeatedly and whistles to himself. He drops the skin peeled from the right body half onto the floor and trims off fat and muscle. Next he cuts into the genital area, then the upper thigh. Afterwards, he cuts the filet out of the loin.

"By then the videocassette was full, but I wasn't aware of it until later. I went downstairs to find a new cassette, but I couldn't locate one. So I drove to Rotenburg and bought two blank tapes at Kruhm EP (Electronic Partner). I drove back home, went to the slaughter room, and continued."

Well then, Meiwes has to take a break from slaughtering to buy a Hi-8 cassette. The Wüstefelder washes off Bernd Brandes's blood, throws on a jacket, and drives to Rotenburg. Fathers holding the hands of their children shopping for the latest video games, and housewives purchasing hairdryers and the like, have no idea they are standing on this Saturday afternoon, March 10, 2001, next to a man-eater at the counter in Electronic Partner. A real cannibal right there in their hometown.

*

Armin Meiwes is wearing his butcher's apron again, secured with a belt. He takes down the remains of the right body half and lays them on the table. He cuts off the foot, picks it up, holds it to the camera, and says, "One foot." He then puts it next to the left foot on the table. With the knife, he works on the remains of the body and cuts off more pieces of flesh. He coaxes the blade out of the shoulder and lays the entire piece of meat on the wooden platter. So doing, he says, "A nice steak."

Meiwes cuts the meat in portions and sets up an ordinary domestic, hand-operated meat grinder. After zooming in for a close-up, he begins to cut the flesh into smaller pieces. That done, he turns off the camera.

AND THE SONGS OF THE TEMPLE SHALL BE HOWLINGS IN THAT DAY, SAITH THE LORD GOD: THERE SHALL BE MANY DEAD BODIES IN EVERY PLACE; THEY SHALL CAST THEM FORTH WITH SILENCE.

(Amos 8: 3)

Chapter 13

THE CONSUMPTION

It is Sunday, March 11, 2001.

At five minutes to ten o'clock, from the tower of Saint James's Parish Church in Rotenburg an der Fulda, the five bells peal, summoning the faithful to Sunday mass.

The oldest bell is the pride of the inhabitants. It was cast in 1482 and regarded to be one of the oldest of its kind in Germany. After the great fire of 1478, the "Jakobi-Kirch," as it is called in Hesse, was rebuilt as a double-nave, late-Gothic hall church. On the west portal, the old units of measurement are still engraved, and on the south wall, are the symbols of the stonemason workshops that erected the house of worship.

The splendid interior is marked by its many structural features: the one-story galleries in the aisles, the two-story galleries in the western part of the nave, and the choir stalls with the organ in the eastern nave. The renaissance organ of Jost Schäffer, from the year 1682, lends to every mass a solemn dignity. The district cantor, who plays it furiously, pulls on its twenty-five registers every Sunday as if his life depended upon it. The intricately carved alabaster altar, supported by six Corinthian pillars, was brought to the St. Jakobirkirche in 1970, when its first home, the chapel of the Rotenburg castle, was pulled down.

The Jakobikirche has been very popular in the province since 2006 among the religious and less religious alike, because of the profound, sometimes entertaining sermons of the new Protestant priest, Michael D. The dynamic young clergyman looks as impressive as the church he presides over. With his short-cut black hair, his laughing eyes, and round glasses, he strikingly resembles a grownup Harry Potter. For a year, the Frankfurt native who studied theology in Bonn has never used notes to help him deliver a sermon. For the Rotenburg "Home and Riverbank Festival," he composed, willingly or unwillingly, the following for a speech (which was published on the Internet): [Translator's note: the verse is rhymed verse in German:]

> *Theology I studied in Bonn on the Rhine,*
> *Beginning there, then I took my leave.*
> *To do my thesis I moved to the Lahn,*
> *Marburg with its university had me charmed.*
> *Life on the Rhine is still in my blood,*
> *And that's why I've rhymed this speech, for good or ill.*
> *The guys on the platform at Carnival time do it better.*
> *I only hope, dear people, you're not sharpening your knives.*

Three miles from the church, Armin Meiwes wakes up in his bedroom called "Meadow." The long night's sleep has done him good after two strenuous days and nights. He opens his eyes to the sound of church bells tolling in the surrounding areas. Until his mother passed away, Meiwes often went to both the St. Jakobi church and the Martin Luther church. But his first thought this morning was not for his creator, but his victim, Bernd Brandes.

Meiwes sees clearly before him the face of the Berliner. He remembers the look of despair in Brandes's eyes when he brought him back to the Kassel train station; a great sadness because he believed his lifelong dream of being emasculated and eaten would never be fulfilled. But, then, Meiwes did come through after all! "Armin, you have fulfilled my dearest wish," the Wüstefelder thinks he hears from The Beyond. "Now, you're happy," Meiwes murmurs to the spirit of Brandes, as he puts his left foot out of bed.

Meiwes wishes to celebrate with a victory meal in a "precious spiritual ceremony." Churchgoers certainly would not welcome an invitation to it. Therefore, Meiwes alone looks forward to consuming, as fast as possible, the remaining flesh of Bernd Brandes.

*

Wüstefeld manor house, Sunday, March 11, 2001, around noon

Meiwes showers, then puts on jeans and a colored shirt. He drinks his coffee and breaks his fast with cornflakes and milk. With a plastic bucket full of warm water strengthened with a few splashes of liquid soap in it, he enters the slaughter room on the second floor. Part of Bernd Brandes's torso hangs from the ceiling hook. The other fleshy parts are piled about ten inches high on the small table. They make up about sixty-five pounds of Bernd Brandes.

Armin Meiwes first wipes up the dried blood on the floor with a cloth. The color of the blood is medium to dark red, not almost black, as on the evening of the deed. The mattress, stained with Brandes's blood and urine, he covers with a plastic sheet and turns it over so the stains are no longer visible. He folds the butcher's apron carefully and stows it on a bookshelf.

Meiwes puts in the washing machine on the ground floor, the blood-smeared clothing (the t-shirt, pajamas, and shirt) he wore to meet, kill and disembowel Brandes. Then he returns to the slaughter room.

With an eight-inch knife, its blade an inch wide, Meiwes painstakingly cuts the flesh of the Berlin graduate engineer into portions. Some pieces he puts through the meat grinder for ground meat. Next, he puts portions in freezer bags, labeling each one "Cator." On the sixty-five pounds of flesh, he writes their exact descriptions: "shoulder," "schnitzel," "ground," "roast."

One by one, he brings the blue bags, about sixty of them, out of the slaughter room into the kitchen. He puts the usable parts of Brandes's body into the freezer chest, where until now French fries, ready-to-eat meals, and bread have been stored. The main compartment of the chest is empty now, but is quickly filled to within a few inches of the cover.

Next, he piles into the side compartments, without any packaging, the two hands, the feet, the remaining skeleton parts, and a few bones. The right arm, boned and skinned, he stuffs likewise into the freezer.

Meiwes lays Bernd Brandes's head in a new white plastic bowl, covers it with a plastic bag, and places it into the left side of the chest. So that the skull will not be discovered immediately, he puts two salami pizzas over it.

The second skinned arm of Brandes, he decides to discard. Meiwes tries to pulverize it into a powder with a chemical cleanser. This doesn't work as well as described in the slaughter instructions on the Internet. So he heats the arm in the oven for several hours at three hundred and fifty degrees until it is dried out. He then rubs the bones into small pieces with a metal grater on a wooden board. The grated bone looks like coarse, white Parmesan cheese. He pours the mound into a plastic bag and stows it in a breadbox on the top floor. Skin, innards and slaughter waste (tendons and fat), he buries in the ground behind the house, next to the former stable. In his computer in the study, Meiwes deletes Brandes's Internet site with the Yahoo password given to him by the Berlin Engineer.

Save for the silver Junghans "Solartec" wristwatch, which Meiwes himself will wear later, and the human flesh in the freezer chest, nothing is left to remind one of Bernd Brandes, externally at least. Armin Meiwes, according to Bernd Brandes's wishes, has "nullified" him, eliminating any physical form of his being.

*

In Bernd Brandes's apartment in Berlin-Tempelhof, at 11 Burchardstrasse, his living companion René J. is already in a panic. From sheer worry about his friend Brandes, the blond baker hasn't slept a wink for the last two nights. Since Friday, Brandes has not been seen or heard from and may as well have been swallowed up by the earth. His cell phone has not been working for seventy-two hours. Only a woman's voice answers, "This connection is temporarily disconnected." That Brandes hasn't called is completely atypical behavior. It has never occurred in the year and a half of their relationship. René telephones friends and acquaintances throughout the weekend. He even calls

Bernd's superior Andreas Kuss, whom he doesn't know. But no one has seen or spoken to Brandes or has a clue where he might have gone.

Finally, René goes to the police at 30 Keithstrasse and files a missing person report. The officials of the Criminal Police, LKA 4125, question the twenty-one-year-old intensively about Brandes, gathering a history and personal details. Only then, when they are convinced he has suspiciously gone missing, will they notify police stations all over the country. They will insert a missing persons notice in the Internet.

The official wants to know, among other things, "Were there quarrels or other unusual events between the two of you at the beginning of the year?"

René answered honestly. "There were no quarrels. We did argue over everyday problems, when differences of opinion arose.... There was nothing to indicate he would do something to himself. He has a great zest for life."

"Can you imagine that he could have done something to himself?"

"No, I cannot."

"Where do you think he might be?"

"Not a clue."

The official queried, "Who, after March 3, 2001, asked you about the whereabouts of Mr. Brandes?"

"Only our friends and acquaintances and my parents. Nobody I didn't know asked about him."

For the police, there was simply no useful information to pursue.

*

Sunday, March 11, 2001, 3 p.m.
The Berlin Criminal Police announces:

Search
Missing person
Name: *Brandes, Bernd Jürgen*
Date of birth: *1/19/1958*

Place of birth:	*Berlin*
Nationality:	*German*
Height:	*5'8"*
Build:	*slender*
Language/dialect:	*Berlin inflection*
Hair:	*short, black*
Eye color:	*gray-green*
Sex:	*male*
Distinguishing Features:	*wears glasses, smokes*
Clothing:	*light blue jeans, size 30/30, gray-green summer jacket, dark-blue gym shoes, size 9, blue socks*
Objects carried:	*Siemens cell phone SL 45, silver-colored, key chain, personal ID cards*
Questions:	*Did anyone see the missing person on March 9, 2001? Does anyone know the missing person's whereabouts or contact persons?*
Facts of the case:	*Mr. Brandes asked his employer for the day off on 3/9/2001 to settle personal matters. Left home in the morning as if going to work.*
Station in Charge of case:	*Missing Persons Office of the Criminal Police, LKA 4125, 30 Keithstrasse, 10787 Berlin, tel. 030/699 32 72 51 or 030/699 32 72 58 will accept information.*

*

After his two-week excursion to the Weiterstadt Penitentiary for detention review, Armin Meiwes has been remanded to Kassel.

The official receiving me at the penitentiary laughs. "Ah, back again," he calls to me. "Yes, I'm one of the few who absolutely want to get in," I reply. We shake hands and clap each other on the back like old friends. Horst is one of the penitentiary officials who has known me from previous consultation appointments. "I have the evening off and beginning tomorrow, two weeks leave," he says, letting me in on his private plans. "I've got to have that, a couple of days in Mallorca with the wife and kids. Going to Mr. Meiwes again?" he inquires, although he already knows the answer.

"Yes," I say curtly.

"Pardon my curiosity, but what are you going to talk about today?"

"His favorite dish."

"In our mess hall?" he asks with a touch of sarcasm.

"No. In his life before incarceration. Today we'll be discussing how Armin Meiwes prepared Bernd Brandes for a meal and why he did it."

The official's smile freezes. I hope I haven't spoiled his vacation mood. "Aha, well, success then with the interview. See you," he says in farewell, promptly moving off at a run.

"Cannibalism taboo." These words of Professor Dr. Beier come to mind. Today Armin Meiwes wants to speak to me in full detail precisely about this taboo. "It can't get any worse," I tell myself encouragingly. Or can it?

Meiwes looks relaxed. We sit down at the table. The condemned man rolls up his sleeves. For me, this is the signal to get started on the next conversation.

"When did you eat Bernd Brandes's flesh for the first time?"

"The first consumption was on Monday evening, March 12, 2001, the beginning of my final week of leave from work. I had a piece from his 'back' in the fridge, a filet. This was the first thing I wanted to eat of Bernd Brandes. I seasoned the steak with salt, pepper, garlic, rosemary, and a green pepper sauce. I pan-broiled it quickly and opened a bottle of good red wine."

"Where did you sit and eat this part of Bernd Brandes?"

"The eating took place in the living room. Quite ceremoniously with a candelabra. I got out the black porcelain and the finest tablecloth from the china cabinet. I sat down at the table and enjoyed the solemn moment."

"Why was it solemn moment for you?"

"I had wanted for thirty years to consume a man. And now it had happened. I was of the opinion that this long-awaited wish was about to be granted."

"What was the first bite like?"

"The first bite was naturally a funny, indefinable feeling."

"Can you describe it for me?

"Human flesh is tasty, similar to pork, but a bit sharper and stronger. The steak from Bernd was rather tough, so that I put the flesh I later ate from him through the meat grinder before cooking it."

*

On the same day, March 12, 2001, his colleagues were still waiting for Bernd Brandes to show at a conference that had begun at nine a.m.

His superior, graduate mathematician Andreas Kuss, recalls in his testimony on 2/11/2003 (Proceedings No. ST/o353947/2002) the sudden disappearance of Bernd Brandes as follows:

> The next day, a Saturday [March 10, 2001], I was called privately by Bernd Brandes's friend, René. René had found my phone number somewhere in Bernd's papers. René was wondering why Bernd had not returned to the apartment. He asked me if I had sent him to some business outside. I told René he had taken a day off. René had no reaction to that. The conversation with René strengthened my suspicion that I was dealing with Bernd's boyfriend. René, however, did not tell me this expressly; he represented himself as a quite normal friend. Now I had already become concerned, and assumed that something could have happened. On the weekend, I also called my superior and told him of the incident. I did nothing myself, however, because I wanted to wait and see if Mr. Brandes would show up the

following Monday at 9 a.m. for a meeting with me. This appointment had already been agreed on before. Mr. Brandes did not appear for this appointment. In the course of the morning, I was called by the Berlin police and questioned about Bernd Brandes. I assume Mr. René J. had submitted a missing person report. Then, as Bernd's superior, I conducted further investigations in the Siemens Company. We inquired of American Express, Lufthansa and the Savings Bank whether a plane fare had been booked, or money withdrawn. The results in all cases were negative. Bernd Brandes's office was unaffected.... About a week after his disappearance, I listened, in the presence of witnesses, to his voice mail, that is, the answering service. No abnormalities were noted. Later on, his computers were checked. In the service computer, it was observed that there were relatively few data files in it from the year 2000. My attention was drawn in particular to the fact that the recent data files from that period had been deleted. These data files are normally saved automatically in the Microsoft software. I suspect that they were intentionally deleted. Bernd Brandes was an expert in this field. He is familiar with these data files, which most computer users would not be.... In conclusion, I may say that to me, the entire matter is inexplicable.

*

"And you then continued cooking the flesh?" I put this question spontaneously, because I cannot imagine handling human flesh. The act of eating human flesh of one's own free will is too inconceivable to me. Armin Meiwes, however, seems to get the impression that I am asking for a cooking recipe. He explains his menu preparation quite succinctly. "I ground the first batch on Tuesday, four days after the slaughtering. I made frisoles. I used kohlrabi, salted potatoes, and the remaining red wine. Then I ate of Bernd Brandes on different days, mostly on the weekends."

"Were there special occasions when you consumed the flesh?"

"No, I ate it now and then, whenever I was hungry. On the day of his death, however, it was especially solemn. Of the sixty-five pounds of flesh, I ate about forty-five."

"Were you the only person who ate from it?

"Yes. I ate from it alone and gave none of it to any other person. It would have made no difference if somebody else had tasted it; he wouldn't have questioned the meat. As I said, it looks different than when slaughtering. During preparation, it is not as dark, but bright and fresh as pork, and tastes so very close to pork."

"How would your mother have reacted if she had lived?"

"My mother would at first have disapproved, but I'm not a hundred percent sure. Perhaps she would have tasted it. I don't know, but it's possible, because in a certain way, my mother's ideas and my ideas of having someone inside us were similar."

"Which body parts were of special importance to you?"

"Really, the chest, the penis, and also the buttocks— not only of Bernd Brandes—have always interested me. They are the only parts I left as they were, that is, with skin on. I was more careful to see that no one was coming when I was eating these. Any visitor could have recognized that they were from a human."

"What opinion do you have of people who want to be eaten?"

Meiwes rubs his palms on either side of the water glass, twisting it to and fro.

"Obviously, it's crazy. It was as with my wish. I think the victims desire this from their childhoods on. Anyway, Bernd Brandes told me that since childhood, he'd had a wish to be eaten. And I believed him. I never had any thoughts about it beyond that."

"Can you imagine yourself being slaughtered and consumed?"

"I have imagined that, too. With people from the Internet like Bernd Brandes, I never knew. Is he coming to let himself be eaten, or is he doing it just the other way around?"

"Weren't you afraid of becoming the victim yourself?"

"I was the one who preferred eating the other person, and did do so. If someone had done it to me, I wouldn't have been angry at him."

"Did sexual desire really play no role in any of this for you?"

"In the killing itself, I felt no arousal, nor in the slaughtering either. The photos and videos I took served only to comply with the wishes of the victims. But when I later watched the video showing the slaughtering of Bernd Brandes, I was aroused. I let the video run on, while eating Bernd Brandes, like background music. The fantasies I had before the event flowed together with video images. I knew even before the day, that it would be so. The act of killing did not arouse me, however. It became burned deep into my brain, so that I no longer needed to look at it. With the part before the act of killing, it was just the same. Consciously or unconsciously, I put the act itself out of my memory."

"What would have happened if, after being unmanned, Bernd Brandes had committed suicide?"

"I don't think Bernd would have been able to do it even if he wanted to, and I don't believe he wanted to die by his own hand. I would much rather he had hanged himself, for example, without any help from me. But it was his fate to have his penis cut off and someone kill him. If one penetrates the psyche of a 'normal' suicide, most often a parting letter is written. The death is usually planned in such a way that the body will surely be found. When it is, everyone the victim feels drove him to his death will have to deal with the manner of his death."

"My victim had prepared to let him self be eaten. With Bernd, this need to show oneself after death was absent. He thoroughly erased all traces of himself. There was nothing to indicate that he had come to me. This was in accord with his wishes. He wanted it never to get out."

"Mr. Meiwes, Bernd Brandes lived in a relationship. To outsiders, he seemed happy. Doesn't that touch you?"

"No, because I know he wanted this end so much. He, himself, set the deadline of March 9, 2001. And he told me relatively little about his life, but the little he did tell me came with corresponding dates. These were dates that signified something of importance in his life, like the date he began working at Siemens, which was also a password of his on the Internet."

Not a word of remorse is to be heard from Armin Meiwes. But if one thinks, however, that in the slaughtering and consumption of Bernd Brandes he had found his fulfillment, he would be mistaken.

*

The following Monday, March 19, 2001, Armin Meiwes drives to his work at the offices of Technology Service, Inc., in Kassel, as if nothing has happened. He tells his colleagues he had a wonderful, relaxing week.

*

Of Armin Meiwes's behavior over the next weeks and months of the year 2001, there are no particular incidents to record. He takes part in outdoor picnics in the village and hangs out with friends and colleagues in the allotments. Witnesses report unanimously, that in this period after March 9, 2001, Meiwes was calm, reserved, and always friendly.

No one from the neighborhood has any idea of Armin Meiwes's cannibalism and the Brandes-filets in his freezer unit. The conspicuously young male acquaintances of Meiwes in this period make this clear during interrogations for the record at the Hersfeld-Rotenburg Police headquarters (Proceedings No. ST/0132109/2002 and ST/0353947/2002).

Witness 1: Yakup N., age 23 at the time, friend

Once or twice a month, I called him up. He came and picked me up and we had a pleasant evening together. We had drinks, watched TV or video.... Around the end of the year 2000, he tried hard to be sexually intimate with me. At the beginning, I always turned his approaches down. At some point, from curiosity, I said okay, I'd try it. This sexual contact, at the outset, didn't go beyond touching and stroking. He also rubbed me with his penis. But we never actually had sexual intercourse. The whole thing, for me, is weirdly embarrassing.... In May or June 2001, my parents moved away. I was there two or three months in Hamburg, when I stayed with Armin for one or two weeks. At the time, he was quite normal as always. I was able to move about in the house freely at any time. He never forbade me to do anything or to enter any room.... I also helped myself to a frozen pizza from the freezer chest. He was at work at the time. In the evening, he asked me if I'd eaten something. I can't say that he was nervous because he was afraid I might have discovered something. He even laughed.

*

Yakup N.'s visit gets Armin Meiwes to take preliminary precautions.

In a handwritten letter dated January 26, 2003, Meiwes sums up the situation to himself:

Video film: Bernd Brandes's foot. Since I had a visitor at the beginning of August, 2001, Mr. Jakob [Author's comment: He means Yakup] N., who at first wanted to stay for four weeks, I had to do something about the bones, the skull, as well as the hands and feet so that they wouldn't be seen. When night fell, I first dug a hole, about 2 x 2 x 3 feet in size next to the stables. When I took the skull, hands, and feet out of the freezer chest, it occurred to me to prepare and photograph a foot, because there were a few foot fetishists on the Internet and such a picture might possibly be put to good use. Meanwhile, I put the already partly defrosted foot under running water to make it thaw faster. Then I got utensils together and laid a tablecloth on the work board above the dishwasher. I spread ketchup and spices on the foot and placed it on a serving platter in front of a bowl of hot water, to make the picture or video look real. Since the perspective didn't work out in the kitchen, I set up the foot in the dining room. This was a room people can see easily from outside, but I didn't want to lower the shutters in summertime. I was very nervous. Also, I wanted to bury the body parts as fast as possible. After taking the video, I wiped the foot off again and ceremoniously buried the parts. I watched that video only once or twice, because I didn't particularly care to eat a foot. Next, I sawed up the rest of the skeleton and buried it. A few days later the visitor came. I had already forgotten the incident

*

In the Kassel Penitentiary, I hand Armin Meiwes a print of Bernd Brandes's foot, as "prepared" by him. In the photo is seen a colorful male foot, standing on a plate. It is decorated with fresh tomatoes and appears to be steaming.

The condemned man takes the picture in both hands and states like an expert, "Here is shown quite clearly, the left foot of Bernd Brandes. I recognize it by its color because I seasoned it."

"Why did you put a bowl of hot water nearby?"

"I heated water and poured it into the bowl so that it would look as if the foot was steaming."

"What was your reason for presenting the foot this way?"

"I did it that way because it looked so nice. But I didn't want to eat the foot. It was still raw and I hadn't cooked it. I liked just the sight of it, not the preparation."

"Did you prepare other parts in interesting ways?"

Meiwes smacks his lips as he talks. "Well, I roasted his ribs in the oven. I left part of his rib cage whole, and after thawing it in July 2001, roasted or baked it. But then I froze the ribs again. I felt they couldn't be distinguished from other flesh."

"What did you do with the hands, legs, and feet of Bernd Brandes?"

"The first time, I froze them for a long time in the freezer chest. But when my visitor announced his arrival, I had to take them out. Originally, I planned to bury Bernd's head in the cemetery. But then I did it at home in the ground and buried the head, legs, feet and arms in all solemnity."

"How may one imagine your solemnity?"

"Well, when night fell I dug a pit, where I laid the head, hands, and feet. I then recited the Twenty-third Psalm."

Meiwes lifts his head and recites the psalm from memory like a lay priest. "The Lord is my shepherd, I shall not want. He maketh me to lie down in green pastures. He leadeth me beside the still waters. He restoreth my soul; he leadeth me in the paths of righteousness for his name's sake. Yea, though I walk through the valley of the shadow of death, I will fear no evil; for thou art with me; thy rod and thy staff they comfort me. Thou preparest a table before me in the presence of mine enemies; thou anointest my head with oil; my cup runneth over. Surely goodness and mercy shall follow me all the days of my life, and I will dwell in the house of the Lord forever."

"I wouldn't have expected that of you, Mr. Meiwes!"

He clasped his hands, his gaze almost gracious. "I also said the Lord's Prayer and then covered the grave."

"Did you also set up a cross on the spot?"

"No. A cross would have been too conspicuous. I put a flower on it, but nothing else, no. The other bones I then buried not far away. No ceremony for them."

Armin Meiwes recounts the burial of the other remains as matter-of-factly as throwing out the trash.

*

Witness 2: Timo B.*, age 16 at the time, neighborhood boy [*Name changed, true name known to the author].

My entire family and I were invited to Meiwes's 40th birthday party at his home. Besides our family, there were office colleagues of his and this Lebanese by the name of Jakob [Yakup N. is meant].... The party wasn't really much fun and went on into the evening, and nobody knew what we were supposed to do. Armin had a collection of videos and we watched the movie "Armageddon." ... He also said I could come by if I had time in the evening, and watch movies with him.... Since then, I've gone there when I had time and I was bored.... Armin, at my request, made the photos [Polaroid photos of Timo B. naked to waist in boxer shorts and boxing gloves], because I had met a girl in the east, I don't know the name of the place anymore..., and I wanted to send her the photos to impress her. He never told me he preferred men. Rather the opposite. Also, I never noticed in Armin a liking for slaughtering, and he never expressed anything of that kind. I would have liked to see the movie "The Silence of the Lambs," and said so to Armin. But he said that such films were not seen there.

Witness 3: Sascha M., age 15 at the time, schoolboy

Then, as it happened last summer...we [Sascha M. and his school friend Timo B.] were up with Armin Meiwes several times at his home in Wüstefeld. It was always on weekends. We were also allowed to stay up there overnight.... When we weren't playing with computers, Armin Meiwes let us watch TV the whole night, which we often did until morning... Armin never told us to stay out of any particular rooms in the house. We could move around freely in the house. Armin only warned us to be careful when we moved about, because in many places there was danger of something collapsing. He meant the ceilings. That was why we stayed most often only on the ground floor and the first floor. There we could pick out a room to spend the night in. I think that on the outside of the door there was a sign saying "Green Corner."

*

One of the questions most frequently asked in connection with punishable offenses of any kind is, "Why did no one notice anything?" In Armin Meiwes's case, this question is obviously difficult to answer, since no one can even remotely imagine a cannibalistic crime in his own neighborhood.

There are two incidents involving Armin Meiwes, however, which could at least have aroused suspicion that something about him was not right.

His first telltale action takes place at a party in the home of acquaintances in Rotenburg in April 2002. On the ground floor of the B. family, their mother observes the following scene and later gives a statement on it for the record to the investigating officials (Proceedings No. ST/0132109/2002):

> *In the course of the party, I noticed that Armin fooled around openly and intensively with Henrik G., 13-14 years old. The two of them rolled about (kicked about) on the grass. Then Armin hid a cigarette lighter or a key ring on his person and made Henrik look for it on him. Henrik spent the night with us and Armin went to his own home. The next morning, however, he was in our home for breakfast. And when they held hands across from me, it was too much for me, and I banged my fist on the table and made a remark that made them pay attention.... I then spoke to Henrik and told him that there were people with different inclinations, and that he had to be careful what he did and what was done with him.... In any case, I spoke afterward*

with his mother and at her request spoke to Armin.... I told him his behavior with Henrik had attracted attention and that I found it objectionable when adults did something with children.... After the conversation, I was glad I had spoken to him and that such things wouldn't happen again.... I have concluded that something sexual had gone on with my son [Timo B.]. I had seen the photos with the boxing gloves.

Of this, Armin Meiwes states, "That was a misunderstanding. I would never touch boys."

*

The second conspicuous incident concerns guests of the so-called "Crossfront" ["Querfront"], a troop of around twelve enemies of the State, who spent three nights at the manor house with Armin Meiwes. This fact is not known to the investigating authorities. A participant in this "journey," who wishes to remain anonymous, sent me a document after learning that I was researching this matter. The document is a twelve-page report by the man and some photographs. One of the photos shows the group of far-right visitors in front of Meiwes's house. Another shows Meiwes on a stroll with the group.

At this point, I publish excerpts from the document passed to me:

During preparations for one of the two Querfront meetings with twelve participants in the home of...in Rotenburg an der Fulda, the question arose where we would all stay. Friedrich said, "Don't worry. I have here a nice neighbor with a huge house where he lives alone. You can all sleep there. He'd be glad to do it."
...It was a bit odd inside, that house. Enormous size, maybe fifty rooms—that's what it looked like—all crammed with old furniture, three

*layers of worn carpets, everywhere plushy old
sofas and armchairs. It wouldn't have raised
any eyebrows if a few crows had been flying
about inside the house.... The beds were
somewhat lumpy and you sank down in them—
ancient beds... We went to sleep soon and some
of us right through until early in the morning.
It's an ideal setting for bad people.... Without
being an anarchist, a Nazi, or something
abnormal of the kind, Armin took part in the
meeting silently but attentively.... Friedrich had
told us, "You can sleep in his home. He's glad
when something's going on and he's well
disposed toward us. He has no problem with
border-crossers or Querfronters." ...He took
walks with us, sat down with us in the evening
at the fireplace, and chatted with some of us....
He told us he had had a somewhat difficult
childhood and especially a complicated
relationship with his mother.... Weren't there
large packages lying in the refrigerator, when we
got a beer for a nightcap out of it?*

So, in Wüstefeld, a meeting took place between
Auschwitz-deniers, chaos-day organizers, and enemies of the
State...and a man-eater, again in our midst.

Armin Meiwes says about this, "I really wouldn't
describe those people as far righters. A few of those who were
there might have been a little more so, but in that area I had
no ambitions of any sort, and they behaved quite normally
and were very nice. But I have nothing to do with the
political views of those people."

*

Certainly, along with giving shelter to enemies of the
State and his acquaintances in "normal" life, Meiwes
maintains his contacts with abnormally inclined Internet
users from the cannibal forums. The urge to repeat this
"kick," as he himself puts it, keeps his soul a prisoner.

At night, he chats on the Internet in his study and is in touch with over four hundred German users who want to be slaughtered or take part in slaughters.

The slaughter fantasies become ever more extreme, as Meiwes tells me. "Jörg B., with whom I kept in touch, wanted to bring his colleague Michael to me in Wüstefeld. He was to be drugged, stripped, and brought into the slaughter room. There we were to hang him up and slaughter him by cutting his throat. He sent me photos of his colleague. Jörg, as he pictured it, always wanted Michael's throat to be cut from left to right because his colleague's left vein was stronger and more easily visible. Then the victim's belly was to be cut open, the innards removed, and the body cut in half. There the chat always ended because Jörg suddenly withdrew. Presumably, he masturbated. We also discussed how the heart were to be prepared and exchanged recipes for the penis and scrotum."

In June 2001, Meiwes meets again with Jörg B., this time in Villingen-Schwenningen. The two men first enjoy coffee in a bistro. Afterwards, they drive to Jörg's apartment in St. Georgen. In the bedroom, the cook strips completely naked. Meiwes rubs him with oil and massages him. Again, Meiwes, as he did in the first "role-playing" in the hotel in Kassel on November 12, 2000, draws with pen and ink on the naked body, demonstrating the planned carving-up.

The third "slaughter-readiness test" takes place on November 3 and 4, 2001, in Armin Meiwes's house in Wüstefeld. The two drink a bottle of beer and then go to the bathroom on the first floor. Jörg runs warm water and climbs into the very tub where Bernd Brandes had lain as he bled to death. Meiwes shaves his underarm and genital hair. Then the cook puts on a bathrobe. Armin ties on the butcher's apron. They go into the unheated slaughter room, with a temperature of fifty-five degrees fahrenheit, on the second floor. Meiwes tries to hang Jörg up by the feet, head down, with the block and tackle, but the victim is suddenly in pain. "My ankles hurt," complains Jörg. The experiment is stopped, and Meiwes and Jörg warm themselves for half an hour in the heated living room. They try it a second time.

Jörg complains again. Thereupon they break off the experiment. They watch TV, chat, and around ten o'clock, Jörg goes to bed in the "Green Corner." At eight the following morning, they have a large breakfast in the kitchen. Jörg then departs. Nothing has been achieved.

*

Although Armin Meiwes has already consumed forty-five pounds of Bernd Brandes's flesh, he searches, as with Jörg B., for more potential victims, and meets with at least four other men. The Wüstefelder says, "Men from the cannibal forums came from all professions and all levels of society. There was a hotel manager, a banker, a student, and a dentist among them. They were well educated and had high incomes."

Meiwes's personal encounters with "slaughter victims," and his perverted activities as well, are briefly summarized in the following pages.

*

Slaughter victim Alexander

On the Internet, September 20, 2001, Armin Meiwes happens upon Alexander K., born in 1975. He is a student and lives in Essen. In his advertisement, he describes himself thus: 6 feet, 1 inch tall, 220 pounds. His passport photo shows a round, friendly face and short, dark hair. His cannibal name is meat4cook [in English]; his Internet addresses are youngmeat2001@yahoo.com and bbq_m69@yahoo.com. His emails to Armin are always signed "Your slaughteranimal" or "The slaughteranimal." Alexander would like to be beheaded and consumed. The student arrives in Kassel-Wilhelmshöhe on Friday, October 4, 2002, and stays in Wüstefeld for six days. In the course of his stay at the manor house, it becomes clear to him that he would not like to remain there forever. Meiwes says, "I didn't slaughter him because he was too fat for me and also not very agreeable. Furthermore, he wasn't sure about this final step and then just no longer wanted it."

*

Slaughter victim Dirk

Dirk M., born in 1976, a bank employee living in London. Height: five feet, eleven inches, weight: 121 pounds, eye color brown. His email address is longpigmeat@yahoogroups.com. The first email contact takes place on June 18, 2001. Dirk M. is a homosexual, and has lived for three years with a friend. He is interested in sadomasochistic games, and for this reason has gotten in touch with Armin Meiwes. They chat for weeks in express terms. Meiwes actually tells Dirk that he has slaughtered a man. On January 10, 2002, they meet at a hotel in Mannheim. Both strip naked in a room. Meiwes fastens the "slaughter victim" with handcuffs to the bed. Meiwes strokes Dirk M., but the Wüstefelder isn't the banker's type. "Nah, none of that." They get dressed, eat burgers at McDonald's, and go to the movies. They sleep in the hotel, take a stroll through the city the next day, sleep another night in the hotel, and then drive home. They don't have sex with each other. On the homeward drive, Dirk has a flat and Meiwes helps him change the tire.

Armin Meiwes very much regrets his departure. Even before the meeting, he had constructed "at his [apparently Dirk's] wish," a lovingly worded judgment. Below a coat of arms with a cleaver, knife, and skull—designed by Meiwes—the following appears:

"Cannibal Court, Germany. In the name of the Cannibals, the following judgment is declared: The accused, Dirk M., is sentenced to death by slaughter. Grounds: The accused has sought numerous times in the past to advertise himself as a slaughter victim. Finally, he voluntarily placed himself at the disposal of this court, in order to make sure that all would take its proper course. The accused is to appear on July 14, 2002, at the Kassel-Wilhelmshöhe train station, in order to be received by the butcher. Death is to occur through the administration of drugs and immediately thereafter by suffocation. Further processing of his body is set forth in the attached Slaughter and Dismemberment Plan. Kassel, March 2002." On the second page of the document is a drawing with the planned carving and a detailed procedure for the slaughter.

But Dirk M. has gotten away once again.

*

Role-playing partner Stefan

Stefan gets a kick out of being chloroformed and, while drugged, putting himself into someone else's hands. This was why he made contact with Armin Meiwes on the Internet forum, "chloroformed guys." They meet on October 6, 2002, in Wüstefeld. Meiwes binds Stefan S. to the bed. They have oral sex and masturbate mutually with their hands.

Alex S. and fur-fetishist Sascha boy

On November, 2002, Armin Meiwes takes photos of a chopping block and an ax for a certain "Alex S.," who wants to be beheaded. He also takes pictures of himself naked in his mother's fox-fur coat for "Saschaboywob," who has a fur fetish.

*

Slaughter colleague Eugen

On February 21, 2002, Meiwes transmits to his "slaughter colleague" Eugen A., by email, two photos from the video showing the killing of Bernd Brandes. On December 5, 2002, he sends Eugen A., on request, two more photos from the video.

*

Slaughter victim Thomas

Thomas L., born 1964. He is a homosexual, lacquer and leather fetishist, and meets Meiwes on the Internet. On December 7, 2001, he drives to Wüstefeld. They go to the slaughter room for half an hour. Thomas L. enters a cage put together by Meiwes and licks Meiwes's dirty boots. Meiwes paints him and hoists him up a little with the block and tackle. But Meiwes doesn't match the preferences of the fetishist, since it is clear that the computer technician doesn't come from the fetish milieu. As a parting gift, Thomas presents Meiwes with a white butcher's apron with a slit for an erected penis, and drives away.

*

Armin Meiwes intensifies his encounters, with the purpose of consuming another "brother." Almost daily, he drives his Lancia to meetings with Internet acquaintances, as he relates to me in the Kassel Penitentiary:

"I made at least thirty or forty trips, as far as Holland, Dresden, and Hamburg. Mostly, however, I got people to meet me at the Kassel-Wilhelmshöhe train station. I did that because I could drive there directly from my office. But these people didn't all appear for the agreed meetings."

"There were many of them, anyway. But was that all?

Meiwes slumps back in his chair, half-closes his eyes, and reflects. Then he says, "Oh, yes. There was also Alexander from Regensburg. I met him not far from Hammelburg. We met at the station. He got into my car right away. We looked for a suitable spot outside the city. There I carried out a slaughter inspection of him in my car. For that purpose, I turned around the load area of the back seat of my Lancia Kombi. I took photos. Alexander wanted me to tie him up. So I tied him up and smothered him with kisses. He wanted to give me a 'blowjob.' Since he wanted to use a condom for it and I didn't have one with me, we didn't do it.

Probably for his own security, he told me that before our meeting, he had sent an email. In it, he informed someone that he was going to meet with me. After about half an hour, I took Alexander back to the station. Then he disappeared on foot."

*

Slaughter victim Daniel

Daniel K., born 1978, domiciled in Kassel. His email address is maedchenfleisch [girl's flesh]@XXX.de. Setting up his website, he gave as his name "Hans Hackepeter," Schlachthof 12 in Kassel. His first email contact with Meiwes takes place on September 18, 2002, on the Cannibal Forum of Armin Meiwes. Daniel K. would like to have a meat inspection done on him. On Sunday, November 10, 2002, Meiwes picks the "slaughter victim" up in the parking lot on Schillerstrasse in Kassel and takes him home to Wüstefeld. In the bedroom, Meiwes, fully dressed, rubs down Daniel's naked body with olive oil. He binds him hand and foot and draws on him with a felt-tipped pen the "slaughter lines." Then he picks up the young man on his shoulders and carries him into the slaughter room. He hangs him by the feet to the ceiling and explains to him how he will bleed to death. When Daniel's feet hurt and he shivers with cold, Meiwes lets his victim down. In the bedroom, Meiwes, like a butcher before selling animal meat, sticks labeled signs into Daniel's body.

Armin Meiwes explains, "I had prepared a bowl with needles and labeled the corresponding flesh parts: 'piece of roast,' 'upper arm,' 'chest.' I stuck fifteen needles with the little signs into him. He felt no pain."

That day they take about one hundred and twenty photos. In the night, they sleep in the same bed, but without having sexual activities. The second meeting takes place on Thursday, December 5, 2002.

Meiwes picks up Daniel at five p.m. at their appointed meeting place in the parking lot in Kassel. In the bedroom, Daniel lies on the bed naked again. This time

Meiwes is also unclothed. He wears only his new butcher's apron with an opening for the penis. The butcher sticks needles again into his guest's body, and now the signs look more professional as they are labeled by the computer. He wraps Daniel's entire body in airtight foil and processes him with the meat hammer. He unwraps him and bites him on his bare bottom, his upper thighs, and his calves.

During their night together in bed, Armin Meiwes wakes up and bites Daniel so hard on his bottom that he screams aloud in fright. At Daniel's express wish, Meiwes ceases his biting attacks. This scene is also recorded by Meiwes with his video camera.

*

Five days remain until the cannibal Armin Meiwes is interrogated for the first time by the police.

FLEE OUT OF THE MIDST OF BABYLON, AND DELIVER EVERY MAN HIS SOUL: BE NOT CUT OFF IN HER INIQUITY. FOR THIS IS THE TIME OF THE LORD'S VENGEANCE; HE WILL RENDER UNTO HER A RECOMPENSE.

(Jeremiah 51: 6)

Chapter 14

THE STUDENT

BERND BRANDES HAS VANISHED. He may as well have been swallowed up by the earth. In truth, he was swallowed—by Armin Meiwes, though putting it this way may seem sarcastic.

His life companion, René J., spends the whole morning on Monday, March 12, 2001, in their shared apartment at 11 Burchardstrasse, desperately searching for clues: a telephone number, a travel reservation, a scrap of paper. He rummages through documents and miscellaneous Post-It notes, even those in the trash can. In the process, he happens upon the blue "Allianz" insurance file folder. In the first pocket, the twenty-four-year-old baker finds a white, sealed envelope. He opens it, reads the few lines, and, in his own words, is "stunned."

At two p.m., a distraught René J. calls police headquarters 4 VB II/5 in Berlin.

The phone conversation is officially noted:

> *Mr. J. called in again and stated that he had just found a will of Mr. Brandes. He promised to fax a copy.*

> *At 2:58 p.m., René faxes the will that so upset him, from Bernd Brandes's fax machine to the police station. The brief, handwritten document makes the following provision:*

> *"Will. I hereby appoint my friend René J...my sole heir to all my property. Berlin, 01/03/2001 Bernd Brandes."*

> *A day later, the officials of the criminal police search the apartment and the basement of*

Bernd Brandes at 11 Burchardstrasse. This action is also entered in the record.

Yesterday, with the KHKS (same office) I searched Mr. Brandes's apartment. There I encountered Mr. J. and his mother. Inspection of the apartment yielded no clues as to the whereabouts of the missing person. Mr. J., whose name is also displayed next to the doorbell, told us he had last seen Mr. Brandes on Friday, 3/9/01, around 6:30 a.m. in the apartment, when he himself went to the toilet. Mr. J. had another day off and lay down again. Mr. Brandes had told him nothing about the fact that he would not be going to work on Friday. Mr. J. thought, therefore, that Mr. Brandes was at Siemens when he got up at about 10 o'clock and Mr. Brandes was gone. There is no attic in this building. The basement was searched without results. According to Mr. J., Mr. Brandes does not own an automobile. From entries in the computer (Internet connections etc.), Mr. J. was also unable to gain any indication as to the present whereabouts of his life companion. From bank statements, however, it appears that on Thursday he withdrew 300 marks [about $75.00] at the Zoo train station. This station, however, is located on his usual route from the office to his home. Mr. Brandes is said to be under stress at the office and to be working in a telephone development area. Signed, W., KHK.

On March 16, 2001, Bernd Brandes's credit card is "marked" by American Express. Its owner can use it only by proving his identity. There is no longer any trace of Bernd Brandes's existence.

*

Tuesday, May 8, 2001

The Provincial Criminal Bureau in Berlin receives a visit, and records the facts in a "Report" without a file Number:

On this day, Mr. and Mrs. BRANDES appeared at this office. Upon questioning, they stated that the mother of the missing person, Bernd BRANDES, was dead. Mr. BRANDES had...remarried.... Concerning their son, they stated that Bernd had lived for seven years with Mrs. Anja B. During that time, they also had many family contacts. Since Bernd is not the kind of man who often leaves the house, has no cultural activities and no athletic interests, they separated. From then on, relations between the parents and their son worsened. On birthdays and holidays, telephone conversations were brief. Even at times when the parents were staying in Berlin, there were seldom any meetings, since Bernd usually pleaded a heavy workload. The Siemens Company had set up a working space for him in his apartment, so that he worked often at home and sometimes late at night. In the fall of 2000, Bernd had revealed to his father that he was a homosexual and lived with a man. His father had no sympathy for this. When Bernd started working at Siemens, his father gave him ten shares of Siemens stock. He has no knowledge of any financial difficulties his son might have, since the latter has a good income at Siemens. Mr. BRANDES had supported his son financially during his student days. The parents do not know any friends or acquaintances of Bernd's. As long as Mr. BRANDES had his medical practice in Berlin, Bernd went to him for treatment. Bernd then switched to a physician who was a friend.... Since Bernd has very good teeth, he does not know of any dentist.... The most recent telephone conversation took place on his birthday in

January 2001. They have no knowledge of where Bernd might be located. Mr. BRANDES does not think his son had chosen to take his own life. He thinks, rather, that because of his workload—constant computer work—he is psychologically disturbed, and might be in a helpless situation.

*

Meanwhile, Armin Meiwes enjoys a deceptive security. He becomes careless and ever bolder. In cannibal forums, he boasts of his experience as a butcher of men. He sends off at least three pictures from the slaughter video, which he alters in a way that distorts them. In one, Meiwes is seen with Bernd Brandes's foot, and in a second, in front of the carved-up, headless corpse. The third photo shows Meiwes with a butcher's knife as he skins Bernd Brandes's right arm.

*

In the Internet newsgroup "alt.sex.snuff.cannibalism," the Wüstefelder inserts this advertisement:

> *Re: Boys sought for butchering.*
> *Text: "Hi, I'm Franky from Germany. I'm looking for young men between eighteen and thirty to butcher. If you have a normal build, then come to me. I'll butcher you and eat your delicious flesh." He offers also a translation in very faulty English: "I am Franky from Germany. I search for young Boys between eighteen and thirty Y/O for butchering. Have you a normal build body, than come to me. I butchering you and eat your delicious flesh. Franky."*

*

Monday, July 8, 2002

Innsbruck/Tirol. The picturesque Alpine town, the capital of the eighth of nine Austrian Federal States, sits among majestic mountain ranges. Every year, hundreds of thousands of German tourists head to this scenic location. Visitors roam along the Karwendel range or gape at the symbolic "Golden Roof," a building with splendid late-Gothic bay windows in the old town. At the command of the Emperor Maximilan in 1497, the roof was covered with two thousand, six hundred and fifty-seven gilded copper shingles. Younger vacationers regularly zoom down the fifteen-hundred-yard-long Olympic bobsled run in Innsbruck-Igls. Celebrities race down the hill on redesigned Chinese cooking pots at fifty miles per hour into the valley.

The twenty-three-year-old medical student Reinhold H., one of 118,500 inhabitants from Innsbruck, lives about a mile from the ice canal near the "Patscherkofel" mountain in a two-room apartment.

Surfing on the Internet in search of "Horror and Nervous Thrills" on the evening of July 8, 2002, he accidentally discovers Armin Meiwes's ad. He replies to "Antrophagus" as an apparently interested person:

From: Reinhold H.
To: Antrophagus@hotmail.com
Date: July 8, 2002

How many boys have you butchered and eaten. Am 23 and from Innsbruck.

Armin Meiwes answers the same day:

Well, let's say I have experience; in any case you wouldn't be the first. 23, that's an optimal butchering age; the body has just matured and is still very tender. Write me more about yourself—your height, and weight? I'm 38, 6 feet, 165 pounds. I look forward to your reply. Your master butcher, Franky.

Reinhold writes on July 9, 2002:

But I don't want to be butchered. I want to live. I wonder what impels someone to kill and eat other people!

Meiwes rejoins:

Hi Reinhold, the question is as old as humanity itself. For myself, I'm not interested in killing someone in cold blood, because then I would be simply grabbing somebody and eating him. And I would be just a common killer. I'm looking for people who have a desire to die, for whatever reason. Some of them dream of being butchered; others simply want to end their lives because they have no future prospects. I then prepare for them a death such as they desire for themselves. My wish since childhood has been to have someone entirely to myself and then to absorb him into me by eating him. Franky.

Reinhold H. answers this email on July 9, 2002:

You are not doing these people any favor by killing them. You look exclusively for young men and exploit someone's life crisis. Everyone sometimes reaches a point where he can't cope with life. Sometimes they have no friends and no family and no one they can talk with. No, what you do is not admirable, but pathologically perverted. People who come to you and whose fate you seal would have done better to go to a psychologist. But not everyone feels comfortable going to a psychologist. And you, too, should go to a psychologist, for even if you won't admit it to yourself, you are a cold-blooded murderer.

With kind regards.

Reinhold H.

*

Tuesday, July 9, 2002

Still up in the early morning hours, at 5:49 a.m., the student writes this email to the Federal Criminal Bureau:

> *Ladies and Gentlemen of the Federal Criminal Bureau, my name is Reinhold H., medical student from Innsbruck. Searching for Horror and Nervous Thrills on the Internet, I happened on something shocking. Namely, Internet forums as markets for human flesh. Among others...Yahoo, Google-Newsgroup and Hotboard. I found ads from people who are eager to have themselves butchered and from people who would like to butcher and then eat. At first, I thought this was to be taken as a kind of erotic game in the realm of fantasy. But, my attention was caught especially by an ad from a certain Franky from Germany, who could not advertise enough how he hankers to butcher a slender man between 18 and 30. I decided to send a short email to "Franky," and he replied promptly. I ask you to look into this. It has already cost me two sleepless nights because I don't know how to handle it.*

*

July 28, 2002

Not until nineteen days later does Chief Criminal Commissioner A. take up the student's report. He first answers Armin Meiwes's ad with a feigned inquiry in order to obtain the data necessary to identify "Franky."

On July 28, 2002, at 1:43 p.m., as "Boy 26," with the email address leto999@yahoo.de, he sends an email to Meiwes:

Hello Franky, just now in search of cannibalism themes, I stumbled on your contribution where you're looking for boys to butcher—I find it fascinating. Write me please how you imagine it. I'm 26 and from Hesse. 'Til then.

Armin Meiwes answers the undercover investigator on the same day at 10:43 p.m.:

Hi, thanks for your email. Now, as I see it, you will come to me, live with me for a week, and during that time I'll really get to know you. One wants to know whom one is eating. During that time, I'll supervise your food. In your last two days, you'll get only liquid nourishment so that the intestines are empty when you are butchered. I'll also enjoy your live body, after all, a little sex is part of it, but only if you want it. Then on X-Day, I'll wake you early and take you to the bathroom to wash and shave you. Next, I will take you to the slaughter room, hang you up by the feet, and cut your throat to let you bleed to death. There are other possible ways of killing and you can choose whether you'd like to experience it all while fully conscious or while drugged. After you've bled to death, I'll take out your innards, cut your body in half, and thoroughly clean it again. Then, when you've been properly taken down, I'll carve you up to prepare many delightful dishes from your delicious flesh. Write me back and tell me your height and weight. Incidentally, I am also from Hesse, near Kassel. Your Master Butcher, Franky.

*

Suddenly, there is a burst of activity in the Criminal Bureau. Twenty-four hours later, the Bureau contacts the

Internet provider, Tiscali, and inquires about the IP name and address of Armin Meiwes. The IP address is a one-time, worldwide address expressly assigned to every Internet computer. A "dynamic" IP address—as in this case—is given only for the period during which Internet access is available through the computers and the telephone connection. IP addresses are allocated by an Internet provider which records in files what IP addresses are assigned to which customers and when the customer logs in. The IP address 62.246.25.129 is assigned on July 28, 2002 at 10:43 p.m. to user Armin Meiwes, and he is now trapped.

But, clearly, the possibility of a cannibalistic crime outstrips even the imagination of the investigating officials. To put it in plain English, the matter is not taken seriously. If a car is parked illegally in front of your door, the police are on the spot in ten minutes. In the case of a man-eater, months pass before the police, despite unequivocal evidence—even from the perpetrator himself—finally swing into action.

Since the alert given on July 9, 2002 by the Innsbruck student to the Federal Criminal Bureau, five months and one day have gone by.

In the meantime, landowners have harvested their fields, Federal Chancellor Gerhard Schröder has been confirmed in office on September 22, 2002 by the 61.2 million qualified voters, and the birches, ash trees and oaks have long since lost their leaves. Armin Meiwes, the man-butcher, plays unwatched with neighborhood children.

*

His good friend Nicole Agaficioaei, maiden name Wurmnest, born September 23, 1963, tells me the following of Armin Meiwes and his life after the deed:

"I have known Armin Meiwes for ten years. To me, Armin is one of the most loveable men in this world. You know, the most precious things I have in my life are my four children. And Mr. Meiwes has very often watched over these four children. We were neighbors and I was alone. My life partner at the time was working. So if something was going on at school or in kindergarten, I called up Armin and he was there immediately. The kids were always glad when he came. He was an easygoing fellow and the kids thought he was fun. I had absolute confidence in him."

"The same person who butchered a man also watched over your children. How can you explain to yourself the fact that he was able to hide this other side?"

"To me, that other thing was inconceivable. I never thought for a moment, 'My God, and you entrusted your children to him?' Naturally, we had already noticed that Armin, as far as his sex life is concerned, doesn't fit the heterosexual norm. We never really talked about it; we all knew it. But that such a horrible thing was a part of Armin's life, naturally no one ever suspected."

"How could you then know that he was not a normal heterosexual?"

"I am a very emotional person and very sensitive. And this was something people noticed—his entire personality. He's not a tough man. There is something soft in the way he speaks, the way he moves, how he sits. You notice then that he differs a little from other men."

"Hand on your heart: on the basis of what you now know, would you entrust your four children to Armin Meiwes again?"

"Considering what is going on now, I must say quite honestly..." she looks briefly at the Fulda River and gathers her thoughts before answering. To my surprise, she says in a steady voice, "Yes, I would again entrust my children to Armin Meiwes, unreservedly, and at any time."

*

Tuesday, October 15, 2002

In the morning, the Innsbruck Student Reinhold H. decides to file criminal charges of Suspicion of Murder under §21 StGB, Suspicion of Manslaughter under §212 StGB, and Presentation of Violence under §131 StGB.

The statement disseminated by the accused that he already has "experience" in the field of cannibalism allows the well-founded suspicion that, at least in one case, he has killed a person. Even if the statements by the accused arose only in his fantasy, gruesome and revolting acts of violence are here inserted in word and text on the Internet, so that at least the factual situation of §131 StGB is realized.

The S. Criminal High Commissioner applies to the Office of the State Prosecutor in Kassel for a search warrant. The Prosecutor's Office refers the matter to the District Court of Rotenburg, which has jurisdiction. German bureaucracy shows its weakest side, for despite unequivocal evidence, despite a criminal charge, despite the name and address of the possible perpetrator, forty-three days go by, and nothing happens.

*

Tuesday, November 28, 2002
141 days after the first report

The District Court of Rotenburg, under File Indicator 5a a GS 2650 JS 36980/02, finally issues a search warrant for the residence house and outbuildings of Armin Meiwes in Wüstefeld 1 for "Suspicion of Presentation of Violence." Quotation:

> *Objects taken into possession during the search are impounded under §§94, 98 stop.... Considering the gravity of the act and the strength of the suspicion, the search and, further, because of the need for investigations, the impoundment, are requisite and appropriate. Signed, H., Judge of the District Court.*

By the time there is a decision to actually investigate the mysterious "Franky" and get a search warrant for his home, one hundred and forty days have slipped by.

*

Tuesday, December 10, 2002, 153 days after the first report, "International Human Rights Day"

At eight forty-five a.m., seven police officials from Police Headquarters in Bad Hersfeld pay the long-overdue visit to the manor house. The official record gives their names:

KOK [High Commissioner's Office] Mrs. W.
KHK [Some other office of the Criminal Police] Mr. S.
PK-A Mr. B.
PK Mrs. L.
PK Mrs. W.
PK Mr. K.

Besides the above, Mr. K. of the town of Rotenburg is also present as a neutral witness to the search. Finally, the owner of the manor house, Armin Meiwes, is there as well.

*

Armin Meiwes sighs. He looks at the barred window of the Kassel Penitentiary. "The sunlight today is really bright," he says melancholically.

"Yes, almost too warm for the season," I agree.

"Very rare, this light coming in. Here inside we live in our own world. From outside we can't bring anything with us," he says, as if trying to elicit sympathy from me.

I offer none. "You lived also in your own world in that former time."

He prefaces his answer with the usual standard phrases. "Well, all right, that was true in a way." With a hangdog look, he lowers his eyelids. If I didn't know why this man is sitting in front of me in the high security block, I perhaps would feel sympathy.

"It must have been entirely clear to you, though, that your deed would, at some time, be discovered, or did you not think about that?"

"Without the student from Innsbruck, it probably never would have gotten out. Never! He accused me. On one hand, I'm mad at him for doing it, but on the other I'm glad, because I'm at last now able to speak about my fantasies."

"After his exchange of emails with you, the student couldn't sleep."

Meiwes grins blithely. "Well, all right, he made an application on the basis of my ad. I then wrote back honestly, telling him how I envisioned it. And then he wrote back again saying, 'Yes, what you're doing is wrong, you're a murderer.' So, I wrote back again, 'Nobody will come anyway; it's only pure fantasy.'"

"But you mentioned on the Internet, didn't you, that you had butchered Bernd Brandes and eaten him?"

"All right, I sent out blurred photos. I told of the deed, in part, but never directly. Anyway, this student filed charges against me, whereupon the police found out my address, and six months later they were standing at my front door."

"What kind of moment was that for you?"

"I can't exactly remember. It was nine days after my forty-first birthday. I was just about to leave for work. Looking out the window, I saw two or three cars drive into the courtyard. Then the doorbell rang. I opened the door and said, 'Yes, hello. What can I do for you?' A policewoman in civilian clothes then said, 'We have a search warrant against you on grounds of presentation of violence on the Internet.' I answered, 'Aha, how so?' The policewoman said, 'On the basis of this advertisement here.' She held the criminal complaint in front of my eyes and I read the text I had published on the Internet under the appropriate cannibal pages: 'Looking for young man to butcher.'"

"What happened then?"

"The whole bunch of officials searched the house, superficially, from eight forty-five to ten-fifteen a.m. I quickly tossed the video film with the butchering of Bernd Brandes into a bookcase in the living room with the other movie cassettes, but they only would have had to open the desk drawer, and there lay the butchery film burned onto a

CD. They did notice the packets of meat in the freezer chest and took a couple of them for testing. I told them it was wild pig meat. Human flesh can't be distinguished at sight from animal meat. In the slaughter room, they took samples. That's all it was."

*

The preliminary report on the search submitted to the High Commissioner of Police for East Hesse, Hersfeld-Rotenburg Police Headquarters, Regional Inspectorate on December 10, 2002, offers the following account:

> *The condition of the house is very bad. The ceilings are broken in places. Almost every room is crammed with old furniture and household equipment. It gives the impression that only a few of its rooms are inhabited. Meiwes's study is located on the ground floor. There, a computer setup, a video camera, a number of diskettes and CD/ROMS, and various computer printouts were impounded. Further, here and in the living room...many videocassettes were found and impounded. In the kitchen, on the ground floor, there was a freezer chest. When it was searched, there was found, beneath many boxes with frozen food, a kind of false bottom. Under it, there were numerous freezer bags with meat, variously labeled. Three of these meat packets were chosen and impounded. In the bedroom of the accused on the first floor, more computer printouts were found, and these were likewise impounded. A book, "Flesh and Blood [title given in English]" was also found here and impounded, along with a Polaroid camera. In the room at the rear of the house, "Green Corner," on a chair by the door, there was a brown paper bag containing pieces of paper labeled variously "lower thigh," "upper arm," etc. and pins. On the second floor...is the former smoking chamber. This room was*

*outfitted as a "butcher room." On a small table lay
three knives, a cleaver, and ax, and tools for
binding, neatly lined up. A butcher's apron was
also lying there. All these objects were impounded.
There were also placards representing male body
parts.... Between the chopping block and the cross,
smudges, which could be blood, were taken from
the floor and preserved. These traces were taken
into safekeeping by Police Officer G. (See separate
report.) All objects seized were impounded or
secured and brought to this office. Signed KOK W.*

*

In the certificate of secured/impounded objects the
following are listed:

*1 Siemens Scenic 600 computer, 1
keyboard, 1 Medion video camera, 4 CD-ROMS,
1 Lexmark printer, 1 mouse, 1 pan with "butcher
tool," 3 freezer bags with meat, 1 Polaroid
camera. Certificate received. KOK W.*

*

Armin Meiwes awaits my next question. He twiddles
his fingers. First, he draws circles on the table with his right
index finger. Then he clasps his hands. Next, he passes his
right middle finger over the fingertips of his left hand. His
nails are polished and neatly cared for.

"Didn't the police notice that a crime had been
committed in your house?"

"No, the officials next brought me—with my
consent—to the police station in Bad Hersfeld. They asked
me to give a saliva sample, voluntarily, which I did. Then,
they conducted an interrogation. Naturally, I gave nothing
away. Some of the questions were really dumb."

"So what did they ask you?"

Meiwes puts on a supercilious expression and states, "I first had to answer a lot of questions about my Internet ads, and also told them I would butcher a person if he expressly wished it. The policewoman then asked me, 'Have you already eaten human flesh?' I answered, 'Who knows?' She then asked me, 'What would you do if someone offered you half a man?' I said, 'As a cannibal, I'd probably eat him up.' The policewoman shook her head and I was set free."

*

The police files record the following:

> *The interrogation of the accused ended at 2 p.m. Mr. Meiwes readily made statements. He only refused to answer direct questions about the meat in his freezer chest.... By agreement with Prosecuting Attorney K. in Kassel, Mr. Meiwes was released and brought back to his home. The undersigned (W., KOK) and PK-A B. arrived there at about 3:10 p.m. In the estate at Wüstefeld, the freezer chest, the office, and the "slaughter room" on the top floor were officially sealed.*

*

The three impounded meat packets from the freezer chest are delivered immediately to the Institute for Forensic Medicine in Giessen, to Mr. H. In a letter, precautionary notice of their delicate contents is given:

> *Telefax   URGENT—Please   deliver immediately!*

> *Investigation for suspicion of a capital offense etc.: Armin Meiwes, accused, born 12/01/1961 in Essen. In aforementioned investigation, several pieces of frozen meat were found in Meiwes's freezer chest. From these,*

three bags of frozen meat were chosen and secured. Since it is suspected here that this could be flesh of human origin, it is requested that they be analyzed as quickly as possible. In opening the bags, care should be taken not to damage the descriptions written on the plastic sheets. If possible, these bags, after thawing, should be held in safekeeping. Should analysis show their contents to be "human flesh," further analysis (DNA etc.) should be undertaken. It is therefore requested that the objects under investigation be kept in cold storage.

Signed S., KHK.

*

Although grave suspicion exists that Armin Meiwes is storing human flesh in the freezer chest of his manor house, the police have to release him. The investigators (still) have insufficient evidence, or none, to justify arresting him. Now, as before, the assumption of innocence prevails.

"What did you do?"

"Well, it was about three o'clock and I made a phone call. I wanted to talk to my brother Ilja, but only his wife was there. I told my sister-in-law the situation. 'Look, I've got a problem with the police.' She asked jokingly, 'Armin, do you have a corpse lying in the cellar or something?' I answered, 'No, in the freezer chest.' She thought I was kidding and laughed."

"Did you tell anyone else about it in this manner?"

"No. I called the office and said I needed leave, but, perhaps, I wouldn't come back at all. Then I called my attorney."

*

On Tuesday, December 10, 2002, at exactly 3:05 p.m., the telephone rings at the reception desk of the law offices of Both & Partner at 4 Gartenstrasse in Rotenburg.

"Law offices of Both & Partner, Jennifer E., good afternoon," answers the young secretary politely.

"Yes, good afternoon. This is Armin Meiwes. I must speak urgently to Mr. Ermel."

"Just one moment. I'll see if Mr. Ermel is free."

For twelve seconds, Armin Meiwes hears the recorded sounds of "Ballade pour Adeline."

The secretary inquires of her boss, Attorney-at-Law Harald Ermel, if she may put the call through.

"Mr. Meiwes wants to speak to you urgently. May I put him on?"

"Yes, okay, put him on."

"Hello, Mr. Ermel."

Ermel replies, "Yes, good day to you. How are you?"

"Can't complain."

"What can we do for you?"

Meiwes tells him, "Well, I have a problem about glorification of force on the Internet. Can I come by right now?"

Harald Ermel's first thought on hearing "glorification of force" is, "I hope Mr. Meiwes isn't fooling around in some politically far-out groups. For God's sake, don't tell me he's a Neo-Nazi!"

"Of course you can come by," he says.

Meiwes adds, "There's something else."

"What's that?"

"Would you represent me, too, if I've killed someone?"

Ermel doesn't quite have an answer. "Oh, Mr. Meiwes, we'll have to think about it. I can't say. I have to hear first what it's all about, in detail. Come by right now, and then you can tell me about it."

"Yes, I'm on my way. See you."

Meiwes hangs up and pulls on a jacket. He drives the four miles to Gartenstrasse, a quiet side street on the edge of Rotenburg. He parks his car right in front of the building, a whitewashed house with several offices under the same roof. The two-story house has a raised ground floor and, on the right, is a garage.

At three twenty-five p.m., five minutes before the agreed time, Armin Meiwes mounts the six steps of the outside stairs to the entrance. He presses the white doorbell on the law firm's sign. The door opens automatically and Meiwes walks in.

The Wüstefelder already knows the office from several visits. The small family firm has existed for three generations and has won a good reputation over the years in construction law, purchase contracts, and notarizing legal documents. Attorney Harald Ermel has been a partner in the firm for thirty-two years and has successfully represented Meiwes in a number of situations, including two traffic offenses and some papers that Meiwes needed notarized.

"It will be just another few minutes," says the pretty blond Jennifer, who is in her third year of training.

"No problem. I'll just sit down on this chair."

The clock is ticking.

In a few minutes, a bomb will go off in Wüstefeld.

*

His bright red hair, the gleaming blue shirt with an azure-blue tie, the jeans and his gray sport coat make the fifty-five-year-old notary and attorney, Harald Ermel, appear dynamic.

The lively Hessian with the laughing eyes scoots about on the five steel rollers of his black leather partner's chair as he works intensively. On the seven-foot wide desk before him, dozens of files are piled. Not quite three feet behind him in the two hundred-square-foot office stands a nine-foot-long antique walnut bookcase. On one of its shelves, eleven matchbox-sized trucks are lined up. One of them bears, instead of "Coca-Cola "or "Nestlé," the advertising sign "Harald Ermel." Every year, on his birthday or for Christmas, he gets a toy automobile as a present from his four colleagues. On the left in the same bookcase stands a somewhat larger model Porsche, a vehicle the modest attorney has dreamt of since his childhood. On the income of a small-town lawyer, he drives to this day, a silver-gray Hyundai, which has seventy-five thousand miles on it.

On the left, within reach, are piled forty fat German law books, bound in black leather, and beside them dozens of transparent briefcases, collections of memoranda stapled together, and a few file folders lying flat.

At the wall opposite the desk hums an air conditioner—probably to keep the files dry—in front of another oaken bookcase three feet wide. The bookcase is crammed from top to bottom with brown-gray hanging folders. Two antique visitors' chairs stand in front of the desk in this overloaded office of law attorney Harald Ermel.

At exactly three-thirty p.m., Armin Meiwes steps into the attorney's room and sits down on one of these antique chairs facing him.

Harald Ermel tells me what happened then:

"Mr. Meiwes came in the door, apparently in total despair. I said, 'Well, Mr. Meiwes, what's up?' He said, 'Well, you're going to hear it right now.' I said, 'Let's talk quietly. We'll manage.' Armin Meiwes then told me again what he had said in our telephone conversation. 'I'm charged with showing violence on the Internet, with sexual motives.' I answered, 'You know what, we'll ask for the police files and find out in detail what has been investigated, and then we can size up the situation.' Armin Meiwes agreed. I handed him a form. 'I need a power of attorney from you, and then we can get on with it.' He signed the power of attorney and I suggested, 'The best thing is for you to come back as soon as I've had a chance to review the investigative files.' Meiwes hemmed and hawed oddly until I asked him, 'Is there something else you wanted to tell me?' Meiwes was quiet until I said, 'My dear Mr. Meiwes, we don't have all day. What have you done?' He muttered, 'Yes, well, I killed a man.' I said sharply, 'And where have you got the body now—in your freezer?' And he said, 'Yes.' Naturally I was stunned at the moment, because I hadn't said it seriously, and then suddenly he came out with the truth. I said, 'We'll have to talk about it now. We can't let the matter rest there. Tell me, what exactly did you do?' Meiwes then confessed immediately. 'Well, then, I killed a man. I butchered him and ate part of him.' Ate him?' I asked, horrified, because I thought I might have heard wrong. 'Ate him,' Meiwes confirmed. My jaw dropped."

Attorney Harald Ermel had already suspected the worst, but a cannibal in his little law office—this was something he had never expected.

"My first thought was that it couldn't be possible," adds the attorney. "But then I had known Mr. Meiwes for many years, and whatever he had told me before had always been true, so that I thought there must be something to it. I was, of course, appalled by what he said since it's not every day that a person is eaten. But a cannibal has just as much right as anyone else to an attorney. I told Armin Meiwes immediately that he was free to choose his attorney. But he wanted to do it with me. 'I trust you,' he said, 'to see it through with me.' I explained to him that a wave was about to crash down on him. 'There'll be an uproar in the media! People will go wild!' But I put it to him straight. 'You've got to deal with it, Mr. Meiwes.' He nodded and replied, 'Of course. That's clear.'"

"What happened then?" I ask.

"He gave me all the details, including the fact that the police had taken flesh from Bernd Brandes into evidence and inspected it."

"How did he explain why he had killed Mr. Brandes?" I went on.

"He said he wanted to eat human flesh. That had been his wish, and it was why he had killed, butchered, and partly eaten his male counterpart."

"Did he tell you also that he'd made a video of it?"

"Yes, that also came into the discussion. The police didn't find the video, which was still in his possession. The house was already partly sealed. It was only a matter of time before he was arrested. It couldn't be prevented any longer."

"What impression did Mr. Meiwes make on you while he was confessing his deed?"

The attorney points to the chair on the right. "Mr. Meiwes sat there, on that chair, like a pile of misery. He was shriveled, lost in his own thoughts. He wasn't the way I'd known him, lively and affable. He had completely changed."

"And when he spoke about the killing?"

"When he was able to recount the act itself, he became somewhat more at ease. It did him good to get it finally off his chest. Later on, he did talk with prison psychologists and that felt like a liberation to him. But the liberation began here in this office."

"Did you also have some idea about the details of the butchering?"

"We discussed the cutting off of the penis. Also the bleeding to death and the events surrounding the dying. The details, how long it all lasted, the whole ten hours, we didn't discuss. It was just about butchering, yes. Eating, yes, but not the details."

"How long was Mr. Meiwes with you?"

"After about forty minutes, I said to him, 'Mr. Meiwes, there's no point in this. Before the mob of reporters descends upon you, you had better turn yourself in. I'll try to arrange for you to be detained immediately for questioning.' And that's how it went. At about four-ten p.m., with his consent, I called the police. I said, 'The accused, Armin Meiwes, is with me and ready to make a full confession. He killed a man. Can you please come and pick him up? Many thanks.'"

*

The police are stuck in rush-hour traffic. At four fifty-five p.m., the police car stops in front of the law office building. Three officers of the criminal police enter the offices and lead Armin Meiwes away, without handcuffs. Harald Ermel promptly informs his colleagues of his client's confession. "Armin Meiwes killed and ate a man." His colleagues cannot, and will not, believe it. Harald Ermel explains, "For the others, it was totally unimaginable. But I said there was something to it. We have to assume it happened."

*

Armin Meiwes is brought at four fifty-five p.m. to the Regional Criminal Inspector's headquarters (RKI) in Bad Hersfeld. Patrolmen from the Rotenburg police station seal the Wüstefeld manor house at five twenty-five p.m. In the service rooms of the Bad Hersfeld RKI, the officials question him at five-fifty p.m. for the second time this day. Excerpts from the record of the interrogation are quoted here:

> *Since Mr. Meiwes has eaten nothing today, he is offered the opportunity to order something to eat. He agreed to have a McDonald's menu brought in. He was granted permission to smoke.*

After the known biographical facts (childhood, youth, parents' divorce, army career) are given, his food is brought to him at six-fifteen p.m. He is permitted to eat during interrogation. During the next five hours, Armin Meiwes gives the story of his life in copious detail, from his birth to the day of the interrogation. After he has laid out in great detail the incident which is incomprehensible to the police officers, the two investigators dig deeper for certainty:

> *Question: "Were you serious in putting this invitation in your advertisement?"*

> *Answer: "Yes. I meant it in all seriousness. I wanted to kill someone and then consume him."*

> *Question: "Did many persons respond?"*

> *Answer: "Yes. There were anywhere from 60 to 100 persons. Most of them, however, weren't serious. There were also letters that seemed to me to show serious intentions. But it was only with Bernd that I had intimate contact. I sorted all contacts, printed some out, or simply saved them in the computer."*

Next come the factual accounts of Bernd Brandes's arrival, the removal of the penis, and the killing. The record continues:

Question: "During your actions, were you sexually aroused?

Answer: "Yes, that too. But I didn't have an erection or any emission of sperm. I did have a hard-on when I watched the video later."

Question: "Were you proud of yourself when you watched the video?"

Answer: "Yes."

Question: "Do you think the whole thing was lawful or right?"

Answer: "Clearly it was not right. And I had feelings of guilt accordingly. From time to time, it occurred to me to give myself up to the police when things were going badly for me. I would have been ready to do something like that if the opportunity had surfaced." ...

Question: "Did you make other changes in the house?"

Answer: "No. At first, I didn't think about it, but on the return trip to Rotenburg, the hopelessness of my situation struck me. When the flesh is analyzed, the only possible conclusion is that it comes from a human. I can't say anymore for the time being. Right now I feel somehow relieved."

The questioning is terminated at eleven-fifteen p.m.

The statement was read, approved, and signed by Armin Meiwes himself. He spends the night at the police station in a single cell.

*

Wednesday, December 11, 2002

Around nine a.m., Armin Meiwes is brought by the police to his manor house. He shows them the video cassettes of the butchering of Bernd Brandes, hidden in his study. He hands over personal belongings of Bernd Brandes: a wallet with his identity card, the cell phone, his wristwatch—that Meiwes wore on his right wrist during the interrogation—as well as a photo and two handcuff keys.

Behind the manure pile next to the stable, Armin Meiwes shows the investigators the three places where he buried the head and other bones of Bernd Brandes. They are immediately dug open. In "Trove 1," the officials find bones and a blue plastic bag, and in "Trove 2," the cut-off head of Bernd Brandes (separately packed in a blue plastic bag). At "Trove 3," the specialists collect many decomposed private parts and innards.

At ten forty-five a.m., Meiwes is questioned briefly again, because—presumably from nervousness—he had made a mistake. He inadvertently gave March 16, 2001, as the butchery day. At eleven a.m., the police officers serve him two buttered rolls and coffee. Directly afterward, the officers watch the video of the act, lasting about twenty-seven minutes up to the moment of the killing.

*

East Hesse Police Presidency

Comment:

> On 12/11/02, 11:05 a.m., the first cassette of the video camera was viewed by the undersigned and police officer S. It is labeled "Cator 03/10/01, 4:15+1/3."
>
> Briefly summarized, the following sequence is to be seen (with time given by the camera's mechanism in minutes):

-00:00 to -00:1:26 p.m. sexual intercourse between accused and victim in slaughter room on the bed

-00:1:26 victim puts his penis on a wooden board on the table, first attempt to cut it. Accused and victim converse. It appears that the victim is in agreement with the actions.

-00:17:26 penis is cut off

-00:20:00 penis is cut up

-00:20:00 victim lies on slaughter table. It is fully evident that the person is still alive— breathing, head and mouth are moving.

-00:26:25 accused kisses the victim, measures his pulse

-00:27:34 accused stabs victim in the neck with knife

At this point, the viewing of the videotape is suspended.

After twenty-seven minutes and thirty-four seconds, the otherwise hardboiled officers break off their viewing of Armin Meiwes's slaughter tapes. Apparently, what they had seen satisfied the evidentiary requirements and they didn't feel the necessity of watching any more of the atrocity, especially so close to Christmas.

It is not until nearly two months later, on February 4, 2002, that police officers S. and F. watch the entire video and download the contents into the computer.

*

The Rotenburg District Court, on the afternoon of December 11, 2002, issues a warrant for Armin Meiwes's arrest:

The accused is urgently suspected of having, on 3/09-10/2001, in Rotenburg an der Fulda, killed a man with desire to murder. On 3/09-10/2001, the accused decided to kill Bernd Brandes, who was visiting him in his manor house in Rotenburg an der Fulda. With the killing, his intent was to achieve his design of seeing a man die and thereupon consuming the corpse. In executing this plan, he cut off the victim's penis with a knife. After the latter fainted because of the injuries suffered thereby, the accused cut the victim's throat with a knife. From the injuries thus inflicted the victim Bernd Brandes died, as intended by the accused. The accused was aware when he cut the victim's throat that Bernd Brandes was still alive at that moment. This act is punishable as the crime of murder under §211 StGB.... During his questioning by the police, the accused substantially admitted the act. He recorded the event in video. The viewing of the video recordings confirmed his statements. To the extent that accused alleges that when he cut the victim's throat, he assumed that Bernd Brandes was already dead, this allegation must be regarded as a lie to cover himself. For it can be seen in the video recording that the victim Bernd Brandes at this point was still recognizably breathing and moving his head. Proof of the act is to be found in the police investigations. There are grounds for arrest of the accused under §112 because in view of the applicable penalty the danger exists that the accused will seek to escape it through flight. He has few, if any, social connections. Considering the crime of which he is accused, a warrant for his arrest is justified also by the fact that the accused engages in an activity regulated by law. (§112 and subsections).

Signed H., Judge on the District Court.

*

Thursday, December 12, 2002

Twelve days before Christmas Eve, at seven in the morning, police officers transport Armin Meiwes in a prison vehicle to the Kassel Penitentiary.

In Bad Hersfeld on the same day, the "Franky" Special Commission is formed. At the outset, it is headed by First High Commissioner S. A week later, the special investigations are taken over by the Hessian Provincial Criminal Bureau (HLKA). The direction of the Special Commission is transferred to High Commissioner where the "Chat" Special Commission begins its work.

*

Friday, December 13, 2002

Tracker dogs of the "Homicide" Special Department from Kassel sniff about on Armin Meiwes's land in Wüstefeld. They start where corpse parts were dug up. According to the dog handlers, the dogs can smell the decomposition fluids that have seeped into the ground. Although the dogs are excited at that location, they find no other area of interest on the property. Relieved that only one corpse is involved, the police withdraw from the property. Armin Meiwes is apparently not a mass murderer.

*

One question will continue to preoccupy the German justice system, the courts, the experts, and the media for another four years: Was the butchering of Bernd Brandes to be considered "Death by Request," "Active Dying Assistance," "Manslaughter," or "Murder"? What exactly, besides a cannibal, is Armin Meiwes? Is he a friend or a cold-blooded MURDERER?

ALL THE WAYS OF A MAN ARE CLEAN IN HIS OWN EYES; BUT THE LORD WEIGHETH THE SPIRITS. COMMIT THY WORKS UNTO THE LORD, AND THY THOUGHTS SHALL BE ESTABLISHED. THE LORD HATH MADE ALL THINGS FOR HIMSELF: YEA, EVEN THE WICKED FOR THE DAY OF EVIL.

(Book of Proverbs 16: 2-4)

Chapter 15

MURDER AND MANSLAUGHTER

IN THE MIDST OF THE PRE-CHRISTMAS holiday mood of the year 2002, the media bomb explodes, ignited by the Deutsche Presse Agentur (DPA):

Report of 12/11/2002, 6:46 p.m.:
Cannibalism: 41-year-old Man Arrested in Hesse on Suspicion of Murder

Kassel (DPA) The police in Hesse have arrested a man, 41 years old, for cannibalism. The man, from Rotenburg in the northeast part of the province, is said to have confessed to killing, carving up, and partially eating a 42-year-old man, with the latter's consent, in front of a running video camera, announced the office of the State's Attorney in Kassel. Because cannibalism, in Germany, is not defined as a crime, the prosecutor's office is investigating the incident as suspected murder. The detainee was arraigned on Wednesday. "The man's confession must be examined and this will take a while," said State's Attorney Hans-Manfred Jung. The victim was reported to the police in Berlin as missing. The deed, committed in the spring of 2000, is reported to be based on cannibalistic and homosexual inclinations shared by both men. The 41-year-old gave a full confession. He is reported to have first cut off the victim's sexual organ with the latter's consent, in order to join him in eating it. Then he is said to have stabbed the 42-year-old and cut him into pieces. He deep-froze the flesh in chunks and later ate most of them. He buried the remains of the corpse. The men are reported to have met through advertisements on the Internet. The police got on the man's trail because he inserted an advertisement again on the Internet. In it, he sought contact with a man who was prepared to let him self be killed and eaten. In the ensuing search of his residence on Tuesday, the police came upon deep-frozen human flesh, skeleton parts, and video photographs. In Germany, the last time a man was thought to possibly be a "man-eater" was in March, 1995: A man aged 33, sentenced to life in prison for the robbery and murder of his 81-year-old life partner, had stated during his trial that he had eaten his victim's innards. It was never determined whether that was true. The most spectacular case occurred 80 years ago in Hannover. A secondhand dealer named Fritz Haarmann murdered, between 1918 and 1924, at least twenty-four young men. At the same time, he was carrying on a prosperous trade in cheap meat, which gave rise to the stubborn, if unproven rumor, that Haarmann sold the flesh of his victims.

The *Die Welt* newspaper seems for a brief moment to be holding its breath after this report while, elsewhere in the world, the story is exploding.

From Alaska to New Zealand, from Japan to the USA, the reports come thick and fast from TV and radio stations, daily newspapers, and online services of how, in the middle of civilized Germany, a man butchered and ate another man. From that moment, Armin Meiwes becomes "The Rotenburg Cannibal," "a flesh-eating monster." On the day of the DPA report, on December 12, 2002 alone, about 2,400 articles worldwide are published about the man-eater. On Google, there are within a few weeks, 80,000 entries on Armin Meiwes. Hundreds of millions of TV watchers of the BBC, RTL, CNN, CBS, or ORF cannot grasp the ensuing reports. Many newspaper readers must reread each line of the headlines and news story to make sure they've read correctly, so unbelievable is the deed to them.

"The most perverted crime! Cannibal devoured Berliner"
(*BILD*, 12/12/2002)

"Man-eater in Germany!"
(*Hamburger Morgenpost*, 12/12/2002)

"A Monstrous Deed on Video"
(*Süddeutsche Zeitung*, 12/13/2002)

"German Cannibal found willing victims on net"
(*The Times*, 12/13/2002)

"This is Armin, he ate Bernd from Berlin"
(*BZ*, 12/13/2002).

"The Cannibal from Next Door"
(*Die Welt*, 12/13/2002)

"Horror in the old manor house"
(*Die Welt*, 12/13/2002)

"This is the weird man-eater. His father: policeman. His brother: priest. Has he butchered more men?"
(*BILD*, 12/13/2002).

"The Man-eater: Free in 3 years?"
(*Bild am Sonntag*, 12/15/2002)

"I want to eat you"
(*Spiegel*, 12/16/2002)

"Appointment for Eating"
(*Stern*, 12/18/2002)

"Lust for Death"
(*Stern*, 12/18/2002)

The news magazine *Spiegel* writes: "What took place in the spring of last year in the basement *[Author's comment: It was on the second floor]* of a large, crumbling half-timbered house in Rotenburg an der Fulda leaves hard-boiled investigators dumbfounded. It forces one to look into the darkest corners of the Internet, where numberless, apparently quite normal citizens, exchange their perversions in ever more blatant forms."

The daily newspaper *Welt,* under the headline "How many cannibals are living among us?" worries, "Toying with cannibalistic fantasies is apparently attracting an increasing number of Internet users world-wide." And quotes High Criminal Commissioner Rainer Richard, forty-one, from Munich.... "It's hard for us to judge whether the advertisements are meant seriously, but experience shows that on the Internet, everything must be taken at face value."

The news magazine *Focus* reports that the police suspect the electronically networked cannibal scenes of being responsible for another killing offense only recently committed and not yet solved.

The *Frankfurter Allgemeine Zeitung* allows itself the assumption: "The police came upon the presumptive perpetrator's trail by researching the Internet. In four or five forums, said the spokesman for the State's Attorney, M. [Meiwes] published his advertisements. He states, 'The ads are still there.' The police apparently acted with dispatch.... As nonplussed as the police, are the residents in and around Rotenburg, after the discovery of the latest bloody deed. No one is prepared to believe that such a thing happened in his neighborhood."

Not a word of thanks to the courageous Innsbruck student who got the information to the police, who needed five months and a day before taking action and searching the house.

The *Times* lets the dean of boulevard journalism, Franz Josef Wagner, speculate that the film *The Silence of the Lambs* or its forerunner *Red Dragon* is to blame: "The cult-star of the year 2002 was Hannibal Lecter, who ate a human brain to the music of Vivaldi."

The *Süddeutsche Zeitung* sums it all up: "It is so improbable. So spooky, that people were sure such cases exist only in films, perhaps in America, but not in Germany, not in Rotenburg an der Fulda.... The forty-one-year-old made a full confession and ran a video of the act. The investigators must have seen it, and for that reason, those involved in the trial will someday be unable to avoid it. The film is too monstrous for words. 'In my entire life, I've never seen anything like it,' says an investigator on Thursday to the Hessian Radio. 'And I hope I'll never again have to see such a thing.'"

*

At the same time, in the High Security Block of the Kassel Penitentiary, Armin Meiwes is talking with the prison psychologist, Dr. Heinrich W. For the first time in over thirty years, he speaks to someone about his emotional life.

"It was as if a huge rock had fallen from my heart. Mount Everest is a pebble in comparison," Meiwes tells me, describing this moment of his "release."

The man depicted by the media as a "monster" tells me about this discussion with the psychologist. "The possibility of talking it all out gave me a feeling of liberation. It was the very first talk with a person in which I could speak about these things uninhibited and without prejudgment. The burden that had built up on my shoulders for over thirty years was gone for good. However strange it may sound to you, after that talk, I came into a so-called access cell. The room was very small, and filthy. I sat behind the bars and blubbered. I felt freer than I had ever felt before in my entire life."

"Couldn't these discussions have taken place before?"

"No. I didn't trust myself! But if they had taken place, for me and also for Bernd Brandes, then this action would never have come about. Neither of us had the courage for it."

*

After the headlines, the enormity of the act of violence becomes apparent to the investigators of the "Chat" Special Commission [hereafter: "Soko"] as well as to the populace at large. Slowly it dawns on the residents of Rotenburg an der Fulda that the story must be true. The sleepy town is stood on its head. Hundreds of reporters, photographers, dozens of TV teams with live broadcasting vans, and the merely curious, besiege the manor house in Wüstefeld. "The dead man must have lain in front of a mountain of earth," reports the FAZ. "The dredger tracks and mounds of earth dug up in the garden of the presumptive perpetrator are easily visible from the street. A neighbor reports having seen the skull, encrusted with earth, which the police uncovered and packed up, together with bones, in blue plastic bags."

Sick individuals send letters like the following to the East Hesse Police Presidency (received December 18, 2002):

> *Hello there, all you police stallions in Rotenburg. Have you gotten lust and appetite for human flesh after the example of your sergeant? Are your cocks standing up, so your flies are bursting open and so raunchy your balls can hardly find room in their sack? ...I'm ready and at your disposal. I'll answer your Internet ads with my cell phone number. You can tie me up, torture me brutally for days, gang rape me, butcher me, and eat me. Your raunchiest cop can first cut off my cock and balls and eat them raw. I'm slim, healthy and hardly 20 years old, willing, no taboos, and appetizing. Hope you have courage and call me soon.*

The letter ends up in the files.

*

At the manor house, where Armin Meiwes until recently was selling computer parts, the "Chat" Soko takes possession of the cannibal archives: 238 video cassettes (twenty-one of them "relevant" as evidence), 221 hard drives with varying memory capacities, sixteen PCs, ninety-five CD-ROMS, 1,210 3.5-inch diskettes, 532 5.25-inch diskettes, twenty-three data tapes. The investigating authorities question about 120 witnesses. The transcripts of the interrogations alone fill forty-three file folders.

After the indictment of Armin Meiwes, other persons are charged, among them Jörg B. under §§ 30, 211 StGB (under suspicion as an accomplice/conspiracy to murder) and Eugen A. under § 131 StGB ("presentation of violence").

*

Bernd Brandes's friend, René J., and his relatives are informed of the forty-three-year-old man's death a few days after the DNA analysis of his mortal remains. They learn the circumstances of his death daily, in grisly fashion, from the media. The killed man's father refuses to organize his burial or to take part in it. The funeral must be performed in secret at a small Berlin cemetery to guard against photographers. Bernd Brandes's life companion, René J., grieves with a handful of friends. Only the head, hands, feet, and a few bones of Bernd Brandes, which were dug out of the garden of the manor house from a depth of a foot and laid in an oaken casket are cremated and lowered hastily into the ground by the pallbearers. The priest tries in vain, during the twenty-minute service, to find comforting words. During the ceremony, René breaks down.

*

From a park bench at the edge of the woods on a hill above Wüstefeld, one can sit and get a broad view of the Hessian woodland. From a height of about thirteen hundred feet, Marion Reich gazes out over the Wüstefeld estate and the surrounding farms. The forty-five-year-old woman was described in the press as "the cannibal's lady-friend" because she visited Meiwes in prison. During our conversation, she wears a wig and dark glasses so as not to be recognized. "The people hereabouts can be very mean," she says. "It's better if they don't hear about my talking with you." Her voice sounds very clear. "Since Armin Meiwes's act, a lot of things have changed in Rotenburg. Envy, rumors, discord fall on fertile soil here. It's best to hush the matter up."

"The deed was presumably too awful to grasp," she comments. "But the crime could just as well have happened in any of the other fourteen thousand towns and communities in Germany. It was just a matter of time before someone translated these abnormal fantasies from the Internet into reality."

"How do you explain that, of all people, your acquaintance Armin Meiwes ate another man?" I ask.

"I've known Armin Meiwes for seven years as a neighbor. You want an explanation?" She shakes her head and buries her face in her hands. Then she continues with moist eyes. "I have only a vague notion. I think the blame belongs to the overbearing influence of his mother, to whom he had to submit for years. Also, he had those fears of abandonment—his father and brother who went away. This left its stamp on him," she says, struggling to find an explanation for the inexplicable.

"What kind of human being is Mr. Meiwes?" I prod.

Marion Reich rubs her hands over her jeans and speaks deliberately. "He's a quiet, sensitive character, that's how I would describe him. Very helpful, very open and honest. He couldn't reveal his other, darker side, of course. It's not something one talks about over coffee. I was shocked when I learned of it, and I thought, no, it couldn't be. Not Armin! It's a misunderstanding! They mean someone else."

"How did you learn about it?"

"I was at work and a colleague, a friend, told me a corpse had been found on Armin Meiwes's property. She had heard it from a baker. Well, I said, 'It must be a mix-up. Who knows how long the corpse has been lying there. Armin certainly wasn't yet living there.' Then, I immediately looked at the news and talked on the phone with friends, and then it really came out that it was Armin."

"What was it like for you?"

"It was as if the ground had been pulled out from under my feet, because during all those months, I had seen a lot of him."

"When did you learn that he had eaten another man?"

She takes a deep breath. "The next day. I called up Mr. Meiwes's attorney, Harald Ermel. He confirmed what wasn't covered by the attorney-client privilege. 'Yes, it's true. Mr. Meiwes consumed a man.' That completely floored me! Of course, everyone in Rotenburg said, 'For heaven's sake, how can anyone do such a thing?' The thought came to me immediately that I must ask him myself. I wanted to talk with him and hear it from him in his own words."

"How did the press get to you?"

"The neighbors told them I was a friend of Mr. Meiwes. Reporters, using false names and false professions, got to my children at their school. They wormed my telephone number out of them and hung around my front door for days and nights. For two weeks, I couldn't send my kids to school. It was just dreadful."

"What did the media call you?"

"Must I say it now?

"Yes, please."

Marion Reich's voice trembles. "The media called me his mistress and beloved. They massacred me, although I didn't have such a relationship with Mr. Meiwes. The press drove me, and my children, out of our minds. They never asked me if I wasn't merely slightly acquainted with him. Only because I was a Christian was I unwilling to turn my back on him."

"What kind of relationship did you have with Mr. Meiwes, then?"

"It was really just friendly. I don't know, if I'd known him longer, how it would have developed. I wrote to him the very next day when he was detained for the search. I got the address from his attorney, Mr. Ermel."

"What was in your letter?"

"I asked if it was really as reported in the media. Then two days later, Armin answered vaguely with a few lines. 'Dear Marion, for the moment I can't write in more detail. Nice to hear from you. Yours, Armin.' I assume he couldn't say any more about it because his mail was censored. In the press, on the same day, I read, 'Today Mr. Meiwes ate pea soup with sausages. 'Sausages' was in boldface type."

Now Marion Reich is talking herself into a rage. "They didn't understand that for Mr. Meiwes, it wasn't about the flesh. His mother, Waltraud, bound Armin Meiwes to her, as I interpreted it. And by eating his friend, Armin wanted to bind Mr. Brandes to himself. It's absolute nonsense, of course. But he worked himself up into a sick world. The Internet offered him a platform where he could contact other sick people. That I find really, really bad."

"How was your first personal visit in the prison?"

"Oh, it was quite, quite difficult. That was on January 14, 2003, from ten-fifteen to ten-thirty-five a.m. I was the first person, after his attorney, to visit him. We were taken to a special room. My heart was in my mouth. I wasn't afraid of him, but I didn't know if I would feel disgusted by him or not. He was glad to see me.

"I remained very serious. I asked him, 'Armin, how can you do such a thing?' Again, he skirted it vaguely. He probably couldn't say more in front of the officials. But he did say, 'Yes, I'm still dreaming about it and imagining such things, only not so often as before. Now I have people I can talk to about it, whether fellow prisoners, the prison psychologist, or Attorney Ermel. One can't talk about a thing like that with anyone else.' After twenty minutes, the visiting time was over. Then I visited him every month. In his letters later on, Armin laid out the facts of the matter in detail. He was very open and honest with me. But it's painful."

Marion Reich interrupts her account and suddenly seems lost in thought. "I often had to cry when I got such a letter from him, because I'm simply sorry when I see how a person is so caught up in himself."

I thank her for the trust she has shown to me, a journalist, despite all the unpleasant experiences before. As we part, she gives me a copy of a letter Armin Meiwes wrote her from his cell.

*

After her first visit, on January 14, 2003, Armin Meiwes writes Marion Reich this letter:

Dear Marion,

I am soooo happy. Back in my cell, I had to cry for joy, and my entire body trembled with excitement. Everything is so hard and happy at the same time, and I thank you for sticking with me just at this time. Somehow I found it funny that the policeman was present, but it was better that we weren't up front in the big room and could talk undisturbed, if only so briefly. You gave me back light and hope. It was just at lunchtime and my neighbor in the next cell said, "You don't have to tell me how your visit was— you're just radiant with happiness." And that's exactly how I feel.

I wish I could embrace you again and kiss you warmly and passionately. With eyes shut, I sit here and imagine you were still here and I see your tender face clearly before me. It is so lovely! [Author's comment: The exclamation point looks like a heart.]

Yours with love,
Armin

Countless letters continue to reach Marion Reich from the prison. Meiwes writes, for example, on January 8, 2003:

All the attendants and inmates are very nice and I have made many friends.... When I

315

think back, the past year seems like a constantly revolving carousel. I couldn't do without my PC and the Internet. It was like an addiction. Then when the police came, it was as if this carousel, from one moment to the next, was stopped. Even though it all came un-hoped for, I'm thankful that it's over and everything is now clarified. You wouldn't believe how many "madmen" there are on the Internet....

*

The main presenter of cannibal excess seems transformed after his confession, so relieved that his arrest has stopped his deeds. In the following weeks, Meiwes reports to the psychologists about his traumas and his father's departure, and speaks openly for the first time in over thirty years about his abnormal fantasies and the butchery he carried out. He is regarded as the "model prisoner," works at first in the prison library, then in the laundry. "Mr. Meiwes was a star for the prisoners," I'm told by one of the officials. "They all wanted to know how he did it. They never saw any danger in him. Mr. Meiwes is by his very nature far too courteous and friendly." Slowly Armin Meiwes begins to put in order the past thirty years of his life.

On January 23, 2003, Meiwes receives a visit from his half-brother Ilja. From ten-thirty to eleven-fifteen a.m., they discuss financial matters such as revolving credits, sale of a property, and sale of the cars. Of the act itself, they speak not a word.

*

Attorney Harald Ermel pores over the investigative files, honing his defense strategy. For the lawyer, the "Cannibal of Rotenburg," the "Man-eater of Wüstefeld," Armin Meiwes, is the case of his life.

"Even in the first conversation with Mr. Meiwes, I assumed that it had to be killing on request," says the red-haired Rotenburg attorney, diagnosing the case. "It was clear at the outset that the Berlin party wanted to die. I could prove that easily, with the films, with the chat exchange, and with Mr. Brandes's assent to his own unmanning."

"Was the video of the act admitted immediately in evidence? That would be unusual for German judges," I ask.

"Yes. The video was shown. In plain view of us all, Bernd Brandes encouraged Mr. Meiwes in this video sequence to do the deed. He requested, 'Please do it this way. Get another knife.' When the severance of the penis didn't work right away, he said, 'Take a sharper knife.' Mr. Brandes actually got my client to do it. It wasn't at all Mr. Meiwes's wish to cut off his penis. His mind was on something else entirely. It was on the flesh, not on such sexual machinations. The Berliner, with certainty, wanted it done the next day. He fiddled with himself throughout the night for the blood to flow out. Bernd Brandes wanted to die, without question."

"But Mr. Meiwes complied with that wish. Do you have understanding for that in some way?"

The attorney counters promptly. "No. It was an action between the two people involved, beyond the comprehension of normal mortals like us. But between those two, it was a death contract, and it worked. They met on the Internet, got all worked up over it, and agreed: One wants to die, and the other wants to eat him. Without the Internet, such a deed would have been unthinkable to Mr. Meiwes. This was the defense strategy for the first trial."

*

On this hot May day of the year 2007, Armin Meiwes presses forward. "Hello, how are you? Today we don't have much time, unfortunately," he announces, coming straight to the point. "It's still Bible time. We have to get out of the room. Otherwise, the priest will go on ranting." Armin Meiwes smiles and we sit down at the table.

"How did you feel after the worldwide uproar in the press?"

"After the whole thing came out, the media reported everything but the kitchen sink. I smiled about it, more or less. I swallowed it."

What a comparison! He gulps it all down, and I cheer up again.

"Smiling and swallowing are perhaps not the right reaction. You ate a man."

"True. But I knew why I had done it. I'm also of the opinion that since the State's Attorney in his press release insisted from the outset that I was a sexually driven criminal, everything got out of control. I had never expected a reaction on such a scale. That there would be some commotion if it came out was clear. But I never dreamed that it would become a global scandal. Considering what came out on the Internet, the Office of the State's Attorney should have declared a ban on news."

"What diagnosis did the prison psychologists assign you?"

"In the Kassel Penitentiary, I spoke with Dr. W., the staff psychologist. He did not give me a diagnosis, other than to certify me as 'normal.'"

"I beg pardon? What's normal about it?"

Armin Meiwes looks at me quizzically. "Well, I didn't come to a psychiatric institution. Instead, I'm sitting here in jail among other quite normal criminals. The reason is, I'm not hurting anyone."

To clarify to myself the meaning of these words, I lay out in my mind the following hypothesis: As long as I don't ask Armin Meiwes to chop off my fingers, he won't do it. If, however, I did express this wish, he might want to comply with it. For an amateur psychologist like me, this is not to be classified as "normal." I refuse to be pinned down, however, to the accuracy of this unscientific stab at an explanation.

"What would you consider a fair sentence for your act?"

"Under §216, Killing on Request, the maximum sentence is five years. Now there's another heading, 'Disturbing the Rest of the Dead.' That would be, let's see, five to seven years."

"Do you think a democratic State should make a cannibalistic act like yours a punishable offense?"

He answers clearly. "In the future, something should be done by the legislature in any case."

"Would you have killed and eaten Bernd Brandes if cannibalism were punishable by death?"

"Yes. The degree of punishment is unimportant. When someone like me has this desire and wants to carry it out, he'll go to any length to bring it about. I have had it for thirty years! Excuse this crude comparison, but for me, the Internet was like the platinum money card, with which I could get whatever I want. It is like when you were a child, you wanted a Jaguar or a Ferrari, and then, finally, when you grow up and could afford it, you finally went out and got it. If the police had shot me in the act, it would have made no difference."

*

Hardly a year later, on December 3, 2003, with rapt attention worldwide, the cannibal, Armin Meiwes, is put on trial. In Room D 130 of the Courthouse in Kassel, State's Attorney Marcus K. reads the indictment. Armin Meiwes submits a comprehensive confession. On the second day of the trial, Monday, December 8, 2003, the judge and two jurors watch the video of the butchery, with the public excluded. Meiwes's attorney, Harald Ermel, who sees the tape in the courtroom also for the first time, thus describes this eerie film presentation. "I was unable to observe how the jurors reacted to the video. Like the others, I was completely in the grip of the scenes in the video. Meiwes worked like a craftsman and explained the butchery; for him it was a mechanical act. But, there were situations in the video that made me wince, where I said to myself, for heaven's sake, it can't be. It was a bad scene when Bernd Brandes's penis was cut off—as a man, you jump. You can't help it. And when Meiwes cut Bernd Brandes's throat, you knew it was final. This man is dead. I think, at that point, everyone present was moved."

After interrogation of witnesses and experts, the State's Attorney, in his summing-up a month and a half later on January 25, 2004, demands a life sentence. Defense Attorney Harald Ermel tries to get a five-year sentence for his client.

After the first trial and fourteen days of hearings, the District Court of Kassel finally announces on January 30, 2004, "in the name of the people" in the criminal trial of Armin Meiwes, born 12/1/1961 in Essen, residing on the Wüstefeld estate, 36199 Rotenburg/Fulda, the following verdict and sentence:

> *DECLARED AS LAW: The accused is guilty of MANSLAUGHTER.*
>
> *He is therefore sentenced to eight years, six months' imprisonment.*
>
> *Applicable penal provisions:*
>
> *§§ 212, 74 StGB.*

In the detailed two-hundred-and-nineteen-page judgment, the Court reasons:

> *Based on the facts established, the accused stands guilty of manslaughter in accordance with §212 subsec. StGB. He killed a man without being a murderer. An innocent assistance to suicide is not the case. For after the victim lost consciousness, the perpetrator had it in his power to act in a manner leading to death.... From the moment Bernd Brandes lost consciousness, at the very latest, the accused held full control, and was thereby the perpetrator and not merely an accomplice. The accused acted also with direct intent to kill.... A killing on request under §216 subsec. 1 StGB is not involved. There was, to be sure, an express request by Bernd Brandes to be killed, of which*

the accused failed to recognize the lack of seriousness, and which he assumed to be serious in the sense of § 16 subsec. 2 StGB. Brandes's request, however, was only one of several motives for the accused's decision to act, and not the dominant and controlling one.... Furthermore, there are no characteristics of murder as set forth in §211 subsec. 2 StGB. The characteristic signs of pleasure in murder are not present here. In killing Brandes, the accused felt no unnatural joy in the destruction of a man's life, but rather saw the moment as a difficulty that had to be overcome to reach the desired goal. The death of Brandes therefore, was not a purpose, let alone the sole purpose, of the act. The accused also did not kill Brandes in satisfaction of the sexual urge in the sense of §211 subsec. 2 StGB.... If the perpetrator is only seeking sexual stimulation, but not the satisfaction of his sexual urge, the murder characteristic must be ruled out.... According to the established facts of the case, the accused felt the act of killing to be a necessary evil in the slaughter and assimilation of Brandes's body.... Also, in the fact that the accused masturbated while viewing the video recording of Brandes's butchery, he did not display the signs of murderous intent in the killing for satisfaction of the sexual urge.... The butchery, carving up and consumption of Brandes, to be sure, was a repulsive act characterized by an extremely coarse turn of mind.... The accused held to what had been agreed with Brandes.... According to the established facts of the case, therefore, the accused is to be sentenced for manslaughter under §212 subsec. 1 StGB, which permits a sentence of imprisonment for from five to fifteen years.... In specifying the penal range of §212 subsec.1 StGB, the chamber took into consideration, in particular, the fact that he was interested only in experiencing his own elation through the anticipated intensity of a relationship, and the processing of male flesh, which he had made into a substitute relationship object. And he acted from self-serving motives in which the death of the man was the necessary intermediate step.... In favor of the accused, it was to be taken into consideration especially that he was motivated to do the deed by a disturbance of his own sexual preference in the direction of a fetishism with a distorted experience of connection, a disturbance that must be regarded as an illness, and for whose occurrence he was not responsible. To this is to be added the circumstance that the accused, with this background, exerted himself energetically to search for a victim. But, from the outset, regarded the consent of the victim to the killing as necessary, even though the killing had no legal justification. Moreover, it rested on a morbid emotional disturbance of Brandes of which, however, the accused was not aware, so that this circumstance cannot be held against him.... After weighing all the circumstances arguing for and against the accused, the penalty should not be fixed in the upper limits of the penalty range. But it also could not remain in the lower range. Accordingly, the sentence of eight years and six months was appropriate to the act and the guilt.... Signed M., Chief Judge of the Provincial Court, Dr. W., Judge of the Provincial Court, G., Judge.

*

In the Kassel Penitentiary, Armin Meiwes awaits my next question with stoical calm.

"How did you react to the first judgment?"

"Well, I was disappointed. I was of the opinion that it was killing on request. Bernd Brandes came to me, he wanted to die, and this is proved, in the chat transcripts and the video. A killing at the wish of the victim, as I understand the law, cannot be manslaughter or murder."

*

Both the State's Attorney, who argues murder, and Armin Meiwes, who claims the crime is a "killing on request," appeal the judgment.

On April 13, 2005, the Federal Court of Appeals in Karlsruhe considers the appeals. Federal Attorney General Lothat S. argues for reversing the judgment of the Kassel court and a verdict of murder. Nine days later, on April 22, 2005, the Court of Appeals reverses the judgment of the Provincial Court of Kassel.

*

Armin Meiwes's second trial begins nine months after reversal of the first judgment.

On January 12, 2006, in the 21st Criminal Division of the Frankfurt Provincial Court, with Judge Klaus D. presiding, begins the first of fourteen trial days, which are set for a period ending at the latest on May 19, 2006.

Before then, on May 9, 2006, Judge Klaus D. pronounces judgment. For Armin Meiwes it is a thunderbolt:

> *The accused is sentenced to life imprisonment for MURDER concomitantly with disturbance of the peace.*

As for the grounds of the judgment, the opinion continues as follows:

> *Judicially, the act is to be considered murder. 1.) This was premeditated killing. That the accused knew Brandes was still alive when he cut his throat, and wanted to kill him by stabbing him, is proved by the hearing of evidence. 2.) The act is not a killing on request. A precondition of that would be that the killer kills, from his point of view, because the person killed wishes it. The fulfillment of the latter's wish for killing must be for the perpetrator,*

therefore, the sole, or at least the principal, motivating reason for the act.... This, however, was not the case with the accused. For him, certainly, the victim's consent to his killing was a condition for it, but not the motivating reason, since he killed Brandes in order to butcher him and thus to come to his fetish of male flesh. This was unaffected by the return to the Kassel-Wilhelmshöhe train station. Hence, to characterize the deed as a killing on request must be excluded.... 4.) The act meets the murder-feature of commission of the deed for satisfaction of the sexual urge. The accused killed, as demonstrated by the evidence, in order to butcher Brandes, to save the scene, and, in addition, to photograph it in video, then eat the flesh and be able to call up the butchery proceedings for sexual stimulation and masturbation into his memory.... 5.) The act also meets the murder-feature of killing for commission of a crime under §168 StGB. That cannibalism is not regulated by law is false. Naturally, the eating of another human being meets the elements of disturbance of the peace of the dead, since in being eaten a human being is put on the same level as a farm animal, which, as the accused put it, "is now only my food"....
The accused realized not only two features of murder. Beyond that, he acted in a self-interested manner and adequately proved, by his behavior subsequent to the act, that to this day he feels no remorse over it. Even during the act, he thought about other victims, and directly afterward looked for other victims. Further, his conduct during the trial, priding himself on the deed, stands in crass contradiction of his final words apparently deploring it. That the accused would commit the deed again today, if he found voluntary victims, the experts convincingly argued. The qualification mentioned by Prof. Beier—if it were possible without penalty— applies only, in the Chamber's opinion, to the

fact that the accused would try to avoid an act of killing by his own hand. Those most endangered are mainly disturbed, suicidal, and sick persons. Precisely with respect to such persons the State has a duty to protect their highest legally protected right, their life, with all the means at its disposal. Signed: D., Dr. K.

*

Gisela Friedrichsen reported on the two trials of Armin Meiwes for the news magazine *Der Spiegel*. The renowned court reporter gave me for this book, the following personal assessment of the case and the second sentence ("life" for murder). I quote it here:

The judges dutifully followed out the pronouncements from Karlsruhe: Let him abandon himself in prison to his abnormal fantasies, let them intensify, alter—the main thing is, behind bars. "It cannot be," according to the presiding judge, "that the State protects its citizens from illegal contracts, but withholds this protection from its weakest members, such as psychically disturbed people." Who will contradict him? But Meiwes is a man and not a monster, although a sick one. In prison, he will not get well, but possibly even more dangerous. Who will guarantee that, left to himself, he will not extend his abnormal inner world? Cannibalistic fantasies do not vanish, after all, by themselves alone.

Hardened as she was after following more than four hundred trials, the two proceedings were, with the laying bare of abnormal details in court, even for the experienced Gisela Friedrichsen, something "more shocking than she had ever experienced." Her personal conclusion was that she "gained the impression that, with the looming dangers of the Internet, people simply look the other way, and don't want to face the truth. Our society must come to terms with the fact that there are such crimes and these 'cannibal scenes' do exist."

Armin Meiwes's attorney, Harald Ermel, sends me in an email the following remarks about the court's judgment:

"We think the intention was to pull Armin Meiwes out of circulation. To tell others, this will not do. We have definitions of murder and so we judge according to these definitions. The sentence is excessive by far. Imagine, by comparison, a child molester who sexually abuses and then brutally kills a child. Quite rightly, he gets life. But if, as in our case, someone kills another who expressly wants to be killed, which is documented and proven, then this man cannot be so treated and put behind bars for life."

In their appeal on constitutional grounds, Armin Meiwes's attorneys argue that the sentence infringes the basic rights of their client. Their office has copied their legal brief to me, and as of interest to law professionals, I repeat it without comment.

By excessive dependence on the factual feature "certain" in § 261 subsec. StGB, the procedural rule that no one be made to incriminate himself is violated. This is an invasion of Mr. Meiwes's human dignity.

If §211 StGB were phrased in conformity with the Constitution, Mr. Meiwes could not have been found guilty of murder, or if found guilty of murder, could not have been sentenced to life imprisonment.

The sentence of life imprisonment on the basis of §211 StGB is out of proportion and violates Mr. Meiwes's basic rights under Article 2, section 1 and section 2 of the Constitution.

The failure to take into consideration mitigating circumstances in sentencing under §211 StGB places Mr. Meiwes without justifiable

grounds on the same level as a man slaughterer.
It thereby violates his basic right under Article 3,
section 1 of the Constitution.

Mr. Meiwes's constitutional complaint is based on the above-cited violations of his constitutional rights. The Constitutional Court has not yet handed down its decision.

The judges of the Constitutional Court will have to decide: Was it MURDER, MANSLAUGHTER, or KILLING ON REQUEST?

*

And what of Armin Meiwes?

The cannibal, who up to now has received no therapy, comments on his life sentence with surprising composure. "In my opinion, the law has been reshaped"—he clears his throat—"so that it could be a murder. I'll go on fighting it as long as I live. Bernd Brandes's wish is decisive for me and I'm fighting for it. He wanted to die. A judge can't just simply say it wasn't for Bernd to decide."

"Did I understand correctly that you are fighting for Bernd Brandes?"

"Yes. We filed an appeal with the Federal Constitutional Court and I hope the justices will respect the arguments that will be presented to it. I will fight for Bernd Brandes's right to die, not mine. I don't care whether it takes ten years or fifteen. My life is screwed up anyway. I've been stamped as the Cannibal of Rotenburg."

Armin Meiwes has destroyed his life, but—and this must never be forgotten—he snuffed out another's life in the most gruesome manner.

*

In retrospect. I think of my conversation with the prisoner's lady friend, Marion Reich. When I asked whether she had ever noticed in Armin Meiwes a hint of remorse, the woman answers in a soft, unsteady voice, "Armin once wrote me in a letter, 'Dear Marion, there are things in life that one imagines one would like to do, and when one has done them, they can't be undone.' In my view, that was a sign of remorse. But Armin never said that to me in person."

"Did you ever see him cry over the deed he committed?"

"No, no, no. He never cried. I've often seen him moved. He is sometimes very depressed. But cry? No. He apparently never learned how. His mother said, 'Armin, a man mustn't cry.' And Armin was very compliant. He always did what others expected of him."

FOR GODLY SORROW PRODUCES REPENTANCE THAT LEADS TO SALVATION NOT TO BE REGRETTED: BUT THE SORROW OF THE WORLD PRODUCES DEATH.

(II Corinthians 7: 10)

Chapter 16

GOD AND DEVIL

O N THE TRAIN TRIP FROM Hamburg to Kassel, to
what is tentatively my last visit to Armin
Meiwes, I am reading in my little lined "moleskin" notepad. It
is a reporter's notepad, the type used by Ernest Hemingway
and Pablo Picasso, and because it is small, measuring just
three-and-a-half by five-and-a-half inches, it fits in an inside
pocket of any man's jacket. It's a present from a friend. Of its
one hundred and ninety-two pages, which are bound in a
black waterproof cloth envelope of "moleskin" (hence the
name), I have almost entirely filled in the last year with
penciled scribbling: sentences, notes, sketches, thoughts, and
Bible quotes. A word and a question in capital letters,
underlined, stand out on many pages, again and again:
"WHY?" and "WHY AM I WRITING THIS BOOK?"

I attempt an answer. First, it was pure journalistic
curiosity. With time, the deeper I researched into the secret
world of the cannibal and his "scene," the more I was forced
to give myself over to this subject. I realized how terribly
bloodthirsty, contemptible, and at the same time, pathetic
were both Armin Meiwes and Bernd Brandes. I had to
complete my task, and this task was, as became ever clearer,
no longer just to write this book, but apparently also to be a
voice. It is like combating pedophilia when no one wanted to
recognize or discuss its existence. The more voices that cry
out, the greater will be the pressure on society to uncover the
"cannibal scene" and to show those involved in it ways of
escape through therapy.

Admittedly, I have no right to pass judgment on
Armin Meiwes and Bernd Brandes. We are all sinners. I
must start with myself to clear away my uncleanness. "Let
him who is without sin cast the first stone," said Jesus when
the Jews wanted to kill a woman for adultery. How would
Jesus, I ask myself, have reacted to the cannibal? I think he

would have forgiven him if he repented this deed. Perhaps he might even have embraced him. I still have much to learn about forgiving, and resolve to speak with Armin Meiwes today about God. Does the cannibal know God?

As I leaf through my notepad, three Polaroid photos suddenly fall out of the folding interior pocket of the little booklet. I snapped them during my first inspection of the house and, thinking them lost, forgot about them. The first snapshot shows a front view of the manor house in Wüstefeld. The second photo shows the slaughter room with the steel bedstead and the wall hooks. The third shows the blue bathtub in which Bernd Brandes bled to death.

Now, I look at the photo of the manor house in detail: the crooked half-timbered walls with the small windows, the rusting golden Mercedes, the garden gone to seed, the rusty child's swing, and the heavy front door by which I entered. I recall how icy cold, eerie, and unreal each of these thirty-six shabby rooms looked to me on my first visit. It was a feeling of dread, revulsion, disgust, fascination—but above all, I felt a deep sadness. I don't think any place has ever touched me as negatively as this house. Was evil, the devil, Satan, present at the act on March 9, 2001, in Wüstefeld near Rotenburg an der Fulda?

I cannot answer with certainty, but I try to explain it to myself thus:

For Christians like me, God is everywhere, at all times. But the decision of which path to take, the good or the bad, is with every person himself. Everyone can weigh the choices. Shall I follow the demonic influences, the sexual drives, the aggressions, hatred, revenge, violence? Or do I turn from these forces and love my neighbor, understand, forgive, and thereby experience the greatest power on this earth, love?

God is love. And Armin Meiwes and Bernd Brandes have obviously received no love, or too little. Both, and on this the experts are agreed, were disturbed in their relationships. How could they have developed a healthy relationship with themselves, let alone with their fellow humans?

The anonymous anarchy of the Internet was clearly the outlet for their unconscious emotional suffering. The "World Wide Web" that we love for Google, Amazon, and *Spiegel* online, lured them, in this case, into sin like a cheap, garishly made-up streetwalker. Just a "click" to the next "kick" and you land, not in heaven, but directly in hell.

Armin Meiwes and Bernd Brandes did not let themselves be guided by God's power. He could not restrain them from this lunatic act. Too powerful were the desires stored up over decades and the devilish addictions they courted. Both men were drawn only to each other and lost in their mutually compulsive worlds.

*

The prison official in the Kassel Penitentiary, who has to deal every day with murderers, killers and one man-eater, drops his hard-boiled professionalism today. "Seems a shame you don't come anymore," he murmurs at the reception desk. "We really got used to your visits."

"It's very kind of you to say so. I'll miss the squeaking noise when the prison door is opened," I respond with a smile, and we climb the stairs to Visitors' Room 3 on the first floor.

"How are you, then?" he asks in a tone of voice that requires an honest answer.

"I've swung open a door to a world that makes me afraid. And, in recent months, I would gladly have shut that door."

"Why didn't you stop?" he wants to know.

"I think it was God's will that I go through it," I answer him and myself simultaneously. "Like the rest of us, I'm only a small light, and at most, I can light a match in the dark abysses."

The official pursues the conversation. "And what will happen when the book comes out?" he asks.

"I can't say. It doesn't matter anymore. I only know that truth takes a lot of courage and strength and that I've reached my physical limits. There was a time in my life when I lived without fear of God. Through this work, it's become clear to me again how thankful I must be for everything: my family, my children, and the love I received from my parents....do you understand?"

The official nods. "Today you can stay half an hour longer than usual. I've arranged it. But at five p.m. you have to be out," he tells me, softly but properly.

"Right," I reply.

"I'll get Mr. Meiwes now. All the best."

"Thank you. All the best to you, too."

In the conference room, I turn on the tap in the washbasin and let the cold water run. I lean over and the water flows sideways through my mouth and into my throat. My body is immediately refreshed. When I straighten up, I see the rubber tree in the mirror. The plant has recovered. Two new soft-green buds are sprouting among the withered leaves. "Life goes on," I murmur to myself.

About five minutes go by and it seems like an eternity. I tarry in front of the barred window with a view onto the interior courtyard. For a moment, I close my eyes to collect myself before the familiar, always courteous voice wrenches me out of my attempt at meditation.

"Helloooo, have a good trip?" calls Armin Meiwes from the door as he enters the room. I turn to him. "Yes, thanks. How are you?"

"Fine, considering the circumstances, quite well," he mutters.

"Glad to hear it."

The prisoner walks up to me at the window and shakes my hand. He peers between the bars out of the closed window. "Broiling heat. Dry today," he remarks.

"Mr. Meiwes, what do you think when you look out?" Today's interview begins at the window.

"It's another world out there. Behind bars, here in prison, time passes differently. Inside here, time practically stands still, while outside it runs on. It's as if the earth had stopped turning. Prison is a completely different world with different laws from those that exist outside."

"Do you feel safe here? Are the other prisoners afraid of you?"

Meiwes waves the question away like a pesky mosquito. "Oh, we have a good community here. I have a full day. I work in the laundry where I have great job that I enjoy. Then, also, I'm the auxiliary worker at the station when our worker is sick. With these jobs, I earn 160 Euros net a month."

What feelings do you have today, now that you've consumed Bernd Brandes?"

"Well then, in my view, he is now a part of me. At least, the thought of him is there, and it's a good thought. He's a friend who stays with me."

"You ate about forty-five pounds of Bernd Brandes. Purely biologically, by cell division, he's been long out of your body. Does that bother you?"

Meiwes pads back and forth. I look down. He wears new, shiny white gym shoes. Noticing my look, he says, "Chic, right? The others were completely worn through. But, to come back to your question. From the biological point of view, yes, this is clear to me. But, the thought of him is still there and that's what counts for me."

"Do you still indulge in slaughter fantasies when you masturbate?"

"Yes. Since I've been doing it for thirty years, I don't see how I could immediately change it or stop it."

"You'll be behind bars for at least fifteen years, unless the judges decide differently. Have you gotten used to the idea?"

The prisoner suddenly becomes reflective. "I had to be sentenced, of course. I've earned punishment. But I don't think about tomorrow. Otherwise I'd go crazy."

"Let's sit down," I suggest to the cannibal.

"Good idea."

We walk the step or two to the wooden table and sit down on the two chairs. Meiwes scratches his chin in embarrassment.

"How do you judge your act from today's perspective?"

"Today, I know what I did was wrong. That it can never be the right way to handle things. These kinds of wishes, the fantasies one has, can never be fulfilled in this manner."

"Is there anything that would have held you back from doing that deed?"

For a few moments, Meiwes looks toward the window at the white clouds floating past in the radiant blue sky. Suddenly he groans aloud—"Aaaah!"—and in a melodic voice continues. "If the little word 'if' didn't exist. At the time when I had a fiancée and wanted to start a family, these thoughts weren't there. They were only latent. Perhaps a good relationship would have saved me."

"Can you rule out, then, that you will again eat a man?"

"A female acquaintance in prison said to me that in realizing a fantasy, one will never experience fulfillment. I took this statement to heart. For what in our thoughts we paint in the most beautiful colors, is in reality different. The killing of Bernd Brandes was horrible."

"Do you think that after thirty years of such fantasies, and having committed the act, you can be cured by therapy?"

"Yes. Since I've been in prison, I have tried to get therapy. First, they said, as long as I was in detention for investigation, it wouldn't be possible because there was no money for it. Now I've applied again, and now they say the plan of execution must first be drawn up. I want therapy, I need it, I know it, and can only hope it will be done sometime."

"What advice would you give to a person with the same fantasies?"

His words come as if shot from a pistol. "Go to a psychologist or a doctor before it's too late!"

"What, in your view, should these people do?"

"Speak! Conversation is always the most important. They have to reveal to someone else the things they fear because if you don't talk about it, then these thoughts eat into your soul."

Meiwes ends his answer and adds one of his typical comparisons. "It's like a record with a crack in it."

"Do you still have a 'crack'?"

Meiwes catches the irony in my question and grins.

"Not to the same degree as then. The emptiness is still there to the extent that what I had imagined would fill it completely did not occur with Bernd Brandes. But the thought of him is there and is always with me. So the emptiness I felt in my childhood is no longer there."

"What do you see in the morning when you look at yourself in the mirror?"

"I see a presentable-looking man, friendly and quite well-liked. Well, we all have warts."

"Is it possible that you have a disturbed self-image?"

"Well, one naturally suppresses certain things, like the interval after cutting Bernd Brandes's throat. The brain doesn't want to accept those things. It happens to everyone, and it's exactly like that with me. In the courtroom, I was told I couldn't have the interview with you because I might play the act down. A man has died and been eaten! How can those things be played down?"

"Do you think many people from the cannibal forums play down their problems?"

"Yes, for sure. Countless people live in this fantasy world. Many of them look for partners, either to be eaten or to eat others. The police have determined that in Germany there are ten thousand potential butchery victims and cannibals. Worldwide, the number is in the area of one million. And if only one of them has the courage not to do it, that's a great success."

"Mr. Meiwes, for thirty years you were locked in your own thoughts. Are you aware that during that period of your life you were completely isolated?"

"Yes."

"That is sad, or is it?"

"I don't see it any differently. Isolated, abandoned, alone; always with the desire to have someone who's nearby and will never go away. That sounds somehow sad." He talks about it as if he were speaking of someone else.

"Have you ever cried about yourself?"

Meiwes swallows. "Often, yes."

"When?"

"Whenever various things were going badly."

"When was the last time you cried?"

"Oofff, when I was arrested."

"And now in detention?"

"No. I brought it on myself. I was ready to go to prison for it. It was clear to me from the outset that what I did has consequences for me. I won't say I'm glad to be in prison. I wouldn't wish it on anybody to be in the clink. But I'm ready to take on this load and I'm carrying it."

"Do you ever cry about your dead mother?"

"Oh, well, no. I assume she's living happily and satisfied in heaven, but I miss her, yes."

"Do you speak with her?"

"No, no, no."

I pull a pocket edition of the Bible from my briefcase, the "Fountain" Bible with "Hope for All."

"I brought this along for you," I tell him, "since you're going to the Protestant Bible Circle every Wednesday evening and to mass on Sunday."

Meiwes takes the Bible in his hands. "That's right. Thank you."

"What does God mean to you?"

"God for me is not someone, the way little children are taught, someone with a long beard who sits on a golden throne somewhere on a cloud."

"What is he, then? Is he a father to you?"

"Yes, that also. Each of us, every grain of sand, is part of him. For me, God is the power that directs and guides everything in the universe."

"Do you hold God responsible, then, for what has happened?"

"No, not responsible, but he permitted it. He looked away! But I don't hold him directly responsible. I also pray that Bernd Brand is getting along all right in heaven."

"God left you the choice whether or not to do it. It was your decision to butcher Bernd Brandes."

"Yes, it's a difficult question. God left me the choice. But, He also left the choice to Bernd Brandes. And if it had been possible for Him, then He would perhaps have been able to prevent it. But He saw that what we had both wanted for ourselves was stronger. When the day has come, when I stand before Him, then He will surely be able to answer these questions."

"You read the Bible. Can it be that you have wrongly understood something in it?"

The convict compresses his lips, and then sucks on his upper lip. "I took, perhaps too literally, the words Jesus Christ spoke at the Last Supper, 'This is my body that I have given for you.' I interpreted it, in principle, in such a way, that with every bite of Bernd Brandes's flesh, he became a part of me, and the memory of him became much stronger and more intense. I probably didn't get it right. I thought that with the flesh sacrifice, I was no longer alone."

"Isn't the eating of Bernd Brandes a sacrifice to an idol?"

"Yes. I thought that he would come a little closer to me. The assumption was probably wrong."

"If I sat in front of you today and said, 'Mr. Meiwes, butcher me,' what would you do?"

"Well, today I'd send you straight off to a psychiatrist. I would ask much more intensively about the reasons and the desires, why it has come to this, and then try to help this person so that he doesn't need to do it."

The cannibal proceeds to the justification. "That's the way it was before. I also had a young man staying with me for five days. After a couple of days, I realized that it was not the right path for him. Before he could ask me, I said, 'Don't be mad at me, but you'd better go home.'" [Author's comment: In the files, however, are also the words, "I didn't care for the young man," and "he was too fat."]

"Right now, there are physicians, lawyers, and teachers who have the same fantasies as you. Our neighbor could be a cannibal."

"Yes, that's right. Other people don't know it. With me, it was known. There are altogether, if you include the estimated number of unreported cases, eighty to a hundred thousand people in Germany alone who are very much interested in this subject matter. But it's quite different than with Hannibal Lecter."

"There was a film with the name, 'Rohtenburg.' Why did you get it banned?"

"In that film, things are presented falsely and in an exaggerated manner. People who see that film may think it actually happened that way and I wanted to prevent that. Such a film is of no help to anyone. And when the 'Rammstein' band makes a joke out of this serious matter with a song like 'My Part,' I find it revolting."

"For many people, your act was revolting. We're asking a lot from people with a book and TV documentation."

"Yes, but I think that's the right way."

"Why did you decide to talk to me, whom you didn't know at all?"

"I looked for someone who would deal seriously with the matter. You wrote me a letter that sounded honest. You explained that you would do it only if it was objective. That was your basic condition. I see many things differently from the way they will be presented in the book. But, as it is, it is truthful."

"Is it true that the police asked you to help them clear up unsolved murder cases?"

"That is correct."

"What are you expected to do?"

"There are two cases where fleshy parts from the victims were missing, and that was naturally a reason for the police to ask whether I could be the culprit myself, or whether I had relevant information from the Internet as to who could be responsible."

"That's almost like *The Silence of the Lambs*, the police coming to you and asking if you can help."

"Well, it's not quite *The Silence of the Lambs*. I'm not sitting in a glass cage with a muzzle. But, except for that, it's comparable. I saw the film for the first time here in prison. The police would have liked to call on me to help, but the State's Attorney refused."

"What for?"

"I can't say. I don't know. I would like to have helped the police. Who knows his way around with cannibals better than a cannibal?"

"What cases are involved?"

"The police are searching desperately for the murderer of two boys. One victim was Tristan B., a thirteen-year-old boy from Frankfurt. In March 1998, he was found dead in an underpass on the Liederbach River. His testicles had been cut off and large chunks of flesh were missing from his upper thighs and buttocks. But the investigators will never find them. The culprit ate them long ago. The other case is an eleven-year-old boy, Tobias, from Böblingen in Baden-Württemberg. As far as I know, his sexual organs were also cut off and not found.

"And what did the investigators want to know about the cases from you?"

"The police officials asked me if I had something to do with it. But I would never do such a thing. It's dreadful to torture and mutilate a child like that." Armin Meiwes lowers his eyes, looking troubled. "Besides, I have always been concerned for voluntariness." He looks back up at me, moving on. "At any rate, I was able to assure the police that they could only be dealing with a cannibal. I had an Internet contact with a man who declared he had butchered three boys. He said he came from near Leipzig and drove a red Renault Mégane. But I don't know if they're taking the clues seriously."

"Why are you so sure the culprit was a cannibal and not a compulsive sexual offender?"

Meiwes looks me straight in the eye. "I'm a hundred percent sure! The river alone was perfect for washing off the blood after the murder. And besides that, chunks of flesh were missing. To me it's so obvious."

Armin Meiwes says it with a knowing certainty that shocks me. The idea that a perverted sex offender is running around free in Germany, carving up children, and eating parts of their flesh, is horrifying. It also confirms, however, that we are dealing with a social problem, and that Meiwes is possibly only one case among many.

It is incomprehensible to me that the State's Attorney declined Armin Meiwes's collaboration in the search for a murderer. I would like, nevertheless, to take seriously in this book, the clues offered by Meiwes, even though they rest on a presumption.

"What does this cannibal look like?"

The prisoner dictates to me the culprit's profile. "Inconspicuous, mid-thirties, regular work, average appearance. Shortly before his offense against Tristan, he had to cope with a traumatic experience, probably the death of a close relative, mother, or father. He is still active today, but more careful. Tristan had to be found because the offender also wanted to demean his victim after his death. It gave him a feeling of power. Now the culprit is probably looking around in the neighborhood of a railroad station, where there are many runaway boys. Presumably, he's committed further offenses since Tristan's murder in 1998. I'm sure he'll strike again."

"Are you glad to have collaborated on the book?"

"Yes, absolutely. Our conversation also helped me get a number of things clear in my mind."

"How do you imagine your life in the future?"

Meiwes takes two or three deep breaths. "Well then, I have two lady friends. A very strong friend whose name is Jutta. I'd be happy to live with her in the future and start a life together. She has problems now with her ex-husband. And according to what she's told me about herself, she had problems with her parents when she was a child, of the kind I'm also familiar with. So we have a common denominator."

"But you aren't going to live together as a cannibal couple?"

"I beg you! That was then."

"And the Wüstefeld manor house?"

"I want to keep the Wüstefeld house no matter what happens. The house is my life. If it collapses, then I'm gone, too. And I may want to leave the slaughter room as it is, but I don't know. Whether I'll live there or not is uncertain. In any event, I won't let the house be used as a welfare home. Nobody in Wüstefeld wants that, nobody in Rotenburg, and I don't either."

Many sides of Armin Meiwes are, now as before, an enormous puzzle.

"Would you like to have children?"

"I wanted children before, but now I don't want any, not of my own."

"Why?"

"I wouldn't want any child to be teased by others as the child of the cannibal. Children are the most important part of society."

It is five minutes to five p.m., and our conversation time approaches its end. "I must go," I say to the cannibal. "Many thanks for speaking about everything so openly and honestly."

As I take my leave, Meiwes seems almost sympathetic, like a reformed person. "Sorry you've had nightmares because of me. I was already aware of it; this business is not for weak nerves."

"As you would put it in your way of speaking, I'll digest it," I answer with a touch of sarcasm.

Meiwes grins again and says, "For people who don't understand it, perhaps it can somehow be made explainable. Not understandable, but explainable. All I can do is try, in having these talks, to prevent something like that in future."

"At least you tried. The decision will be made by each of the people who are inclined that way for himself. And let's hope that He up there will help them to stop it," I reply, looking up to the ceiling of the room. Meiwes remains silent. An official comes to take him back to his cell. In the corridor, we shake hands. "See you soon," he says. "See you sometime," I say as politely. Armin Meiwes's eyes shine in farewell, but at the same time are oddly veiled.

As I leave, I think, the Cannibal of Rotenburg doesn't really live. He exists only in himself. I think that a long, long time ago, Armin Meiwes locked his soul and his feelings into a room constructed by his own mind. He forgot where the exit was and threw away the keys. There was no one there to help him build ties and feelings toward others. As he himself says, he is "a soul imprisoned in itself." The Wüstefelder has, in part, excessively brightened and reshaped his life history in his own thoughts—relationship to his mother, father's departure, loving relationships with women—in order to have supports, like a handicapped person who has to go down stairs. Meiwes searches for explanations, for causes and reasons, to understand in part the unexplainable in his cannibalistic behavior. He won't be that lucky. Only therapy, which he himself wants and urgently needs, can possibly help him prevent fantasy from being translated into action.

Everything I asked him, and everything he answered, changes nothing of the facts, but at least we were able to appreciate the reality of the matter. That was why I wanted to talk with him.

My wish for Armin Meiwes is that someday, with the aid of therapy, he can break out of his cage, but I fear that as long as he lives, he will remain a prisoner of his body. In his basic nature, apparently nothing will change.

I dreamed one night, after digesting Armin Meiwes's descriptions of his act, that I carved up two friends at their request. I came into the scene when I threw accusations at myself after the bloody deed. I screamed in despair, my heart was racing, and my whole body shuddered with horror at myself. "I'm a murderer! I'm a murderer!" my voice echoed unceasingly. I awoke in fright from my nightmare. My face was wet, but not from sweat, as I thought at first. My face was wet with tears. I wept bitterly. Then my mind suddenly asked me two decisive questions: Why is Armin Meiwes always able, after this deed, despite supposed remorse, to sleep with an easy conscience, and, how is it possible for someone to butcher a person and then not carry these dreadful memories, eventually, into his sleep? I think this deed was for Meiwes so repulsive, so frightful, that he pushed the visual memories of the killing far down into his subconscious where they could no longer reach him. His dreams, however, of Bernd Brandes, of the brother he had always wanted, whom he finally butchered and assimilated into himself, continue in beautiful, romantic pictures.

*

Shortly after five p.m., I step through the lacquered olive-colored revolving door of the Kassel Penitentiary and look back briefly at the building. I feel a deep liberation, while at the same time there remains a sort of apprehension.

Two boys are playing football on the other side of the street. The taxi I've ordered is already waiting. I get into the cab, lost in thought. At the wheel is the same Turkish driver who chauffeured me to my very first meeting with Armin Meiwes. "Aah, you! We know each other!" he declares, seemingly glad to see me again. "Heard it from colleagues that you are the journalist with the man-eater. You still all there?" He grins, his gold tooth gleaming at me. I reply, "Outwardly I am, but inside I feel somewhat corroded." The Turk understands nothing but laughs heartily and drives me to the Kassel-Wilhelmshöhe train station. Suddenly, on a side street, I see, in block letters on a wall like a sign of hope, an advertisement for a house of worship: "Whoever comes to me, him will I not send away. JESUS."

I think, after all this, I'll have a talk with my pastor.

THOUGH I SPEAK WITH THE TONGUES OF MEN AND OF ANGELS, AND HAVE NOT LOVE, I AM BECOME AS SOUNDING BRASS OR A TINKLING SYMBOL. AND THOUGH I HAVE THE GIFT OF PROPHECY, AND UNDERSTAND ALL MYSTERIES, AND ALL KNOWLEDGE; AND THOUGH I HAVE ALL FAITH, SO THAT I COULD REMOVE MOUNTAINS, AND HAVE NOT LOVE, I AM NOTHING. AND THOUGH I BESTOW ALL MY GOODS TO FEED THE POOR, AND THOUGH I GIVE MY BODY TO BE BURNED, AND HAVE NOT LOVE, IT PROFITETH ME NOTHING. LOVE SUFFERETH LONG, AND IS KIND; LOVE ENVIETH NOT; LOVE VAUNTETH NOT ITSELF, IS NOT PUFFED UP. DOTH NOT BEHAVE ITSELF UNSEEMLY, SEEKETH NOT HER OWN, IS NOT EASILY PROVOKED, THINKETH NO EVIL. REJOICETH NOT IN INIQUITY, BUT REJOICETH IN THE TRUTH. BEARETH ALL THINGS, BELIEVETH.
ALL THINGS, HOPETH ALL THINGS, ENDURETH ALL THINGS. LOVE NEVER FAILETH: BUT WHETHER THERE BE PROPHECIES, THEY SHALL FAIL; WHETHER THERE BE TONGUES, THEY SHALL CEASE; WHETHER THERE BE KNOWLEDGE, IT SHALL VANISH AWAY.

FOR WE KNOW IN PART, AND WE PROPHESY IN PART. BUT WHEN THAT WHICH IS PERFECT IS COME, THEN THAT WHICH IS IN PART SHALL BE DONE AWAY. WHEN I WAS A CHILD, I SPAKE AS A CHILD, I UNDERSTOOD AS A CHILD, I THOUGHT AS A CHILD: BUT WHEN I BECAME A MAN, I PUT AWAY CHILDISH THINGS. FOR NOW WE SEE THROUGH A GLASS, DARKLY; BUT THEN FACE TO FACE: NOW I KNOW IN PART, BUT THEN SHALL I KNOW EVEN AS ALSO I AM KNOWN. AND NOW ABIDETH FAITH, HOPE, LOVE, THESE THREE; BUT THE GREATEST OF THESE IS LOVE.

(Corinthians 1: 13)

My Imprisoned Soul

These first interviews, which I have given for documentation and the book, are not a justification for the act.

I have resolved to collaborate in it in order to show what can happen when one cannot speak about his feelings and problems.

I know there are thousands of people on the Internet who have fantasies and imaginings similar to those I had.

My goal in this book is to show these people where silence, or burying problems in one's inner self, can lead.

Most people who hear of my act cannot grasp it, and comprehend with difficulty what happened. In consequence, through half-truths or assumptions, many things that are not true are read into it.

In my childhood, I had wished for a younger brother with whom to share the problems I had at the time. I did not wish to add them to my mother's other burdens.

Thirty years later, when I was in a similar situation, isolated and alone, I tried to solve these problems through the Internet. There I dealt intensively with the subject of death, and at various sites happened upon cannibalism. At some point, I took courage and developed contacts. In the process, one was mutually worked up. For me, what for others is "abnormal" became "normal." Instead of help and liberation, everything became more and more narrowed down. Day after day, I spent at least an hour on the Internet. It became an addiction.

I answered advertisements and inserted some myself. That was how I discovered Bernd Brandes's ad on a cannibal site. This developed into the subject of this book.

One can exchange fantasies, but must not let oneself be taken over by them.

Whatever his problems, one should always seek out someone impartial with whom one can talk about one's fantasies. For reality is never fantasy. A fantasy one can talk about does not need to be translated into action.

—Armin Meiwes

PROFILE OF A CANNIBAL

Armin Meiwes is a puzzle to many people, including the author of this book, Günter Stampf. They want to know if he is an evil man or just a disturbed individual, if he is dangerous or if he is only bizarre, if he feels no guilt for what he did, or if he truly has had a change of heart as his final statement to Stampf concerning his motives for allowing the interview seems to exhibit. Furthermore, people want to know why Meiwes became a cannibal, and they seek an explanation for his "condition" in the trials and tribulations of his childhood and in the perverse cyber world of the Internet. Some want to know if Armin Meiwes should be pitied and helped, or if he should be left alone and ignored. Should he be let out of prison at some point and welcomed back into society, or should he be locked away until death ends the prison sentence for him?

As a criminal profiler, I have to conclude that Armin Meiwes should remain where he is and be left to his own fate. I believe Armin Meiwes is a psychopath who cares nothing for the rest of us on the planet and is only ever cooperative or pleasant when he needs to use us to get something he wants. I say we should wash our hands of this cannibal because he is beyond repair, but we should not fail to recognize that the existence of Meiwes is representative of certain social ills within society that should be addressed.

Some of you may consider me harsh and overly judgmental concerning this man, Armin Meiwes, whom you have come to know through his many meetings with Günter Stampf, and you possibly believe this man is should be given help and another chance in life. Let me assure you that a thorough analysis of Meiwes will lead you conclude as I have, that this man is not, and has not been since his childhood, a decent human being. He is psychopathic through and through, and the following profile will leave no doubt in your mind as to the real nature of Armin Meiwes and the threat he may represent to innocent people if he were ever to regain his freedom and be allowed to live among us once again.

Was Armin Meiwes once a victim to be pitied? There is no doubt of this, which the evidence proves. The young Armin had a less than desirable upbringing and parents to whom most of us wouldn't wish to have been born. Yet many people have had similar misfortunes, and they don't become cannibals. We can be grateful that humans tend to be resilient, and a good many can overcome less than perfect circumstances in their youth to grow up to be responsible and law-abiding citizens. However, it has been my experience that those individuals who do grow up to be walking disasters usually have had relatively dysfunctional families, stubborn personalities, and a myriad of negative environmental factors in their lives. When all these factors combine, the result may be an increasingly disaffected individual who eventually becomes a social nightmare.

While it is not easy to predict when all these elements will come together in a way that spells catastrophe, one can certainly recognize early on if a child is failing to be accepted and loved within his family and community. Such a child may eventually morph into an outcast, a loser, and a malcontent. As these children grow towards adulthood, they find alternative methods of "success" through manipulation and lying. They gain power and opportunities with the increase of their physical size, experience, finances, and freedom of movement. They may eventually desire to create a new game of life in which they can be the masters and winners instead of the pawns and patsies. They then begin to fantasize as to which acts will turn the tables on their "enemies" and how they can work this to their advantage. These disturbed individuals may go on to become con-men, domestic abusers, robbers, rapists, and serial killers, or they may become clever enough at their game to become stockbrokers, politicians, and clergymen, who will bilk their followers out of millions before the latter realize that they are dealing with wolves in sheep's clothing.

But in order to arrive at the point where society and all that it represents is to be hated, manipulated, and beaten, the psyche of an individual must take a major deviation from normal psychology and completely disassociate itself from the rest of humanity. In other words, one must become a psychopath.

To analyze the evilness of the crimes of Armin Meiwes and the evilness of Armin Meiwes himself, we must determine if he is a psychopath or not. For if he is not a psychopath, then perhaps he is simply a confused, deranged man. On the other hand, if he is a psychopath, he is going to be a much less defensible individual. He would be the very kind of being who could cold-bloodedly and with clear intent commit a heinous crime and then do it again given another opportunity. Any remorse or guilt he expresses over his crimes would then be nothing but a ploy to achieve some hidden agenda he is pursuing.

It is important to remember that although Meiwes may have once been an innocent little boy (as were all psychopaths and criminals at some time in their lives), we cannot allow this vision to influence our present evaluation. We can feel sad for the once cute and loveable tot, Armin Meiwes, but our tenderness for the child who existed decades ago does not matter in addressing the question, "Is Armin Meiwes now a psychopath?" For once one becomes a psychopath, one remains a psychopath for all of one's life, and there is no treatment in the world that is going to change this fact. Deciding if Armin Meiwes is a danger to society outside of prison hinges more on his psychopathy status and his ideation than on the actual crimes committed. We must rely on more than just an offense report to evaluate the likelihood of Meiwes committing another homicide and mutilation.

The key traits of psychopathy are as follows:

glib and superficial

deceitful and manipulative

emotionally shallow

egocentric and grandiose

lacking empathy

impulsive

poor behavior controls

need for excitement

lack of responsibility

early behavioral problems

adult antisocial behavior

By the time Armin Meiwes became an adult, all of these traits were present in his character, even if they were not apparent to all around him. There were certainly neighbors and coworkers who found him polite, helpful, kind, and friendly. However, Meiwes himself brags in one of his prison interviews that all this niceness and friendliness is but a cover for his private cannibalistic "hobby."

"I learned to suppress my emotions completely in company. Always be nice and polite, and don't talk too much. That way I get along without stumbling into a trap. None of my friends or colleagues got wind of my pleasure in cutting up a man. Not one."

This glib, superficial exterior of Meiwes's is characterized by the lack of any true friends who can verify that there is any depth to his character, relationships, or conversations. There is one neighbor with whom Meiwes went to Lebanon a few times and a group of coworkers who vacationed with Meiwes. None of these men comment on the lack of emotions expressed by Meiwes but believe that he is simply shy and awkward. They set him up with occasional dates and urge him to use a dating service in order to develop a meaningful relationship. He goes along with their suggestions, minimally, and makes a couple of very feeble attempts at "getting married and creating a family." However, his dating life consists of very few interactions before he considers the women inappropriate and unpleasing (at least this is his side of the story). The reality is he cannot connect with healthy human beings, because there is a requirement in such relationships to give and take, something psychopaths find totally unacceptable.

We can see through Armin Meiwes's phony friendliness and cooperativeness the manipulative nature of the psychopath. No true emotion engenders his relationships; rather it is a self-centered egocentricity that is the motive behind any kind of human interaction. Meiwes cares little for how others really feel or think and he does not do anything for them for the sake of their well-being or happiness. He does only what is beneficial to his own purposes. Helping the neighbors, for example, is a way of distracting them from being suspicious of what is taking place at the house next door. Following up on advice of "friends" gives Meiwes the appearance of similar (and normal) aspirations and goals. The occasional outings with the boys, dates with women, and offers of help with babysitting or meetings, etc., serve purely as a smoke screen to distract from his odd lifestyle and his bizarre ideations.

Even the relationship with his mother has nothing to do with love or even obligation. Meiwes needs his mother for his own survival. This parasitic relationship between a psychopath and a female is very common. Women are more tolerant of peculiar male behavior in their own homes than are men (who are more tolerant of weirdos in their social lives). This is especially true of a mother's capacity to put up with incredibly horrible behavior from her male offspring. Meiwes's mother was also dependent on Armin for her needs, and so this symbiotic relationship worked for both for mother and son. She needed him to be the man in her life, the one man who would obey her, and he needed her to frame his existence, provide a home for him, and give him a modicum of respectability in the community. She was even useful in disapproving of women that Armin might on rare occasion bring home. His ill and needy mother was a good excuse for Meiwes's inability to live like other mature men, thereby allowing him the freedom to continue his secret world of cannibalism without interference. She served his purposes, and this is the only reason he did her bidding.

Meiwes, even with his mother, exhibits shallow emotions. There is no affection between them, and he wishes more than once he could do her in. When she does eventually die, there is no grieving for this woman who was such a major part of his life for decades. He refuses to ever speak or bother about her again, and simply closes his mind and the door to her part of the house and moves on.

Meiwes also shows no shred of romantic love for any other woman, no deep friendship with any man, and no particular feelings even for his brother, Ilja, the real brother he is trying to replace with another through assimilation. Ilja is still alive, still nearby, yet Meiwes hardly even speaks of him with the author, except in connection with a failed business matter and some assistance he receives from Ilja after his arrest. He shows no great love for his brother, no desperation to gain his brother's attention; in truth, Ilja really means very little to Meiwes at all.

We can further see this lack of interest in any real intimacy as Meiwes attempts to gain a "brother" to eat. He claims he wants first to establish a relationship with his "meat." He says he does not want to rush into the killing and the cannibalism but, first, he wants to get to know his "brother" and establish a close bond. Then he will be ready to devour him. However, Meiwes hardly learns a thing about Bernd Brandes before ending his life. Their chats on the Internet are purely sex- and fetish-based. Even when they meet, they only speak of personal matters in unimportant small talk. It is purely Meiwes's self-serving fantasy that he imagines he will only eat someone with whom he has a deep connection. It is his way of minimizing his behavior and the heinousness of his actions. It is also part of his particular psychopathic need for power and control that he tells himself these men have "chosen" him as the perfect man to give themselves over to. This voluntary surrender provides Meiwes with the ego boost he needs, which is why, even after he has killed and is consuming Brandes, he carries on conversations with the dead man and makes a big deal over their "relationship." He is merely attempting to get as much pleasure as he can out of his act for as long as possible.

Eventually, though, the feeling diminishes and Meiwes goes on the search for a new "brother."

One very telling example of Meiwes and his shallow emotions is in his letter to his lady friend who is visiting him in jail.

> *Dear Marion,*
>
> *I am soooo happy. Back in my cell, I had to cry for joy, and my entire body trembled with excitement. Everything is so hard and happy at the same time, and I thank you for sticking with me just at this time. Somehow I found it funny that the policeman was present, but it was better that we weren't up front in the big room and could talk undisturbed, if only so briefly. You gave me back light and hope. It was just at lunchtime and my neighbor in the next cell said, "You don't have to tell me how your visit was—you're just radiant with happiness." And that's exactly how I feel.*
>
> *I wish I could embrace you again and kiss you warmly and passionately. With eyes shut, I sit here and imagine you were still here and I see your tender face clearly before me. It is so lovely!*
>
> *Yours with love,*
> *Armin*

What bunk! This is a homosexual man who had never on the outside shown any true interest in a female. He also has little likelihood of living on the outside ever again. Yet now he is professing grand and undying love to Marion Reich after just one visit! Meiwes, I can guarantee, feels none of these emotions, but has learned what he should tell a lady in order to show he cares for her. Meiwes does not know any true emotion of love and can only play-act. In these cases, psychopaths often do so inappropriately, at the wrong time or the wrong place, because they are not really experiencing these emotions at all. Psychopaths often profess love upon first encounter because they are trying to achieve some goal (sex, security through marriage, attention) and therefore don't see any need to waste time waiting for a real relationship to actually develop.

In spite of the fact that some people, including his lawyer, seem to believe Armin Meiwes is a truthful, honest man, there is much evidence to the contrary. A pathological liar is not necessarily a person who never tells the truth, for even a psychopath will tell the truth when it is beneficial to him. First of all, sometimes telling the truth gains one more than lying, and secondly, telling the truth enough of the time convinces people that this person is telling the truth when actually he is now telling a lie.

Meiwes obviously told his mother many lies in order to continue with his perverted activities in the home. He clearly admits lying to her to cover up his vacation on the boat with his work friends. He also lies about his sexual activities with women. He claims he had sexual intercourse with them, while they state he did no more then kiss and pet them. He lies to the court when he says Brandes is the one and only; and then they find witness after witness to prove he went right back out in search of the next victim. He even tells lies to Stampf a number of times, and when caught, quickly changes his story, as though he never said the falsehood in the first place. It is likely Meiwes spent much time telling falsehoods to his friends and coworkers, and they simply did not realize they were being lied to, or they couldn't prove he was not telling the truth. They may have questioned some story he related, thought it unlikely, but then shrugged their shoulders and left it alone, chalking up such talk from Meiwes as expected, because, well, he is a bit odd after all, and he is just being Armin. Then they forget the incident.

Armin Meiwes does not take responsibility for his own behaviors but blames most of his poor life choices and events on others. He blames his cannibalism on his father and brother leaving him, not on his teenage and adult choices to pursue creepy thinking. He blames the army for tossing him out, and does not admit his irresponsible use of alcohol.

He blames his mother for his bachelorhood and for myriads of other problems, and he blames the women he has met for breaking off their relationships for unfair reasons. He blames the student who got the investigation going that resulted in his incarceration for being unfair to him. In truth, Meiwes is responsible for his own arrest, as he broke his cardinal rule of never carelessly speaking of his hobby to others. It is his bragging to this new Internet acquaintance that does him in. His impulsiveness and his need for excitement, coupled with arrogance, causes Meiwes to respond foolishly to the young man.

Meiwes blames his victims for coming to him and "making him" kill them. He blames them for the lack of satisfaction he receives in the act. He blames the system for giving him such a long sentence, and he blames "circumstances" for the fact that he never sought psychiatric help. Armin Meiwes never does anything wrong; well, he admits to doing nothing wrong, unless he is forced into a partial admission by the courts or Stampf, but these admissions are reluctant, not truly acknowledged by Meiwes. He only "confesses" to something if he can't squirm out of the issue of culpability, and, even then, he will offer up a number of excuses or justifications for his behavior. Finally, he has the audacity to blame God for not preventing him from killing and eating Bernd Brandes! Even this horrific act, as premeditated as it was, is still something for which Meiwes takes no responsibility for committing. The commission of antisocial, immoral, and illegal acts is not an issue for Armin Meiwes, as he cares nothing for what others think and what society views as right or wrong. For Meiwes, right is what makes him feel good, and wrong is anything that prevents him from feeling that way.

A lack of empathy and remorse is the number one hallmark of psychopathy. Armin Meiwes has exhibited neither empathy nor remorse in his entire life. His violation of social norms and general disrespect for society's values is evident. He sneers at them, willingly breaks the laws, and flaunts the values of the society in which he lives. He exhibits no empathy towards the women he dates. He has no sympathy for their needs to have relationships with their own parents; he is miffed at any woman who is reluctant to move into his bizarre home with his overbearing mother, and he feels no remorse for any part he might have played in the failure of his involvement with these women to move to a deeper level.

Meiwes has no empathy for the sick individuals who want to be eaten. He doesn't even begin to think about these men's families and what killing the men might do to them. Even though he "befriends" Brandes, Meiwes never urges him to get help and never feels bad that Brandes is now dead. Rather, he is proud that he provided such a great death for Brandes. He feels no sympathy for his victim's life partner, who is devastated by the murder of his lover.

Armin Meiwes feels no remorse for the murder of Brandes or his act of cannibalism. Although sometimes he claims (lies) that he feels remorse and that speaking to a psychiatrist has been so freeing and cathartic, he then admits he still constantly fantasizes about killing and cannibalism. The fact that he continued in his pursuit of more victims after Brandes and thinks still of getting more victims (and he even wants to keep his torture room intact back at the manor) means he would undoubtedly be back to his crimes should he ever be released.

Furthermore, serial crimes may escalate in violence and perversion as one continues to commit them (as the stimulation needed to reach the previous level of excitement must be ratcheted up). Meiwes is an extreme danger to the community because he is already fantasizing about acts of violence he has not yet experienced. He may also get frustrated waiting for men to offer themselves to him (if he hasn't already and is actually responsible for those two victims the police asked him about—surely, they thought that he himself might be guilty, because they were unlikely to really want him to "profile" for them). While he did release men from his torture room when they wished to go home, this does not mean he released all of them. Sometimes, perpetrators of violent crimes will let some victims go, either because they would have been linked too strongly to them, or because it makes them look "safe" to be around. This latter is a very popular technique with serial killers of prostitutes. The serial killer picks up a different girl each week over a period of time. He pays them for the sex act, treats them nicely, and then returns them safely. Then, one day, when one of the girls is all alone and there are no witnesses to see her get into the serial killer's car, she disappears. But all the girls will vouch for the killer when they are interviewed by the police, because he has always been a standup fellow and never hurt any of the girls in any way. It could be likewise with Meiwes.

Meiwes is a liar when he states that he simply wants a brother in him. He is obsessed with mutilation, gore, and even sadistic acts while the victim is alive or dead. His thrill is not merely in the consumption. For this, he could do without all the perverted fanfare and sexual orgasms. Meiwes is a sexual sadist and a serial killer (even though there is no proof of other murders connected to him at this point in time). All serial killers are dissatisfied with just one crime because they enjoy gaining power and control in their lives through their crimes. Most serial killers are psychopaths who are massive failures in life and they kill because it makes them feel like somebody. Each serial killer picks a different way of expressing his power and control, whether through a violent assault and rape that takes less than ten minutes, or keeping the victim in a basement prison and torturing them to death over the space of a month, or by luring in victims to kill and eat them. Like with Lay's Potato Chips, I bet Armin Meiwes can't eat just one.

What mostly differentiates psychopaths from one another is their method of societal revenge and the vehicle used to accomplish that revenge. The revenge fantasy starts in childhood and becomes more elaborate in the teen years. The revenge fantasy is always one of power and control, but which particular scenario is selected, which fantasy one wants to develop into an actual physical act, is dependent on the psychopath's own experiences and environment.

Needless to say, it is quite impossible to fantasize about something that does not exist. As King Solomon once said, "There is nothing new under the sun," and this would be true for all our thoughts and ideations. Armin Meiwes, for example, apparently became enamored with butchering as it was practiced in his locality, when he was able to see the process firsthand as a child. He saw in this act that a man could take the life of another being, and then do the most dramatic things to its body by butchering, cooking, and eating it. For these acts of killing and eradication, the man was then treated as a hero! For the fatherless, powerless young Armin Meiwes, this scenario may have been extraordinarily exciting and enticing.

However, becoming a butcher of animals did not rise to the level of reward Meiwes needed. He wasn't trying to gain the favor or admiration of his fellow human beings; he wanted to revenge himself on them. He had no gripes against animals, but only the human beings around him who abandoned him, subjugated him, or ignored him. If he could only reenact the butchering of the animal with a human being, then he would do the same things to them that he believed had been done to him, only he would trump them in the act. He would pay them back, and then some. Of course, such contempt for society, and this level of willingness to break its rules and mores, requires that Meiwes be the type of psychopath as described above.

Armin Meiwes loves the feeling of destroying and obliterating another human being. He likes to cut off their penises, because as a weak and sexually impotent man (within relationships with either males or females), he can commit the ultimate act against a man, thereby creating the most macho feeling he will ever achieve in life. Meiwes's greatest moment, however, appears to be when he guts his victims, removing from them their very inner existence (the innards represent the depth of the person). Finally, by eating his victims, Meiwes has his great last laugh, and in the consumption, which he draws out as long as possible, the feeling of power and control continues unabated.

Yes, not only is Armin Meiwes able to cut off a man's penis, take his life, and disembowel him, but he can then eat up every part of him. Armin Meiwes is God, and as God he has indeed decided to allow this act to occur. This grandiose thinking is the stuff that psychopaths dwell upon. The desire to be above all others, above the law, and even above God is what makes their crimes worth the risk. The desire is so strong it can lead to impulsiveness that eventually causes carelessness and their downfall.

Everyday activities lack the excitement of being an outlaw, and delaying gratification is seen as a sign of weakness, a submission to society's rules. Therefore, while it may seem as if psychopaths have poor behavioral controls, they actually simply don't want to control their behavior. Meiwes discusses over and over with Stampf how he could have prevented the deed from occurring, but then admits that, quite frankly, he didn't want to stop himself from committing the crime. Meiwes also appears impulsive in his aggressive victim search, and the speed in which he answers emails and sets up dates increases his risk of being found out. Psychopaths, however, do not think taking immediate action without much planning signifies a lack of patience or an immature need for instant gratification, but rather see such behavior as a sign of strength and power.

Armin Meiwes came up with a good story to tell his victims, the court, the media, and even himself. He presents himself as a nice man who simply struggles with the desire to be linked with one person through time. Nothing could be farther from the truth. Armin Meiwes is a violent, psychopathic serial killer. He is taking out his rage on society for his failure as a man by breaking one of the greatest taboos of humankind. By becoming a cannibal, a man-eater, Armin Meiwes is no longer a "nobody." He is the Cannibal of Rotenburg, and he has feasted on the citizens of his country. He has become God through his ability to control life and death. Finally, while psychiatrists, journalists, and citizens try to understand Armin Meiwes and even feel sorry for him, Armin Meiwes is laughing at their foolishness and doing everything he can to convince society to let him go. It is my job as a criminal profiler to implore society to keep Armin Meiwes behind bars, where he belongs.

But more than this, both Günter Stampf and I hope this book helps educate society about the cannibals in our midst. We would like to see society address the issues that encourage the development of psychopathy in children who one day may turn into dangerous criminals. We would like to see society and its citizens take a stand against the use of the Internet by perverted sexual predators, including cannibals trolling for their next meal. We want society to recognize the damage that is done to impressionable juveniles when they are lured into repulsive, anti-life, soul destroying ideation of the sort that is prevalent in cannibal chat rooms. All of the citizens of the world need to face the growing role of the Internet in spreading and validating violence, sexual perversion, and other acts against humanity and society. Hopefully, we will all work together to ameliorate the problem through whatever methods we find to be most effective.

Otherwise, Armin Meiwes, or someone "inspired" by him, may become the cannibal next door. For that matter, he may already be there.

—Criminal Profiler Pat Brown

June 24, 2008

A few hours before this book went to print
A new instance of cannibalism
Hits the ticker tape.

BILD, August 28, 2007

New Cannibal Case:
German Eats Austrian

It's the strangest, most gruesome crime of the year! A nineteen-year-old German is reported to have killed a homeless man in Vienna, and possibly to have eaten him.

As reported by the Austrian news agency APA, the dismembered body of Josef S. (age forty-nine) was found in a homeless shelter in Vienna.

A cleaning woman discovered the disemboweled body of the homeless person in the morning. The actual time of the deed might have been one or two days earlier, according to initial investigations.

The presumed culprit was found in the same room. He said to the police, "Just look at what happened."

The scene of the act—a picture of horror!

The victim's skull was cracked open with a twenty-two-pound dumbbell in order to take out portions of the brain.

The body was slit open in many places. Inner organs and intestines hung partly out. The innards of the forty-nine-year-old were arranged on a plate by the suspect and set down in an adjoining room. There was blood everywhere in the room.

The dreadful suspicion of the investigators: The culprit may have eaten the innards of the corpse raw. He was found and arrested with blood dripping from his mouth next to the corpse.